Ford & ISO 14001

The Synergy Between Preserving the Environment and Rewarding Shareholders

by **Tim O'Brien**

McGraw-Hill, Inc.
New York   San Francisco   Washington, DC   Auckland   Bogotá
Caracas   Lisbon   London   Madrid   Mexico City   Milan
Montreal   New Delhi   San Juan   Singapore
Sydney   Tokyo   Toronto

Copyright © 2001 by McGraw-Hill, Inc. All rights reserved. Printed in the United States of America. Except as permitted under the United States Copyright Act of 1976, no part of this publication may be reproduced or distributed in any form or by any means or stored in a database or retrieval system without the prior written permission of the publisher.

ISBN 0-07-137463-9

The executive editor for this book was Paul Scicchitano. It was set in Galliard and Frutiger by Suzanne DuBose. The contributing writer was Alan Dessoff. The author has assigned all royalties from this project to the Edison Institute in Dearborn, Michigan, for the establishment of an environmental curriculum at the Henry Ford Academy of Manufacturing Science.

Printed and bound by Automated Graphic Systems, Inc.

As shown on the cover, the sun has been
incorporated into a special logo commissioned
to represent Ford's Environmental System and its
commitment to ISO 14001. The seven continents of
the world are embodied within the sun as a daily reminder
to the many thousands of Ford employees that the sum of
their actions can have a positive and profound impact on
the road to global sustainability.

> **Our Environmental Pledge**
>
> Ford Motor Company is dedicated to providing ingenious environmental solutions that will position us as a leader in the automotive industry of the 21st century.
>
> Our actions will demonstrate that we care about preserving the environment for future generations.
>
> *Ford Motor Company*

Ford's Environmental Leadership

Ford's decision to pursue ISO 14001 certification and to require the same of its business partners benefits the environment and makes good business sense. Here, we will share Ford's vision of environmental leadership.

Since its founding in 1903, Ford Motor Company has reflected Henry Ford's legacy as an industrialist and conservationist. From using agricultural products, such as soybeans in automotive components, to manufacturing alternative-fuel vehicles for more than three decades, Ford has been committed to conservation and the environment. Henry Ford's dedication to the environment is carried over to this day.

Ford Motor Company's environmental leadership commitment is based upon the belief that environmental performance can enhance financial and operational performance and support the company's vision to be the leading company for automotive products and services. Its experience with ISO 14001 is a powerful example of this philosophy.

Contents

Preface	3
Chapter 1. Overview of Ford's ISO 14001 Program	7
Chapter 2. The Ford Decision to Lead	15
Chapter 3. Implementation and the Certification Experience	23
Chapter 4. Ford's Road to Sustainability	61
Chapter 5. Supplier Program	97
Chapter 6. The Ford Retail Program	105
Chpater 7. Reflections of Senior Management	109
Chapter 8. The Future of ISO 14001 at Ford	119
Chapter 9. Ford's Approach to Implementation	125
Chapter 10. Sample Documentation	167
Ford's Registered Sites	261
Glossary	275
Acronyms	283
Index	285
About the Author	293

Preface

It takes strong management leadership to support an environmental management program (EMP) if it is to truly succeed in promoting environmental stewardship. This commitment must include a strong belief in what the system is capable of accomplishing and carry sufficient organizational commitment to mobilize resources, challenging the status quo where necessary to find smarter ways of doing things.

This is no small task in any organization, but especially one the size of Ford Motor Company. With more than 335,000 employees on six continents we produce passenger cars, trucks, engines, transmissions, castings and forgings and metal stampings of all kinds at 112 wholly owned, equity-owned and/or joint-venture plants. Our automotive brands include Aston Martin, Ford, Jaguar, Lincoln, Mazda, Mercury, Volvo and Land Rover. Our automotive-related services include Ford Credit, Quality Care, Hertz, TH!NK and Qwik-Fit.

Despite the sheer size of the institution, there never was much question about getting top management commitment once a decision was made to pursue ISO 14001 implementation in 1995. Our program had many early champions but especially Ford President and CEO Jack Nasser, former President of Ford Automotive Operations Ed Hagenlocker, Vice President of Powertrain Operations Roman Krygier, Group Vice President of Global Manufacturing Jim Padilla and Environmental and Safety Vice President Helen Petrauskas. Since stepping up to become chairman on January 1, 1999, William Clay Ford, Jr. has been one of the most ardent supporters of ISO 14001. A self-described lifelong environmentalist, Mr. Ford sees ISO 14001 both from the perspective of the world's second largest automotive manufacturer as well as from the vantage of environmental organizations. He makes no secret of the fact that he wants Ford to play a leadership role with respect to ISO 14001, both internally and among our value chain of suppliers.

Ford & ISO 14001

What's more, he regularly shares this vision in speeches and public appearances. He uses many platforms to deliver this message to audiences that might not otherwise be familiar with ISO 14001 and in so doing has set the standard for other automotive companies to follow. Perhaps his most powerful statement to date was in his letter to shareholders in the company's 1998 annual report, in which he predicted that ISO 14001 would save millions of dollars over a five-year period:

> [W]e see no conflict between business goals and social and environmental needs. I believe the distinction between a good company and a great one is this: A good company delivers excellent products and services, a great one delivers excellent products and services and strives to make the world a better place.
>
> Great companies understand that to fully meet the expectations of consumers, they must address the concerns of society. That is the only way to ensure sustainable development and growth. It also is the best way to richly reward shareholders. How does social responsibility support shareholder value?
>
> At Ford plants around the world, we are lowering emissions and reducing waste, and in the process saving money. Last year Ford became the first and only automotive company to certify its plans around the world under ISO 14001, the international environmental management standard. By meeting ISO 14001 standards, we will continue to improve our environmental performance and also reduce our costs by hundreds of millions of dollars over a five-year period.
>
> That helps consumers, investors and the community. We will create more overall value like this for all our stakeholders in the future by sharpening our consumer focus and transforming and growing our company. This report explains what we mean.
>
> I've worked for Ford Motor Company for 20 years, and served on its Board of Directors for 10 years. It's more than a job to me — it's my heritage, and my way of life. I view the company and its employees as an extended family...

At the Convergence 2000 International Congress on Transportation Electronics held in Detroit on October 18, 2000, Mr. Ford reiterated his belief that environmental programs like ISO 14001 constitute more than just corporate philanthropy:

> [A]t about the same time I became chairman, Ford Motor Company became the first automaker to certify all its plants around the world under

> *ISO 14001, the international management standard that regulates and independently audits air, water, chemical handling and recycling.*
>
> *All of our factories around the world are held to the same green standards, and now we are requiring our suppliers to meet them, too.*
>
> *Anyone who thinks there is a conflict between preserving the environment and rewarding shareholders should take a look at this program. It's saving us millions of dollars in energy, water, material and waste-handling costs. It's confirmed my strong belief that — in addition to being the right thing to do — preserving the environment is a competitive advantage and a major business opportunity...*

In the company's first Corporate Citizenship report under the Global Reporting Initiative's Sustainability Reporting Guidelines in May, 2000, Mr. Ford stated that ISO 14001 would help get his message across to financial analysts who question how corporate citizenship might build shareholder value:

> *[A]nalysts are focused on the next quarter's report and, at most, your next year's report. And the kinds of issues we've been discussing today have payoffs five, 10, 20, 50 years down the line. I do believe that I'm building a stronger Ford Motor Company for my children and my grandchildren. But that's not a theme that resonates very well with most analysts. What really helps is when you can point to things like ISO 14001, where the environmental case and the business case mesh together...*

Mr. Ford's interest in social responsibility and giving back to the community actually has its roots with Mr. Ford's great-grandfather, Henry Ford. The younger Ford, in a speech to the Los Angeles Ad Club, said his grandfather was an environmentalist long before the term was coined.

He used hydroelectric power to run many of his auto plants and his own home. He recycled wooden shipping crates into running boards, and the leftover scraps into charcoal. He experimented with soybeans as a renewable resource for making lightweight auto parts. He had a strong ethic of preserving the natural environment, as well as reducing, reusing and recycling. His vision was to create technology that complemented and benefited both mankind and the natural world. The younger Ford points to specific cost savings and resource reductions as a result of ISO 14001 that shows the company's continued commitment to environmental leadership:

> *[I]n this cynical age, it would be naive of us to expect people to take our word for it when we say we are committed to being an environmental*

leader. But I am convinced that our actions will convince them that we are sincere. We've taken a lot of actions recently to back up our words: We are the first and only automotive company to certify all of its plants around the world under ISO 14001, the international environmental management standard that regulates air, water, chemical handling and recycling. Nobody else has done this.

Disposable packing is down by 25 percent per vehicle. We've kept 17,000 tons of paint sludge out of landfills. We're also saving billions of gallons of water and huge amounts of electricity annually. All of this not only protects the environment, it saves us hundreds of millions of dollars. We are changing the definition of an industrial company. In the process we've made a real reduction in our impact on the environment worldwide. This program has been so successful that we just announced that we're going to require all our supplier plants worldwide to meet ISO 14001 standards. We're also looking for ways to take our facilities around the world to the next level of environmental friendliness...

I'd like to recognize all of the efforts of the Core Team, the Environmental Quality Office (EQO), the Environmental Management Group as well as all those responsible for implementation and certification at all the Ford facilities. Also, I want to especially acknowledge the contribution of John Connor, principal facility environmental control engineer, to this book. The Ford employees who contributed to this effort did so because we are proud of our company's leadership in this area and excited about the opportunity to share our vision and experience.

My wife, Diane, and I plan to donate all royalties from the sale of this book to the Edison Institute for the establishment of an environmental curriculum at the Henry Ford Academy of Manufacturing Science.

Overview of Ford's ISO 14001 Program

During the last decade, the implementation of quality management systems within the manufacturing sector has escalated to an all-time high. As a means of securing their competitive edge in the marketplace, industry leaders worldwide are intent on achieving customer satisfaction, and are implementing such systems as a means of demonstrating their ability to satisfy customer requirements for quality.

The foundation for much of this activity has been the internationally accepted ISO 9000 series of standards on quality. Since the ISO 9000 series was published in 1987, acceptance of the standards has been so swift and widespread that ISO 9000 registration has become a virtual prerequisite for doing business in the global marketplace, particularly in the European Union. At this writing, an estimated 343,000 third-party certifications have been issued to the standards, with users on every continent and in 150 countries. Countless other organizations have implemented ISO 9000-based systems but have elected to forgo formal certification, or registration, as is the preferred term in the United States. While demand for ISO 9000 registration remains strong from manufacturing sectors, more service organizations also are adopting the standards and pursuing registration. In recent years, hospitals, advertising agencies, military units and even schools are counted among the newest users.

Though the ISO 9000 standards are little more than a decade old, this dynamic series has literally transformed international trade practices by providing a single common registration scheme for quality that is applicable to any organization, from any industry, anywhere in the world. By harmonizing quality requirements on an international scale, ISO 9000 standards have satisfied market needs across the board, leveling the playing field for global competition. Various industries are adapting the basic framework of the standards to industry-specific interpretations like the automotive standards QS-9000 and ISO/TS 16949.

Ford & ISO 14001

Following the remarkable success of the ISO 9000 standards, the focus of international standardization in the field of management systems has expanded to address protection of the environment. ISO 14001 is the world's first internationally accepted environmental management specifications standard and, according to a recent industry study undertaken by *Quality Systems Update* and Plexus Corp., is poised to become the next great management phenomenon after ISO 9000. In late 1999, roughly 14 percent of US and Canadian respondents registered to ISO 9000 reported plans to seek ISO 14001 registration over the following 18-month period.

Ford Motor Company was the first automotive manufacturer to certify a manufacturing facility and the first to achieve certification of all facilities worldwide to the ISO 14001 standard. All of Ford's manufacturing facilities have been ISO 14001-certified by independent third parties. Ford facilities in Germany also are certified to the European Union's Eco-Management and Audit Scheme (EMAS), which has a broader scope than ISO 14001.

Ford's decision to pursue ISO 14001 certification benefits the environment and makes good business sense as well. The establishment of an environmental management system (EMS) and the discipline that goes along with it has allowed the plants to identify opportunities to reduce energy and resource use and minimize waste, resulting in significant cost savings in addition to reduced environmental impacts.

As a result of our success, Ford became the first US automaker to require ISO 14001 EMS certification of all of its suppliers with manufacturing facilities in 1999. We have found considerable value in certifying our own facilities to the ISO standard and felt that asking suppliers to obtain certification would help improve competitiveness and promote sound environmental management throughout the company's value chain.

The requirement, which applies to about 5,000 organizations worldwide, asks suppliers to certify at least one manufacturing site by the end of 2001. Also, the requirement states that all of the suppliers' manufacturing sites shipping products to Ford must be certified by July 1, 2003. We have offered support to suppliers pursuing certification, including developing and sponsoring ISO 14001 training for suppliers and trainers in the United States, United Kingdom, Germany, Australia, Mexico and Latin America.

ISO 14001 establishes universally accepted requirements for environmental management that have been adopted and sanctioned by standards bodies in most industrialized nations. While ISO 9000 registration provides assurances that companies have a system in place to control the quality of their products and services, the presence of an ISO 14001 certificate tells purchasers that companies have a general policy to address, among other things, prevention of pollution and compliance with all relevant laws and regulations. Purchasers will be assured that a company has a management system to achieve its environmental objectives and targets, and a structure to help it improve the management system through corrective and preventive actions and training. What makes ISO 14001 different from other environmental programs (EMPs) is that it promotes a systematic approach to environmental management. It is an approach that has proven to be highly valuable in the quality arena.

ISO 14001 identifies the essential set of elements that an EMS should have, but does not dictate how the system should be established. Individual organizations are responsible for deciding how to implement the system and tailor it to meet their own specific needs.

The environmental management specifications document is but one of a family of standards comprising the ISO 14000 series of standards. The series addresses everything from environmental labeling to lifecycle assessment, environmental auditing and environmental performance evaluation. Applied to an ISO 14001-based EMS, several documents in the series can provide valuable suggestions and recommendations for implementation and maintenance of your system. Some even relate to specific industries or industry sectors.

Who Created ISO 14000?

Both the ISO 9000 and ISO 14000 standards were created by the International Organization for Standardization (ISO). Based in Geneva, Switzerland, ISO is a worldwide federation of 137 national standards bodies dedicated to facilitating global trade through the creation of international standards applicable to a broad range of industry and economic sectors.

While ISO 9000 is the organization's best-known work to date, ISO's many technical committees have produced more than 13,000 standards. Prior to 1987, the organization was known primarily for its work in standardizing product characteristics to promote international trade — the speed of photographic film, thickness of bank and telephone cards, dimensions of freight containers, even universal symbols for automotive controls.

As the first ISO standards written for environmental management, ISO 14000 represents a new direction in establishing consistent, universally accepted standards, with equal relevance to companies that manufacture sophisticated components, say for passenger vehicles, and those providing overnight delivery services.

Benefits of Implementation

Implementing an ISO 14001 EMS provides the framework for an organization to manage those aspects of its operations and activities that can affect the environment. By learning to manage these aspects, harmful activities and potential liabilities are greatly reduced. To this end, ISO 14001 works well because it fosters ongoing compliance with national and international requirements.

ISO 14001:

- Establishes a high level of corporate commitment to the prevention of pollution.
- Identifies legal and regulatory requirements.
- Determines environmental aspects and significant aspects — the ways in which an organization may interact with the environment. Typical environmental aspects for a manufacturing plant include air emissions, discharges to water, odors, noise, energy use and storage and handling of hazardous material associated with an organization's activities, products and services.
- Encourages environmental planning throughout the complete lifecycle of a product, service or process.
- Establishes a process for achieving targeted environmental performance levels.
- Allocates resources and training necessary to achieve the desired level of environmental performance.
- Measures an organization's overall environmental performance against its environmental policy, objectives and targets to determine adequacy.
- Establishes an auditing and management review process for the EMS to identify opportunities for improvement.
- Establishes lines of communication with interested parties, internally and externally.
- Encourages suppliers and contractors to establish consistent environmental management techniques, thereby also providing protection against unintended negative impacts from external activities.

All of these functions work together to improve an organization's overall environmental performance.

Implementation Process

ISO 14001 is the only specification standard in the ISO 14000 series that describes the requirements for certification/registration and/or self-declaration of an organization's EMS. The ISO 14001 document defines the requirements that an organization must incorporate into its EMS to meet internationally recognized standards for sound environmental performance.

To achieve ISO 14001 certification, a facility must identify all of its environmental aspects. The next step is to identify which of these aspects are "significant." A significant aspect, for example, may be one that is regulated by a government agency, uses a material that is toxic or consumes natural resources. Objectives and targets must then be established for significant aspects. An objective is a general statement of an overall environmental goal that the facility sets out to achieve, (e.g., reduce air emissions). A target is a detailed performance requirement that is set in order to achieve that objective (e.g., reduce emissions of volatile organic compounds [VOC] by 10 percent by 2001).

The result of the analysis is a structured review of the aspects a facility must manage, procedures for their management and objectives and performance targets — similar to the management of any significant business issue. A significant feature of the certification process is the employee engagement that is necessary for its success. It is not a "top-down" mandate from senior management that filters down to all employees, but a grassroots "bottom-up" commitment to environmental stewardship. Every employee in the manufacturing facility is responsible for knowing the plant's environmental policy and implementing it. At Ford, we brainstormed some innovative methods to raise employee awareness, including pocket guides, videos and even a video game called "ISO Mania" (see page 57).

Once a facility has gone through the process and established its EMS, it can then either self-certify or obtain certification through an independent third party. After the initial certification, the facilities go through an annual or semiannual reevaluation (surveillance audit). During the evaluation process, the third party audits the facility's performance against its environmental policy, objectives and targets.

When a company can demonstrate that its EMS conforms to ISO 14001, it is eligible to apply for certification/registration. With that distinction, a company earns credibility as having an EMS that satisfies universally recognized requirements for environmental management. It is this level of recognition that opens doors toward a significant competitive advantage in the global marketplace.

Registration to ISO 14001:

- Promotes continuous improvement.
- Maintains flexibility for product sourcing to export markets or customers who may make registration a condition of purchase.
- Positions an organization to take full advantage of any regulatory flexibility that may develop.
- Enhances an organization's image and competitiveness.
- Establishes a common EMS for manufacturing facilities with multiple sites.

The standard itself does not establish absolute requirements for environmental performance beyond an organization's commitment to achieve conformance with applicable legislation and regulations and to continually improve its EMS. The standard does, however, mandate that you meet the requirements of your own environmental policy, objectives and targets.

The standard applies to those environmental aspects that an organization can control and can be expected to influence. It contains only those requirements that can be objectively audited for registration and/or self-declaration purposes.

The ISO 14001 standard is applicable to any organization wanting to:

- Implement, maintain and improve an EMS.
- Assure itself of its conformance with its stated environmental policy.
- Demonstrate such conformance to others.
- Seek certification/registration of its EMS by an external organization and/or make a self-determination and declaration of its conformance with the standard.

The extent to which the standard is applied is dependent on such factors as an organization's environmental policy, the nature of its activities and the condition in which it operates.

ISO 14001 includes these elements:

- Environmental Policy — Creating an environmental policy for the organization that states its overall environmental goals.
- Planning — Identifying environmental aspects, legal and other requirements and establishing environmental objectives and targets.
- Implementation and Operation — Establishing and/or conforming to environmental training requirements, communication processes, documentation and document control, environmental operational controls, materials management, regulatory compliance, emergency preparedness and emergency response procedures.
- Checking and Corrective Actions — Providing for monitoring and measuring environmental aspects, identifying nonconformance and procedures for corrective and preventive actions.
- Management Review.

While the language in ISO 14001 is fairly straightforward, implementing organizations should keep the following in mind:

- Mandatory requirements are identified by such words as "shall," "must" or "is required."

- Recommendations are identified by such words as "should," "is suggested" or "it is recommended."
- Although references to procedures appear in 14 places in the standard, documented procedures are required in only three places.
- Aside from the obvious word "record," words such as "identify," "document" and "documentation" indicate the need to create a record.
- Nonprescriptive words are words such as "appropriate," "suitable" or "where necessary" that allow for flexibility in their interpretation. Such words allow organizations to adapt portions of the standard to suit their own business needs and drivers.

2 The Ford Decision to Lead

William Clay Ford, Jr.'s basic philosophy is that there is no inherent conflict between doing well environmentally and doing well as a business. We can accomplish both at the same time, the chairman reasons, and indeed, each complements the other. We have demonstrated repeatedly, much to our satisfaction, that there is a synergy of interest between the ISO program and our business agenda. Our aspiration is that, over time, we will break down the habit of characterizing somebody as either an environmentalist or a business person and come up with another term that combines the two — perhaps a "responsible" person.

We chose to pursue a strategy of ISO 14001 registration for all our plants worldwide even before the standard was published in September, 1996. It was a draft international standard (DIS) when we made our decision to proceed. The standard itself is a brief document. But when we set out to apply it on the scale we envisioned for our global company, in what were then 140 enormously complex manufacturing facilities in 26 countries in different parts of the world, we knew that we would encounter many issues that we had not foreseen. We were doing something that no other organization of our scale had done.

So, going through the process required considerable invention on our part and by our registrars. Actually, we made some of it up as we plowed our way through uncharted waters. We knew where we wanted to go, but it was not clear how we were going to get there or what all the implications were of what we were doing.

Historically, Ford Motor Company has been an analytical company, not unlike other successful businesses. That means that before we undertook a strategic initiative, we analyzed it thoroughly. Before we made a decision, we wanted to understand each and every issue that we were about to face and know where that issue would take us.

Ford & ISO 14001

> "Corporate citizenship is one of our five sources of competitive advantage, and we cannot be a truly great company without helping to develop great communities."
>
> —Jacques A. Nasser
> President and CEO, Ford Motor Co.
> January 22, 1999

In some ways, that strategy of deliberate analysis no longer can serve us as well as it once did. Times are different and we see many signs of that now in the company, on environmental matters and in other areas. The fact is, if we want to be a leader in a particular area, we can't spend five years thinking about it before we act. We have to follow our basic instincts and to some extent take a leap of faith.

That was very much the case with ISO 14001. We adopted the standard and just took off and ran with it and trusted that we were going in the right direction. Ultimately, of course, it turned out that we were.

We chose to certify to ISO 14001 for three key reasons:

- The mid to late 1990s was a period of transition at Ford as we moved from a multinational company to a global company.
- To support this globalization, there was a need to be consistent in our approach to environmental issues.
- We saw a need to provide support to Ford corporate strategies such as corporate citizenship and employee empowerment.

Globalization

In 1994 we were going through "Ford 2000," the company's strategic decision to globalize its business. Before that time, Ford Motor Company essentially was a loose affiliation of national companies — Ford in the United States, Ford in Europe and so forth. They were related from a legal standpoint, but they operated more or less independently of each other.

Ford decided in 1994 that this strategy just wasn't going to work any more. The world was becoming a smaller place; "globalization" was the new word. The demands of business — our business — required us to operate globally. So we reorganized and became a global company.

In that process, we brought together, for the first time in the same organization, the environmental professionals of what had been the national Ford companies around the world. They were asked to sit down together and spend some time understanding one another's issues and where they saw their mutual environmental interests going.

Our European colleagues brought up something called "environmental management systems." At the time, two EMS models were in place: in Great Britain, BS 7750, developed by the British Standards Institution (BSI); and EMAS, which was very popular in Germany. ISO 14001 was just being developed by ISO, but as we continued our series of meetings to discuss environmental issues, our European colleagues continued talking about it.

As Americans, we thought we had it all figured out, but we listened politely to our European colleagues anyway. Then one day, one fellow said something that really caught my attention. He said, "You know, some of our major fleet purchasers are beginning to ask about our EMS certification status as part of fleet bids; they're not conditioning bids on certification yet, but they're beginning to ask about it."

If that didn't wake us up, nothing would have done it. In the automotive business, the fleet business — selling large numbers of vehicles to governmental or private-

Why ISO 14001 Certification?

- Transition from a multinational company to a global company — Ford 2000

- Desire for consistent global systems including environmental systems

- Supports Ford strategies: corporate citizenship, empowerment (delegated responsibility)

sector purchasers — is a huge element. And now we learned that some of the major governmental fleet purchasers in Britain were beginning to ask about our registration status to ISO 14001 or another EMS.

It became evident to us at that point that our decisions on adopting an EMS would be important from a business perspective as well as from an environmental perspective; it was going to be necessary for us to compete effectively on a global scale. That was reinforced when we saw that even some emerging countries were beginning to use ISO 14001 almost as a de facto regulatory program. They didn't have decades of regulatory history, as we do in the United States; they just started picking up ISO 14001 and running with it.

Finally, the light bulb came on for us here in the United States, and we identified ISO 14001 as something in which we needed to be engaged. Then, as we began to explore it we also began to understand our new global business responsibilities. We realized that not only was it something in which we *needed* to be engaged; it was something in which we *wanted* to be engaged.

Consistency

One important factor in the recognition process was that the environmental requirements for our then 140 major manufacturing facilities in 26 countries (some of them have since been spun off into a new company) were highly localized. They addressed the same subjects — water discharges, air quality, solid waste disposal and so forth — but they applied mostly on a localized basis. That was the case even here at home. An extreme example was in Wayne, Michigan, where two of our plants — the Michigan Truck Plant and the Wayne Assembly Plant — are located next to each other. But to some extent, each had different environmental requirements and different management teams that addressed them.

Multiply that for a corporation of our size and it meant that we had 140 plants that essentially were managing the same environmental issues 140 different ways. That meant we probably had varying levels of performance and maybe even some compliance concerns. That was not where we wanted to be.

So one of the things that globalization brought to our attention as we looked at ISO 14001 was that the standard offered us a terrific opportunity to put in place a process that established a level of consistency across the company. That doesn't mean that we do everything exactly the same way everywhere. It means that we have the same disciplined, analytical approach to determining what our environmental issues are and what our approach to managing those issues should be. It provides a level of assurance that environmental issues are looked at in a disciplined, thoughtful way at every Ford plant around the world.

We did not have that assurance before. On the contrary, we were sure that with 140 plants in 26 countries, there probably were places on any given day where environmental issues were not being considered in a disciplined, thoughtful way.

The external registration infrastructure, that to a large extent already had been developed for ISO 9000, strengthened the assurance that we are looking at issues thoroughly and thoughtfully. Having an outside auditor come in periodically helps to maintain the discipline of the ISO process.

It also helps us from a resource standpoint. The Ford Environmental Quality Office (EQO) is comprised of about 70 people scattered around the world. That means we cannot be global police officers. We cannot run around to all Ford plants on a daily basis to be sure they are doing what they are supposed to be doing.

I don't mean to suggest that plants try to avoid their environmental requirements. That's not in human nature. People don't want to do bad things environmentally. But in the course of a day's work, they might shift their attention elsewhere as they deal with a variety of competing issues. The ISO auditing process helps bring them back into focus.

So those are the two global realities we recognized in 1995: that the ISO 14001 program, although not well recognized in the United States at the time, was becoming well recognized and accepted in almost all other parts of the world, particularly in Japan and Germany; and that in our particular corporate circumstance, ISO 14001 gave us an opportunity to instill a common environmental approach across a geographically and operationally disparate organization.

Corporate Strategies

We did not make the decision to adopt ISO 14001 based on financial factors. We certainly saw that there might be customers out there — fleet purchasers and others — who would like our plants to be registered to the standard, and so registration might enhance business opportunities for us. Also, we certainly believed that we could achieve some operational savings from the disciplines that ISO 14001 imposed. Ultimately, however, we decided that whether or not we proceeded that way would not be determined by a financial analysis.

Rather, it was an operating discipline that drove our decision and, to some extent, a matter of our reputation as a company. We thought it would mean something to be the first company in our industry — and the first company of our scale in any industry — to go this route. If you're interested in the reputational aspects of leadership, coming in second or third doesn't quite cut it. People might remember the name of the gold medal winner, and perhaps the silver, from an Olympic event, but virtually no one remembers who won the bronze. We thought it was important to be the gold medal winner in this instance. We also felt that it was important that this not be a top-down decision from senior executive ranks, but rather a bottom-up initiative from the grassroots of the company. If you have a strong enough force of personality or organization, you can compel people to do things without taking the time to explain to them why they should. That often happens in top-down initiatives. The problem is, it doesn't lead to effective implementation of a program.

So we took our time, through most of 1995, to go around to the operating committee of every Ford business organization that would be affected by this decision and make the case to them explaining why we thought they should want to do this. Everybody agreed. Some agreed because they really believed it and were strong environmental advocates. There probably were some who agreed because they figured, "How can you disagree on an environmental program?" And there may have been some people who agreed even though they didn't really understand what it was they were agreeing to. The important point is that we got everybody to agree.

Ed Hagenlocker, who was president of Ford Automotive Operations (FAO) at the time, signed a letter at the end of 1995 committing the company to conclude its registration of all plants worldwide by the end of 1998. How did we settle on 1998? We pulled the date out of the air. Some people who had been involved in the program said it was a reasonable target date. Also, if we wanted to be first, we had to have a deadline. So we picked the end of 1998.

The letter read as follows:

> *There is an increasing global demand for companies to demonstrate their commitment to the environment by obtaining independent certification to an internationally recognized environmental management system standard known as ISO 14000. To meet these business needs, FAO will pursue ISO 14000 Environmental Management System certification in a phased program commencing in 1996; expected completion will be by year-end 1998.*
>
> *The ISO 14000 certification process involves documenting and managing business operation systems with an emphasis on environmental matters. Manufacturing Operations are primarily affected, but related Product Development, Purchasing and other processes will be included in this initiative.*
>
> *FAO will implement ISO 14000 in an integrated manner, with other key initiatives such as ISO 9000, Quality Operating Systems and the Ford production system, in support of the company's Ford 2000 strategies.*

Mr. Hagenlocker, like just about everyone else at Ford Motor Company at the time, didn't know much at all about what ISO 14001 was, in substance or detail. But he knew it was an environmental program. And as part of Ford 2000, the company had just articulated a corporate strategy that contained several components. One was corporate citizenship, and environmental responsibility was a key element of that. So Mr. Hagenlocker sensed that it was the right thing to do. He agreed, intuitively.

Intuition is an important characteristic. There's a sense as you get involved in the program that you're doing the right thing. But in 1995, the Ford decision to lead was largely intuitive. Mr. Hagenlocker signed the letter, and the second largest automotive company in the world was committed for better or worse.

3 Implementation and the Certification Experience

Now that we had a letter from Mr. Hagenlocker authorizing us to proceed and committing us to have all Ford plants registered to ISO 14001 by the end of 1998, what were we supposed to do next? How were we going to accomplish this at more than 140 plants in 26 countries that didn't even speak the same language? English is the basic language of Ford Motor Company, but we also had plants in parts of the world where the native language was Spanish, German, Chinese, Vietnamese or something else.

We recognized the need for a common, disciplined approach to environmental management at all our manufacturing facilities. To address this need, we decided to develop and implement a system designed to address the requirements of ISO 14001 as well as existing environmental programs including regulatory compliance assurance, waste minimization/pollution prevention, energy management and others.

Corporate Environmental Policy

Our approach was based on maintaining and reinforcing the environmental requirements as stated in Ford's Corporate Environmental Policy Letter No. 17, issued August 28, 1996, on the subject of protecting health and the environment:

> *Sustainable economic development is important to the future welfare of the company, as well as to that of society in general. To be sustainable, economic development must provide for protection of human health and the world's environmental resource base. It is Ford's policy that its operations, products and services accomplish their functions in a manner that provides responsibly for protection of health and the environment.*

Ford & ISO 14001

Ford is committed to meeting regulatory requirements that apply to its businesses. With respect to health and environmental concerns, regulatory compliance represents a minimum. When necessary and appropriate, we establish and comply with standards of our own, which may go beyond legal mandates. In seeking appropriate ways to protect health or the environment, the issue of cost alone does not preclude consideration of possible alternatives, and priorities are based on achieving the greatest anticipated practical benefit while striving for continuous improvement.

Ford's policy of responsibly protecting health and the environment is based on the following principles:

Protection of health and the environment is an important consideration in business decisions. Consideration of potential health and environmental effects — as well as present and future regulatory requirements — is an early, integral part of the planning process. Company products, services, processes and facilities are planned and operated to incorporate objectives and targets which are periodically reviewed so as to minimize, to the extent practical, the creation of waste, pollution and any adverse impact on health or the environment.

Protection of health and the environment is a companywide responsibility. Management of each activity is expected to accept this responsibility as an important priority and to commit the necessary resources. Employees at all levels are expected to carry out this responsibility within the context of their particular assignments and to cooperate in company efforts.

The adoption and enforcement of responsible, effective and sound laws, regulations, policies and practices protecting health and the environment are in the company's interest. Accordingly, we participate constructively with government officials, interested private organizations and concerned members of the general public toward these ends. Likewise, it is in our interest to provide timely and accurate information to our various publics on environmental matters involving the company.

What to call the global EMS we were about to develop was a key decision to be made. ISO already was a familiar term within the Ford Motor Company in terms of ISO 9000, the quality management system. We didn't want the Ford environmental system to be viewed as another ISO system. We decided it was Ford's environmental system, and that was what it was named initially, with the possessive "Ford's." But we ultimately dropped the possessive part and it became the Ford Environmental System (FES).

We wanted people throughout the company to connect with it and not consider it

Chapter 3

Ford's Environmental System

Common global EMS implemented at all company manufacturing facilities by the end of 1998:

- Strives for continuous improvement
- Establishes metrics to measure performance
- Captures requirements of ISO 14001

---

to be only a program of Ford headquarters. We wanted to show that there was ownership that went beyond ISO and that the system containted things that were important to Ford.

Core Team

To accomplish the goal of developing one common EMS, we formed a global Core Team early in 1996. The 12 to 20 members of the Core Team — the number varied throughout the process — were experienced with the implementation of management systems and certification activities. They represented:

- Environmental Quality Office (EQO) — the corporate environmental staff with offices in the United States, Europe, Canada and Latin America.
- Powertrain Operations — casting, engine and transmission.
- Visteon — electronics, fuel systems, plastics, air conditioning, etc.
- Office of the General Counsel — legal support on environmental issues.
- Quality — provide the experience of ISO 9000 implementation.

The Core Team's job was to read the new ISO 14001 draft, interpret it and put it into a context that we could use in every one of our plants worldwide. Some of the main goals of the team were to design a system that:

- Supported corporate environmental goals and objectives.
- Integrated existing policies, programs and practices.
- Satisfied the requirements of ISO 14001.
- Allowed flexibility, giving each plant the latitude to adapt the system to meet its own particular needs.

Global Core Team Formed
First Quarter 1996

Twelve to 20 members representing:
- Environmental Quality Office (US, Europe, Canada, Mexico/SA)
- Vehicle Operations
- Visteon
- Office of General Council
- Quality

We believed that by maintaining conformance to ISO 14001, the FES would carry greater credibility and recognition as a system that met standards for environmental management that were upheld on an international basis. This recognition, in turn, would open doors to improved competitive advantage through Ford's global marketplace.

In a key move, members of the Core Team were trained together as ISO 14001 lead auditors. That training, completed by the summer of 1996, served to jump-start team members on at least understanding what the new standard — still a DIS and not yet in final form — was all about. Everyone on the team had different opinions about what it meant, and each organization in the company that was represented on the team had operated differently over the years. For example, everyone had a different way of reviewing projects and performing other business functions.

Core Procedures

The Core Team wasn't able to resolve all the differences with respect to some business practices, because different ways of doing things made sense to different business units. So the team had to craft procedures that would allow units to operate in a way that continued to make sense to them. They had to provide structure, but also some flexibility. We wanted to tell plants what they needed to do but not necessarily how to do it — a blend of "do it this way" and "figure it out for yourself." It was a difficult challenge.

In intensive meetings in our Dearborn headquarters, the Core Team developed a global EMS consisting of 17 corporate-level core procedures. They became the main vehicle that Ford utilized in its plan to harmonize environmental management practices among all our manufacturing facilities worldwide.

The core procedures consisted of individual procedures intended to instill consistent environmental management practices among all Ford operations worldwide by defining how to satisfy the requirements of ISO 14001.

As an international standard, ISO 14001 is intentionally generic in its language so that it may be applied to any organization, from any industry, anywhere in the world. The subjective language of the standard allowed Ford, as an individual company, to interpret how the standard's requirements should be applied to its own unique operations.

Ford's core procedures also were designed to give individual plants a best fit in adapting the requirements to their own activities and needs. The core procedures were intended to be used as a basis for the creation of facility-specific procedures for each plant. We tried to provide guidance to plants without being too prescriptive. We walked a fine line, trying to provide enough guidance without stifling a plant's creativity.

While we were flexible in some areas, we were inflexible in others. Again, our goal was a common approach. If we moved a plant manager from Europe to Asia Pacific, we wanted that manager to be able to walk into the new plant and find exactly the same EMS and immediately be able to understand it.

Ford's ISO 14001 Program

Second quarter 1996: Began system development

Third quarter 1996: Developed core procedures and implementation tools

Third and fourth quarter 1996: Launch phase at two European sites, five North American sites

1997-1998: Launch and implementation at more than 140 manufacturing facilities

The following is a brief description of each core procedure that was integrated into each plant's own site-specific environmental procedures:

1. Creating, Issuing, Numbering and Controlling Environmental System Documents, Regulatory Communiqués, Procedures, Standards and Guidelines.

Specifies requirements and guidelines for amending and creating EMS documentation, including formatting guidelines.

2. Environmental Aspects and Significant Environmental Aspects and Establishing Environmental Objectives and Targets.

Establishes a general procedure for identifying the environmental aspects and significant environmental aspects associated with a facility's activities, products and services that it can manage, control or influence. Includes development of objectives and targets and EMPs.

3. Internal Environmental System Audits.

Establishes criteria for planning and carrying out internal environmental system audits, including the assignment of responsibility and the frequency at which these audits should be scheduled.

4. Corrective and Preventive Action.

Defines the responsibilities and actions for applying corrective and preventive actions.

5. Management Review.

Provides general requirements for conducting management reviews, including how often facility management should review the EMS and who should participate.

6. Environmental Emergency Planning and Response, Incident Response and Corrective Action.

Establishes the mechanism for preparing and maintaining emergency plans and dealing with emergencies involving potential environmental spills/releases and the taking of corrective actions. Also defines the mechanism for responding to and reporting environmental incidents.

7. Environmental Regulations and Other Requirements, Obtaining and Maintaining Information.

Defines the major elements required for maintaining current environmental regulations and company policies and other environmental requirements against which each facility must comply.

8. Environmental Regulatory Compliance Assurance Program.

Defines the major elements required for implementing an Internal Environmental Regulatory Compliance Assessment Program.

9. Environmental Review of All Projects.

Defines general criteria for evaluating and planning for the environmental implications of new projects in order to assure that appropriate consideration is given to the environmental aspects prior to granting project approval and funding.

10. Agency Approvals.

Describes corporate requirements for securing approval from regulatory agencies for processes affecting facility air emissions, waste management, water discharges and other environmental approvals.

11. Prevention of Pollution/Waste Minimization.

Establishes a worldwide, coordinated company procedure for implementing and documenting a site-specific prevention of pollution/waste minimization program.

12. External Communications.

Defines how communications from the public and other interested parties concerning the environmental aspects of a facility should be received, documented and responded to, including communications with regulatory agencies.

13. Contractor Management.

Defines corporate requirements for managing the environmental aspects of contractors and their subcontractors.

14. Document and Data Control.

Defines responsibilities and actions for providing assurance that documents, data and records are controlled, including the need to make relevant documents available at the locations where they are needed.

15. Records Maintenance.

Defines responsibilities and actions for assuring that records are properly retained and accessible.

16. Materials Management.

Establishes corporate requirements for identifying and monitoring materials and chemical substances that may be of regulatory significance.

17. Energy Management Efficiency.

Defines corporate requirements for implementing an Energy Management Efficiency program at a Ford facility, including information and reporting requirements.

The Core Team also laid out these generic steps for implementation at each plant:

- Obtain management commitment.
- Establish and train a Cross-Functional Team (CFT).
- Identify aspects and their significance.
- Create an environmental policy.
- Identify organizational responsibilities.
- Provide awareness training.
- Complete work procedures and work instructions.
- Provide training on procedures and work instructions.
- Conduct internal audits.
- Conduct a second-party review.
- Conduct a registration audit.

The Core Team developed an implementation flow chart and sample project schedule that described the path for implementing the FES and gaining ISO 14001 registration (see Figure I, pages 58-59). The flow chart was based on a 10-month schedule of activities from management commitment to final certification. Stars indicate management review, to underscore the importance of management in the process.

The Core Team also developed the tools to implement the program in individual plants. We knew that each plant would need materials to deliver the message of the FES to its own people. From Ford's experience in implementing ISO 9000, we learned a valuable lesson.

Managers of the ISO 9000 implementation allowed each plant to develop its own

Generic Implementation Steps

- Get management commitment
- Establish/train CFT
- Identify aspects/ significance
- Create environmental policy
- Identify organizational responsibilities
- Conduct awareness training
- Complete procedures/ work instructions
- Conduct procedure & work instruction training
- Perform internal audits
- Conduct second-party review
- Complete registration audit

---

materials. The cost proved prohibitive and this approach did not ensure consistency in delivery of the message. For the FES, the Core Team decided to create one standard package of materials.

Obtain Management Commitment

The first step in beginning implementation at each plant was to gain the commitment of management at that plant to subscribe to the principles of the FES and ISO 14001. A directive from top management would provide the needed push for lower-level managers. Obtaining management commitment was easy at some plants and difficult at others. Initially, EQO and Division Staff conducted an Operating Committee meeting with a plant's senior management team to explain the principles behind the new FES and the company's plans to streamline the environmental management activities of all Ford plants worldwide.

Environmental Management Representative

After securing the commitment of senior management, an Environmental Management Representative (EMR) was appointed at each facility to oversee and guide all aspects of the project. The EMR was responsible for attaining the cooperation of other plant functions and departmental managers in implementing the EMS and securing the ongoing maintenance of the system. Specifically, the EMR's responsibilities were to:

- Ensure that EMS requirements were established, implemented and maintained.
- Report on the performance of the EMS to senior plant management for review purposes and as a basis for making improvements to the EMS.

For large or complex organizations, additional individuals were designated to share the responsibilities of the EMR.

Cross-Functional Team

To assist the EMR(s) with implementation activities, a CFT also was established at each facility, with representatives from key departments and functions. We believed that such an arrangement would instill cooperation and shared responsibility across departmental and functional lines. The main responsibilities of the CFT were to assist the EMR(s) with the development of:

- An implementation plan and timeline for the facility.
- Facility-specific procedures.
- Roles, responsibilities and authorities for the EMS.

In forming the CFT at each plant, we found it effective to align team members with significant aspects in their areas of responsibility. For example, someone from the wastewater treatment plant was assigned responsibility for wastewater. In some instances, facilities could assign a system element of ISO 14001 — documents, for example — to different team members. So each CFT member was responsible for an element of the standard as well as the significant aspect that was their area of

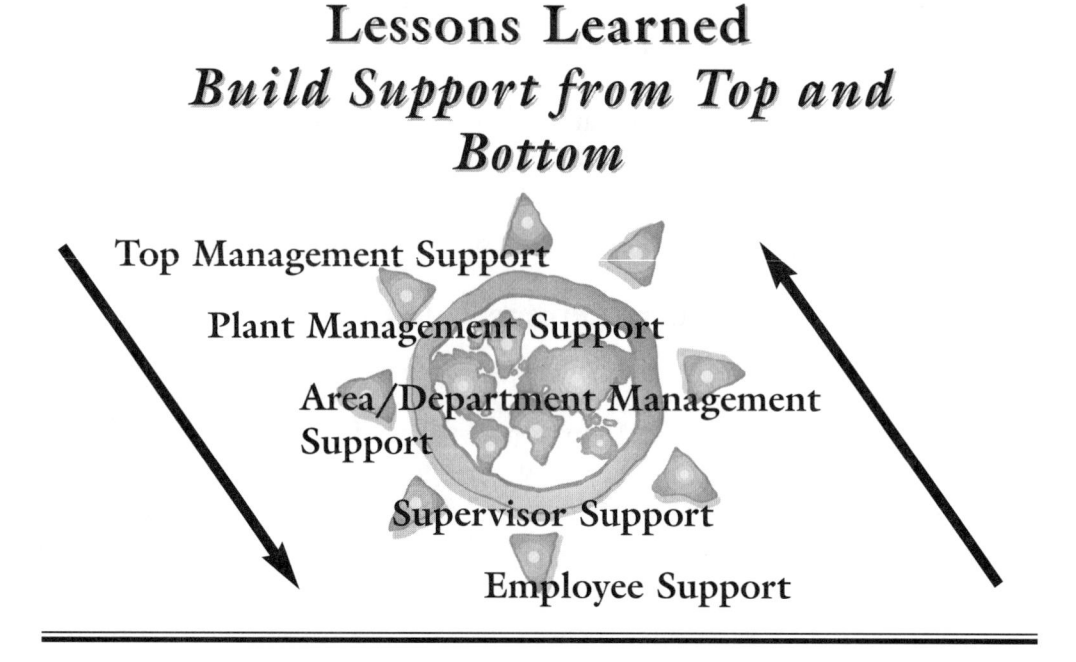

Lessons Learned
Build Support from Top and Bottom

Top Management Support

Plant Management Support

Area/Department Management Support

Supervisor Support

Employee Support

responsibility. There was flexibility to allow for different approaches.

Forming the CFTs provided some valuable lessons. If you go to a plant and say, "Ok paint area, I need a guy from your area to come to a meeting once a week for 10 months," who do you think you're going to get? They usually assigned somebody they thought they could do without for a couple of hours a day. At the beginning, some team members weren't too happy about it themselves. "Why did I get this assignment?" they grumbled.

Then, a curious thing happened. They began to realize that they could make a real difference. They began to feel that they were indeed part of the program, and at the end, they would receive recognition for their part in the program. They loved it. They came out of the process proud of what they had accomplished and with a wholly different attitude.

Implementation Training

Initially, CFT members had to receive appropriate training on the ISO 14000 standards, EMSs and implementation techniques. Members participated in training workshops, sponsored by EQO, to become knowledgeable about:

- The components of the FES.
- The concepts, requirements and terms of ISO 14001.
- What implementation of such a system entails.

EMS Implementation Plan

Once a general working order was established, the first vital task of the CFT was to develop an EMS implementation plan for its facility. To create the plan, the CFT referred to the flow chart developed by the global Core Team. After adapting the flow chart to the facility's specific needs, the CFT had to determine how each implementation activity was to be accomplished by developing a strategic plan of action. Implementation plans answered questions such as:

- How will a particular task/requirement be met?
- How much effort will be involved?
- What decisions need to be made and who should provide input?
- What resources will be required (materials, personnel, professional consultation, etc.)?
- Who will be responsible for ensuring that the task is completed according to plan?

Identifying Environmental Aspects

After finalizing the implementation plan, the CFT conducted a facilitywide evaluation of all the plant's environmental aspects — those elements of a plant's activities, products or services that can interact with the environment. Interactions can result in positive (e.g., paper recycling) or negative (e.g., water depletion) impacts on the environment.

The impact of Ford's operations and products on the environment is significant. These include consumption of nonrenewable resources and generation of waste and emissions to the land, air and water. Although Ford does not have a complete inventory of its environmental impacts, it has tracked and reported progress on a number of key environmental, health and safety indicators.

Environmental Regulations and Other Requirements

Along with the identification of environmental aspects associated with a plant's activities, products and services, the CFT also reviewed all legal and other requirements applicable to the facility. Not everyone on a plant's CFT was an environmental expert, at least at the beginning, but we wanted everyone to have an understanding of whether an aspect was regulated or not.

Maintaining regulatory compliance plays a large role in effectively managing the environmental impacts of a plant's operations. Thus, facilities needed to be fully aware of their legal obligations and requirements for environmental protection.

Legal requirements include county, regional, federal, state, provincial and local environmental laws and regulations, operating permits, licenses, ordinances, authorizations, consent orders, insurance policies, contractual requirements, memorandums of agreement and other such items.

The "other" requirements refer to industry associations, commitments made to the public, company directives, policy requirements, etc.

It also was crucial for facilities to have a system in place for identifying and accessing applicable requirements. A procedure established for that purpose in each plant included a system for obtaining and maintaining current environmental regulations. It also included a system for tracking changes and communicating those changes to employees accordingly.

Many Ford facilities maintain a master list of all laws and regulations pertaining to their operations. The plant EMR or designated environmental engineer keeps a list of local regulations and ordinances. The Ford EQO maintains current regulations at national, state, provincial and regional levels for company locations worldwide.

Significant Environmental Aspects

Once all environmental aspects were identified, the CFT had to conduct an extensive evaluation against legal requirements and other criteria to determine which activities, products or services were the most important to manage. ISO 14001 identifies these environmental aspects as "significant aspects." The standard requires that an EMS address them as priority items. They should form the basis for establishing process and management controls, environmental improvement programs, investigations and studies.

The Ford EQO and Operations/Divisions required facilities to maintain lists of all identified environmental aspects and significant aspects. Those lists were to be reviewed by the CFT semiannually and whenever a new or changed process or activity was introduced and once a year during management review. For most significant aspects that were identified, a plant was to establish objectives and targets designed to:

- Control or manage the activity.
- Improve the activity.
- Study the activity.

One of the most difficult and time-consuming exercises for the CFT in each plant was understanding and developing their lists of aspects, determining the significance of the aspects and developing objectives and targets. Although ISO 14001 does not require objectives and targets to be developed for each significant aspect, the Core Team agreed that developing them anyway would reduce inconsistencies and reinforce a plant's commitment to continual improvement.

We gave a blank copy of a form (see Chapter 10 for sample forms) to each CFT member and had them interview people in different departments and say, for example, "We think you have water usage in here," and then verify the sources of the water. We collected all of these forms and put them through a filtering process to determine what aspects were significant. That way, we came up with a list of the significant aspects in the plant.

To ensure consistency when identifying environmental aspects, the Core Team developed a system-level procedure to address aspects, objectives and targets and management programs. General aspect categories included:

- Air emissions
- Liquid and solid waste

- Stormwater discharges
- Storage tanks
- Wastewater discharge
- Energy usage
- Water usage
- Material usage
- Noise
- Natural environment
- Odor
- Land conditions

The Core Team included in the aspects procedure specify minimum criteria for evaluating the significance of aspects. The procedure stated in part that environmental aspects may be considered significant when:

- Subject to relevant legislation, regulation, permit requirements and/or other requirements.
- Subject to environmental regulations or other requirements that specify controls and conditions.
- Information must be provided to outside authorities.
- Subject or potentially subject to periodic inspections or enforcement by authorities.
- Aspects are addressed in the facility business plan.
- Subject to a potential accidental release (liquid or gas) that is regulated or that could be of sufficient quantity to cause environmental concern.
- Subject to high environmental loading due to one or more of the following:

    —Toxicity.
    —Ford restricted substance standard.
    —Volumes and masses of releases.
    —Consumption of renewable and nonrenewable resources.
    —Frequency of releases.
    —Severity of actual or potential impacts.

The significant aspect identification process was based on:

- Identifying similar aspects that could be found in all or most departments within the plant.
- Identifying aspects specific to a department or location.
- Reviewing the facility list of legal and other requirements.

In determining the significance of a plant's environmental aspects, the CFT in each plant also established an evaluation system based on the corporate approach. It addressed those aspects that were under the control of the facility and those that were under the influence of the facility. The evaluation system attempted to answer key questions such as:

- What is the scale of the impact?
- What is the severity of the impact?
- What is the probability of occurrence?
- What is the duration of impact?
- Does the impact pose any potential regulatory or legal concerns?
- What costs are associated with changing the impact?
- What are the concerns of interested parties?

Independent of criteria the CFT set in determining the significance of an environmental aspect, any activity having one or more of the following characteristics was more than likely to be categorized as significant:

- Regulated by permits, certificates or licenses.
- Having the potential to cause accidental releases (e.g., gases and liquids).
- Subject to environmental regulations specifying controls and conditions.
- Tracked by authorities (e.g., reporting information/data).
- Subject to periodic inspections or enforcement by authority agencies.
- Associated with energy consumption.
- Part of a company business plan or initiative.
- Having a high environmental toxicity or load.
- Presenting actual or potential environmental impacts.

Figure II. Aspects: Environmental Interactions

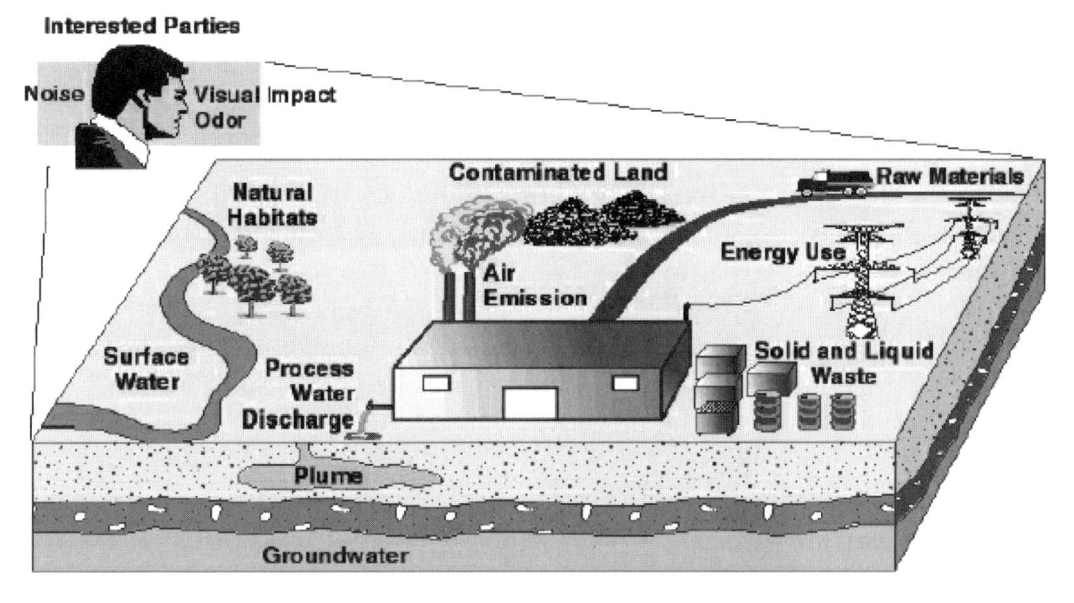

Figure III. Aspects & Significance, Filtered Approach

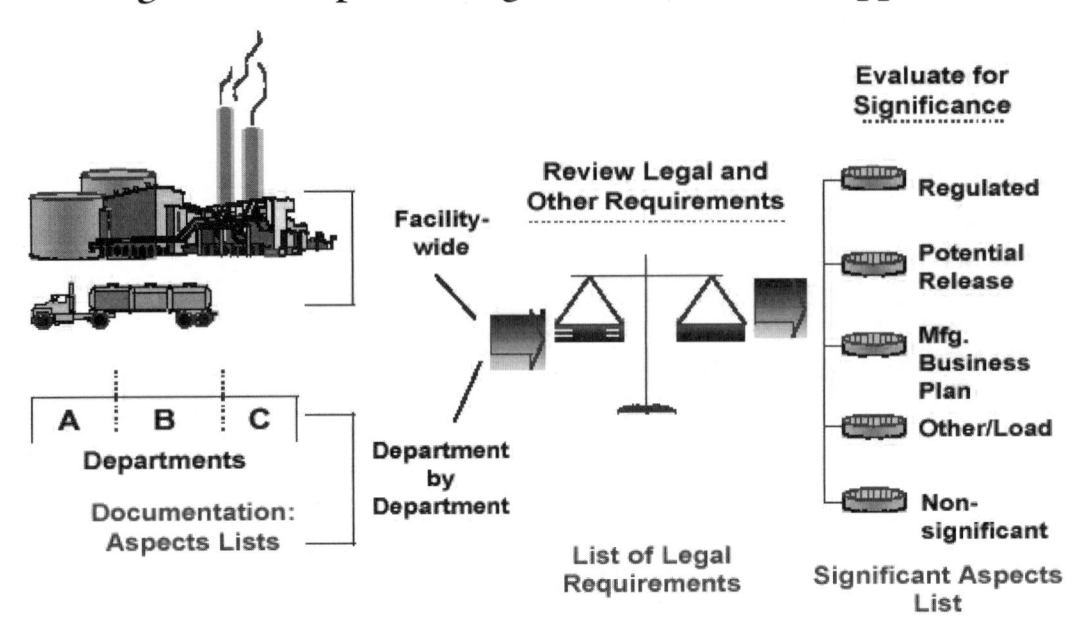

Implementation training provided detailed examples of typical aspects and their interaction with the environment, or impacts (see Figure II, page 37). To visualize the requirements of the procedure and to provide a simplified approach to documenting significant aspects, implementation training also included a "filtered approach" diagram (see Figure III, page 38). Using this approach, the CFT was provided details and examples to assist with determining significant aspects in its plant.

Objectives and Targets

The core procedures required the CFT to establish and maintain environmental objectives and targets for all significant aspects (see Figure IV, page 40).

Objectives and targets are overall environmental goals established at each relevant function and level within a plant. They answer the question, "What do we want to accomplish?"

For each objective that was set, at least one environmental target was to be established. Where practicable, targets were to be expressed in terms of quantity, with a time frame set for achieving the objective.

The setting of environmental objectives and targets represented the turning point of the implementation process. It was the phase where specific plans for improved environmental performance were set into motion.

The core procedures required the CFT to place objectives and targets in one of three categories: control, improve or study. The procedures required the CFT to consider the following when establishing objectives and targets:

- Environmental, legal and other requirements.
- Technological options.
- Financial, operational and business requirements.
- Views of interested parties.
- Environmental policy.

The CFT was required to review objectives every six months. The facility management team including the facility/plant manager was required to approve changes in aspects and significant aspects as part of its management review at least annually.

Along with objectives and targets, facilities were encouraged to consider establishing measurable environmental performance indicators to track their progress in fulfilling specific objectives and targets. Performance indicators were to be quantifiable measurements taken by a facility to gauge the progress made in achieving objectives and targets. For example:

OBJECTIVE	Reduce water use.
TARGET	Reduce water use by 10 percent by December, 1998.
PERFORMANCE INDICATOR	Quantity of water used per unit of production.

Environmental Policy

After the CFT identified those environmental aspects that should be of top priority to its plant, an environmental policy was created for that plant to provide focus and direction throughout the work force in achieving the facility's desired level of environmental responsibility. Each local environmental policy letter was based on the corporate letter. A plant's environmental policy embraced the concepts of the corporate policy but also included key aspects unique to the plant. The CFT modified the letter to make it specific to the activities, significant aspects, objectives and targets at each plant.

Typically, the plant manager and the union representative at the plant signed the policy to underscore their joint commitment to it. The environmental policy embodied the ideas and commitments of management to environmental protection and served as the foundation on which the EMS for a plant was built by answering the question: What is our facilitywide goal for environmental responsibility and performance that is required of the organization? In defining the environmental policy, top-level management had to ensure that it:

- Was appropriate to the nature, scale and environmental impacts of the facility's activities, products or services.
- Included a commitment to continual improvement and prevention of pollution.
- Included a commitment to comply with relevant environmental legislation and regulations and other requirements to which the organization subscribed.
- Provided the framework for setting and reviewing environmental objectives and targets.
- Was documented, implemented, maintained and communicated to all employees.
- Was made available to the public.

Environmental Management Program

The CFT also was responsible for establishing and maintaining EMPs for its facility to help achieve the objectives and targets developed for the significant environmental aspects by describing how they would be achieved.

The EMP took the shape in most facilities of a summary document defining basic responsibilities, actions, means and time frames for achieving multiple objectives and targets, or multiple action plans for individual projects. It addressed key issues, including:

Figure: IV. Environmental Management Programs

- Program Plan: What tasks need to be accomplished to achieve the objective and target?
- Operational Controls: What needs to be controlled to achieve the objective and target consistently? (e.g., create procedure/work practice, conduct management review meetings, perform routine maintenance, etc.).
- Responsibilities: Who is responsible for carrying out specific tasks?
- Resources: What equipment, personnel, materials, etc. are needed to fulfill the objective and target?
- Schedules: What time frames were set to complete specific tasks?
- Performance Indicators (optional): How is progress made in achieving the objective and target to be tracked?
- Miscellaneous: Any additional issues that are deemed necessary to fulfill specific goals (e.g., design considerations, disposal activities, use of materials, operation, etc.).

For organizational purposes, a project summary list of all EMPs was to be established and maintained for individual departments and functions. EMPs were to be revised regularly to reflect changes in environmental aspects, significant aspects, objectives and targets. Revisions might include adjustment of time frames, allocation of additional resources, reassignment of responsibilities, etc.

When a new activity, product or service was introduced, the facility was required to complete an environmental review to identify associated aspects and impacts, set potential objectives and targets and develop EMPs accordingly. Before any project was granted approval and allocated funding, the project originator was to conduct

Objectives, Targets and EMPs

- System level procedure specified criteria — objectives and targets for all significant aspects
- Training helped visualize the requirements and provided a simplified approach to documentation
- Objectives and targets categorized in one of three types:
    - Control
    - Improve
    - Investigate or study

> **Lessons Learned**
> *Engaging the Team*
>
> - Beware of information overload
> - Delegate responsibilities
> - Involve hourly employees, contractors

an evaluation to characterize the associated environmental and energy-related implications.

EMP templates provided in the Implementation Training required the CFT to identify the means, time frames and responsibilities for achieving associated objectives and targets.

The diagram shown in Figure IV (see Figure IV, page 40) was used to assist the CFT in visualizing Ford's approach to developing categories of significant aspects (control, improve or study), and to develop project plans to address these significant aspects, including the identification of resources, responsibilities, specific tasks and operational controls (local procedures and work instructions).

Other illustrations and examples such as Figure V (see Figure V, page 42) were used to assist the CFT in visualizing the type of information required on a typical EMP program sheet.

Figure V. Environmental Management Program(s)

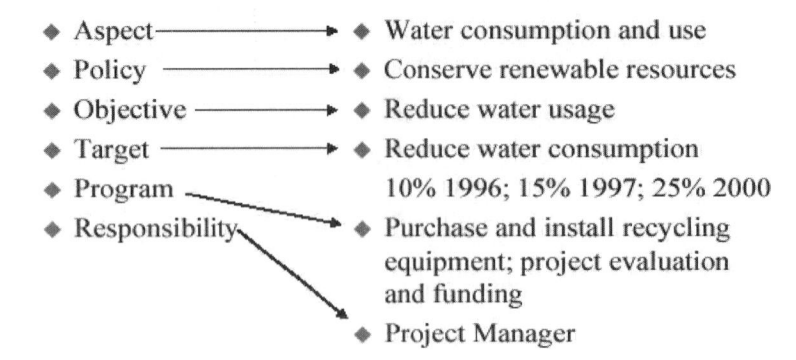

- Aspect ⟶ ◆ Water consumption and use
- Policy ⟶ ◆ Conserve renewable resources
- Objective ⟶ ◆ Reduce water usage
- Target ⟶ ◆ Reduce water consumption 10% 1996; 15% 1997; 25% 2000
- Program ⟶ ◆ Purchase and install recycling equipment; project evaluation and funding
- Responsibility ⟶ ◆ Project Manager

Additional samples and templates were provided to identify typical facility/plant organizational structures as well as responsibilities for implementing and maintaining the FES. Master document and record templates served as guides for maintaining information. Examples of completed templates were provided in the Implementation Training. System-level procedures that were provided defined the mechanisms for controlling, accessing and maintaining up-to-date EMS documents and the requirements for retention of records.

Structure and Responsibility

A management system that is not properly structured is destined to fail. For every department, function, area or activity, there must be clear understanding of who is responsible for what and who reports to whom. For an EMS to operate effectively, roles, responsibilities and authorities must be assigned, documented and communicated to employees.

At individual plants, roles and responsibilities were divided among four levels:

- Management.
- EMR and CFT.
- Relevant committees or teams (e.g., energy, waste minimization, etc.).
- Employees with specific EMS responsibilities.

While job descriptions and organizational charts are useful tools, the most effective way to document roles and responsibilities is through procedures and work practices. They define roles, responsibility and authority, help employees understand what their involvement is in performing a specific task and define exactly what equipment and resources will be needed to accomplish the task.

EMS Documentation

Of all the activities that took place in implementing the FES at individual plants, the most extensive and time-consuming by far was to document the system. To meet the directives of the FES and ISO 14001, facilities were required to establish adequate documentation.

The FES is driven by these key documents:

- Corporate environmental policy, which outlines the organization's intentions and principles in regard to environmental performance.
- Facility environmental policies, which support the philosophy of the corporate policy, but also reflect the characteristics and principles of the individual plant.
- Core environmental procedures that are intended to (1) serve as the basis for the development of facility-specific procedures, (2) satisfy the requirements of ISO 14001 and (3) ensure global consistency.

- Facility-specific procedures, which embrace the principles of the core procedures and address the individual needs of plant-specific operations and activities.
- Facility-specific work practices, which provide detailed instructions for completing specific tasks in specific work areas.

Training

Once requirements for carrying out EMS-related activities were established at a facility and roles, responsibilities and authorities were defined, job-related training was provided throughout the plant. Training plant personnel to carry out EMS activities competently and consistently was essential in ensuring that the day-to-day operations of the EMS conformed to planned arrangements.

These steps were taken to meet the specific training needs of a plant:

1. A training needs analysis was conducted to determine training needs among departments and job functions.

2. EMS-related job skills and qualifications were defined and documented, including the amount, type and level of training to be provided in carrying out specific tasks and the required level of competence for employees in education, skills and experience.

3. Training procedures were established and/or revised, specifying:

    - The importance of conforming to requirements.
    - Significant environmental aspects.

Lessons Learned

- **Implementation requires effort and commitment**
- **Excellent opportunity to heighten environmental awareness within the facility/plant**
- **Program maintenance involves the continued support of the plant**

- Roles and responsibilities.
- Consequences of departing from procedures.
- Competency (training, experience, education).

4. A training schedule was developed.

5. Appropriate training was provided.

6. For evidential purposes, training records were created to document the training that individual employees received.

While each plant was responsible for developing its own training agenda, the underlying goal for every facility was the same — to ensure that employees:

- Understood the importance of attaining conformance to EMS requirements.
- Understood the potential consequences when departing from procedures and work practices.

As a means of ensuring that training needs were being met at least minimally, internal auditors needed to find answers to these questions:

- Were employees aware of their roles and responsibilities in achieving conformance with the environmental policy, procedures and requirements of the FES?
- Were employees aware of the significant environmental aspects associated with their work activities?
- Were employees aware of the FES objectives and targets that had been set for their department or work area?
- Did employees understand the consequences that might result when FES procedures and work practices were not followed?
- Were employees aware of the benefits that might result from improved FES personal performance?
- Did employees understand their roles in responding to FES emergency situations?
- Did employees know how to access FES information relevant to their jobs?
- Were records on file to demonstrate the competence of individual employees and the FES training they received?

Awareness

While most of the training provided at a plant was related to job activities associated with significant environmental aspects, all employees with a role in maintaining the EMS needed to receive general EMS awareness training.

Awareness and communication became a key part of rolling out the FES. We had

General Employee Awareness Training

Campaign Material Package

—Environmental Policy Cards
—Pocket Guide Flip Books
—Commercial Show Reels
—Cascade Videocassette
—Salaried & Hourly Training Material
—Campaign Posters

---

to find a way to communicate to plant employees what the company *and they* were doing with respect to ISO 14001 and why. There was a "people" aspect in launching the FES. We had to get people's attention. It was important that the people in a facility knew there was a company environmental policy and were able to describe it in their own words.

While EMPs traditionally have been directed at the company's environmental specialists, the FES captured a broader audience. All employees were responsible for supporting the overall system. A corporatewide slogan, "Protecting the Environment Is Everyone's Job," was developed to deliver this message.

Each plant received a campaign material package for an employee awareness campaign. The kit included:

- Environmental Policy Pocket Cards, to build employee awareness of Ford's policy and to provide quick reference to the policy during ISO 14001 audits (see Figure VI, page 47). We had the basic card translated into at least 11 other languages, and variations of some languages: Spanish and Spanish as spoken in Mexico, for example, as well as versions of the Chinese language.

- Pocket Guide Flip Books, to provide quick reference to major elements of the FES and ISO 14001 and to prepare managers for audits.

- Commercial Show Reels, containing 10 "commercials," each 70-seconds in length, on the FES and ISO 14001.

- Cascade Videocassette, to build employee awareness of the FES, promote the Ford Environmental Policy and highlight key elements of ISO 14001. Plants could run the videotape on their local systems with segment modules to be shown as posters and other materials were distributed.

- Salary and Hourly Training Material, based on a train-the-trainer concept, salary and hourly supervisors were provided materials and instructional techniques to conduct general employee awareness activities and present information on procedures and work instructions to targeted employees during normal departmental meetings.

Each element of the campaign material was developed to achieve a specific communication purpose. All elements were designed to work together to create maximum

Figure VI. Environmental Policy Pocket Card

Ford issued pocket cards (above) enscribed with Ford's Environmental Policy to all employees as a training aid. The cards also carry special graphic logos created to promote program recognition.

Ford & ISO 14001

Training videos, flip books (see page 49) and pocket cards (see page 47) along with a series of promotional materials, including mugs and hats, were all used for ISO 14001 training for Ford employees.

awareness of the FES. The campaign material promoted new concepts, including integrating environmental responsibility into everyday business activities and decision-making at plants, and the key message that "Protecting the Environment Is Everyone's Job."

We provided awareness training to some people who had worked in a plant 20 or 30 years, and it brought unexpected reactions. When we said, "These are programs we've had for a long time," they responded, "I never knew that." Some people told us that when they went home at night and sat at the dinner table and said, "I had a discussion at work today on the environment," their children would respond, "Oh, dad, we do that all the time." Then dad asked, "Do you recycle?" And the kids answered, "Of course we recycle." One plant worker said the next day at work, "You know, that's the first time I sat for an hour with the kids at the dinner table. They never moved." Through his job, he had gained a new way to relate to them.

External Communication

In addition to employees, there was a need to develop a process for informing other groups of people of a plant's environmental values. They were the interested external audiences — neighbors, regulatory agencies, suppliers, customers, shareholders, environmental groups, registrars that certified the plants and anyone else

Ford's Environmental System
ISO 14001

INTRODUCTION

MOVING TO THE NEXT LEVEL:
FORD'S ENVIRONMENTAL SYSTEM

Dear Colleague,

This Pocket Guide summarises the significant elements of Ford s Environmental System, which will be implemented by Ford manufacturing facilities around the world by the end of 1998.

Ford s Environmental System will incorporate and build on the many environmental quality achievements made by Ford. To commonize this System at our facilities worldwide, each plant will apply for certification to ISO 14001, the international environmental management standard.

Ford s conformance with ISO 14001 will be assessed by an independent certification organisation, through interviews and follow-up with employees involved in manufacturing operations. Successful certification will depend on cooperation and all employees knowing Ford s environmental policy and demonstrating conformance to all ISO 14001 standards.

This Pocket Guide is being issued to engineering, manufacturing, and support staff to ensure that employees are aware of Ford s Environmental System and in conformance with ISO 14001 standards. It includes Ford s environmental policy, the reasons why Ford is implementing our global environmental management system, how it relates to ISO 9001 and other initiatives, an overview of the ISO 14001 standards, and information about audits.

Please take advantage of every opportunity to support the implementation of Ford s Environmental System in your area and your plant s certification to ISO 14001. Protecting the environment is everyone s job.

E.E. Hagenlocker
President, Ford Automotive Operations

Helen Petrauskas
Vice President, Environmental and Safety Engineering

Ford created flip books for employees that contained ISO 14001 essentials. The flip books included the introduction seen above, an overview of ISO 14001, information on audits and an explanation of Ford's Environmental Policy.

interested in a plant's ability to manage its environmental aspects. ISO 14001 requires that procedures be established not only for internal communication between the various levels and functions of a plant but also for receiving, documenting and responding to relevant communication from external interested parties.

Communication was a key in promoting the success of the FES. Good communication instilled credibility that a facility was operating in an environmentally responsible manner and that it was not attempting to hide information from the public. Good communication also provided a proactive way for a plant to respond to complaints and concerns raised by external parties.

Internal Audits

Once a facility's EMS was implemented, an internal evaluation system was established to ensure that the system was properly implemented and continued to perform effectively. The internal evaluation system consisted of periodic internal audits conducted by trained personnel and management review sessions conducted by the plant's senior management team. Regularly scheduled audits and management reviews are requirements of ISO 14001.

Internal audits were and still must be conducted periodically to determine:

- Whether the EMS conforms to planned arrangements for environmental management, including the requirements of ISO 14001.
- Whether the system has been properly implemented and maintained.
- Whether there is a need for improvement, as determined through the discovery of nonconformances.

Lessons Learned
Conduct Second-Party Reviews

- Prepares for registration assessment
- Identifies gaps in the system
- Identifies strengths and weaknesses
- Promotes best practices
- Provides a coaching opportunity

The primary focus of an internal EMS audit is to verify whether procedures and work practices are being followed according to planned arrangements. Auditor findings are subsequently incorporated into management reviews.

It was the responsibility of the EMR in each plant to plan, schedule and implement internal environmental audits. An EMS audit schedule was developed for each plant specifying the frequency of audits for various departments and activities.

Ford developed and provided internal auditor training at all the plants. Material used for the training was specifically designed to familiarize personnel with the procedures that formed the core of the FES as well as the requirements of ISO 14001. Training was presented in an open and active workshop format in which personnel developed audit questions based on the EMS at their facility. They also gained knowledge and experience performing actual audits under the guidance of the instructor.

Key personnel with responsibility to assist in implementing the FES in a plant were encouraged to take an ISO 14001 lead auditor course from outside trainers to give them a strong foundation and understanding of the standard and its requirements.

Management Review

At least once a year, a plant's manager and the facility's Operating Committee meet to review all elements of the EMS at their plant, including the requirements of ISO 14001. Management review sessions are held to evaluate identified problem areas and to make recommendations for continual improvement to the environmental policy, objectives, programs or other elements of the EMS. It is a decision-making process, conducted by a plant's senior management to authorize changes to the EMS, including investments, revised objectives and targets, new projects and so forth.

Preparing for Registration

Implementing the FES at a plant was a tremendous accomplishment in itself. But there still was a final step to be completed if the plant was to fully realize all the benefits of having the system in place and also meet the corporate objective of registration of all plants worldwide. That final step was the process of registering each plant.

Before proceeding with the final third-party registration assessment, a second-party audit was conducted to determine if a plant's EMS conformed to ISO 14001 and was consistent with the FES requirements. The second-party review was considered to be a "dry run" for the registration assessment. The audit was conducted by

Ford & ISO 14001

Ford personnel who had completed a five-day lead auditor training course and passed a test. They included members of the global Core Team and representatives from the EQO and operations/division environmental staff.

We developed a generic three-day audit plan for second-party audits, assigning

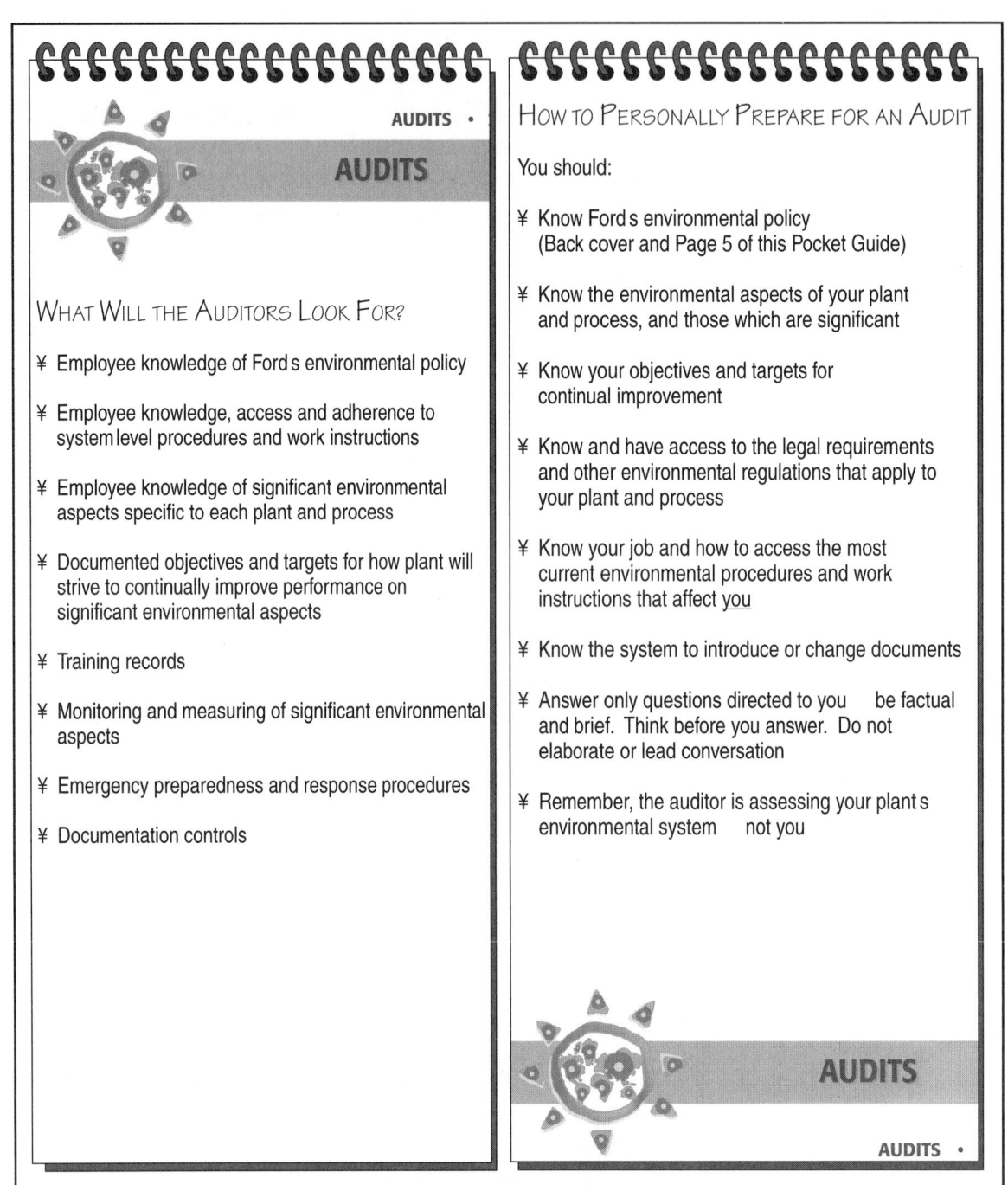

AUDITS

What Will the Auditors Look For?

- Employee knowledge of Ford's environmental policy

- Employee knowledge, access and adherence to system level procedures and work instructions

- Employee knowledge of significant environmental aspects specific to each plant and process

- Documented objectives and targets for how plant will strive to continually improve performance on significant environmental aspects

- Training records

- Monitoring and measuring of significant environmental aspects

- Emergency preparedness and response procedures

- Documentation controls

How to Personally Prepare for an Audit

You should:

- Know Ford's environmental policy (Back cover and Page 5 of this Pocket Guide)

- Know the environmental aspects of your plant and process, and those which are significant

- Know your objectives and targets for continual improvement

- Know and have access to the legal requirements and other environmental regulations that apply to your plant and process

- Know your job and how to access the most current environmental procedures and work instructions that affect you

- Know the system to introduce or change documents

- Answer only questions directed to you — be factual and brief. Think before you answer. Do not elaborate or lead conversation

- Remember, the auditor is assessing your plant's environmental system — not you

AUDITS

These two pages from Ford's training flip book describe the auditing process to employees and explain how to prepare for a third-party audit.

different members of the audit team to look at different elements in a plant. At the end of the three days, they produced an executive summary of the major items that needed attention. They left it up to each plant to go through the details.

When a plant passed this review, it was ready for the final third-party registration assessment to be performed by an accredited ISO 14001 registrar. This is an important distinction because not all ISO 14001 registrars (and ISO 9000 registrars for that matter) are accredited. In fact, even some accredited registrars may offer unaccredited registration certificates if asked to do so.

The National Accreditation Program operated jointly by the American National Standards Institute (ANSI) and the Registrar Accreditation Board (RAB), the United Kingdom Accreditation Service (UKAS) and the Dutch Council for Accreditation (RvA) accredit most of the registration certificates issued in Canada and the United States at present. A recognized accreditation provides assurances that the registrar conducts its audits in accordance with defined criteria and is itself subject to scrutiny by an outside body.

Pilot Plants

In the summer of 1996, after all Core Team members had completed lead auditor training, the team decided to select some plants to pilot the environmental program. Five plants participated in the pilot program:

- Oakville Assembly, Ontario, Canada.
- Van Dyke Transmission, Sterling Heights, Michigan.
- Lima Engine, Lima, Ohio.
- North Penn Electronics, Lansdale, Pennsylvania.
- Windsor Aluminum Plant, Ontario, Canada.

As we worked with the pilot plants on implementation, we found that they were moving faster than the Core Team itself. Plants wanted to know when procedures would be finalized. As each core procedure was finalized, we started to implement it at the pilot plants.

Although it was early in the implementation process, we also started talking to registrars. We told them what we were planning to do — register all Ford plants worldwide to ISO 14001 by the end of 1998. We did not believe at the time that there were enough resources in any one firm to do that, so we considered engaging two or three registrar organizations. We looked at firms with global resources, a strong reputation in the industry and trained personnel. We put together a scope of work and interviewed six firms. We wanted to be sure that they had the necessary computer and language skills and resources to perform registration audits on a global basis. After the review, we selected Lloyd's Register Quality Assurance (LRQA) and the Vehicle Certification Agency (VCA). Some plants also used TUV Rheinland. There were a few exceptions due to regional or country registrar availability.

Case Study: Lima Engine

The *Lima Engine Plant* in Lima, Ohio, is a good example of how the implementation process worked at the pilot plants. In March, 1996, Lima Engine began a 10-month process to implement the FES steered by a CFT that included members from all the plant's operating areas.

One of the first items on the agenda was a study of Lima Engine's environmental aspects — once again, plant activities, products or services that interacted with the environment. This represented a major undertaking for a 40-year-old, 2.4 million-square-foot facility where 2,100 hourly and salaried employees build more than 900,000 engines a year.

Eventually, Lima Engine identified 30 significant environmental aspects, ranging from wastewater discharge and material handling to solid waste disposal. Objectives and targets were established to control, improve or further study these aspects.

After developing facility-level environmental policy and management programs, the CFT defined how departmental work teams would implement the FES.

By the summer of 1996, the focus shifted to developing procedures and writing work instructions. The wealth of individual employees' environmental knowledge was documented. This step ensured that each employee had immediate access to up-to-date and approved environmental procedures and work instructions.

In the fall of 1996, the employee education and awareness effort at Lima Engine shifted into high gear. Everyone received a pocket card summary of the company's environmental policy. Pocket-size flip books were distributed to make key information readily available on the ISO 14001 standard.

Training on the standard was provided during weekly safety training sessions and at individual worksites. Videos, posters and newsletter articles promoted the advantages of the FES and ISO 14001 registration. Lima Engine's internal auditors checked how well the FES was understood, implemented and documented. After corrective and preventive actions were taken in response to the internal audits, plant management reviewed the FES, as it had throughout the spring and summer. A pre-assessment review was completed in late fall.

All that remained was a plant visit by VCA, the independent auditing organization that would conduct the ISO 14001 certification review there.

In December, 1996, Lima Engine received ISO 14001 certification, along with the Van Dyke, North Penn, Oakville and Windsor plants. These five Ford plants became the first automotive manufacturing facilities in North America to receive ISO 14001 certification.

To achieve registration, Lima Engine invested more than $220,000 in direct training costs and devoted more than 5,600 employee hours to meetings, training, internal audits and third-party audits.

Three critical factors made a difference in Lima Engine's ISO 14001 certification. The first and most important was teamwork. Everyone in the plant made a personal commitment to the environment as Ford employees and as members of the community.

The second success factor was that Lima Engine was already registered to ISO 9001. Many parts of ISO 14001 are closely related to ISO 9001, especially in policy development, document control, record keeping, training, auditing, monitoring and measurement. Both ISO standards also promote continuous improvement of the management system.

Lima Engine's third success factor was leveraging the power of the corporate intranet — the Ford Web — and using information technology to develop, document and disseminate the FES. By putting the system on the Ford Web, Lima Engine reduced its need for paper documentation. Lima Engine shared its "environmental intelligence" over the Ford Web, giving other Ford plants around the world a head start on their own system development and ISO 14001 registration efforts.

Within a year of putting its system in place, Lima Engine had:

- Reduced its consumption of water by nearly 200,000 gallons per day.
- Eliminated its production of boiler ash, the largest single component of the plant's solid waste stream.
- Increased the use of returnable packaging from 60 percent to 99 percent on its newest engine product.

The employees of Lima Engine are proud of the FES and their ISO 14001 registration. The plant has forged close ties with environmentally related organizations in the surrounding community. A Lima Engine representative serves on the North Central Ohio Solid Waste Management District Policy Committee and the Allen

County Local Emergency Planning Committee. Neighbors from the community have visited the plant and seen how the FES supports waste minimization, pollution prevention and emergency response.

Lima Engine is an example of how much time and effort went into implementing the FES and achieving ISO 14001 registration at the local level. At the global level, this effort was repeated by more than 200,000 employees in 140 plants in 26 countries.

The *Ford Halewood Assembly and Transmission Plant* in Liverpool, England, was working toward registration to the British environmental management standard BS 7750 before ISO 14001 was developed. Similarly, the Saarlouis Body and Assembly Plant in Germany was following the European EMAS requirements. Both switched to ISO 14001. In March, 1996, the Halewood plant became the first major automotive manufacturing site in the world to receive ISO 14001 certification. Saarlouis followed in April, 1996.

In July, 1997, the *Ford Lio Ho Assembly Engine and Casting Manufacturing Complex* became the first ISO 14001-certified automotive facility in Taiwan. In December, 1997, Ford was the first automaker to have all its facilities in Australia registered to the standard. The first passenger car plant in Mexico to receive ISO 14001 certification was the Ford Hermosillo Stamping and Assembly plant.

On December 8, 1998, Ford Motor Company became the first automotive company to complete registration of all its plants around the world to ISO 14001. The environmental milestone was marked at a ceremony at the Michigan Truck Plant in Wayne, Michigan, where representatives of LRQA and VCA presented a giant certificate representing certification of all 73 North American manufacturing plants. Similar ceremonies were held in other Ford regions around the world.

Ford Motor Company Philippines, Inc (FMCP), located in Santa Rosa, became the first Ford plant to achieve ISO 14001 certification simultaneously with a new plant launch in September, 1999. In the words of FMCP President, Terry Emrick, "We are proud to join all of our ISO 14001 plants around the world and are even prouder to have reached this standard before launch."

Chapter 3

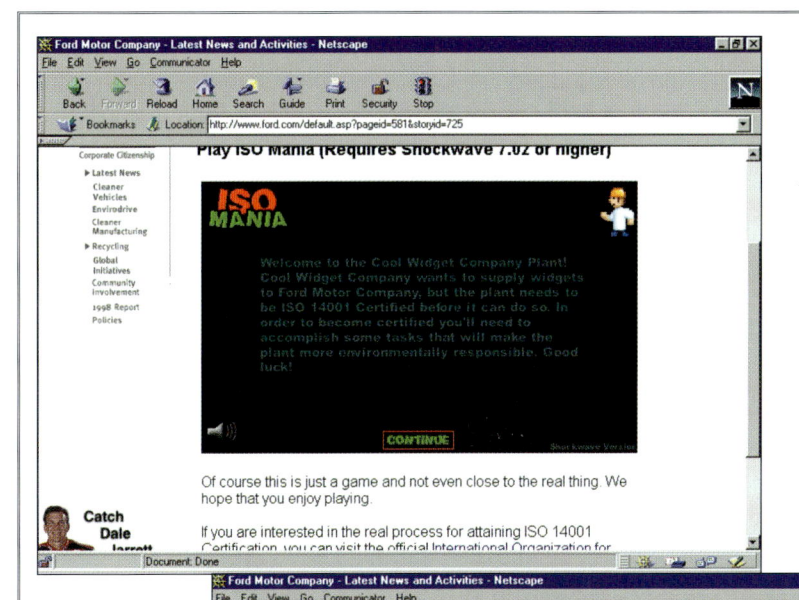

Whoever says ISO 14001 training is boring certainly hasn't played ISO Mania, Ford's Internet-based awareness game in which players negotiate an electronic maze to locate CFT members while evading a roving Neanderthal from the Evil Widget Company.

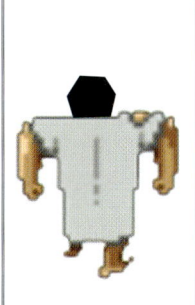

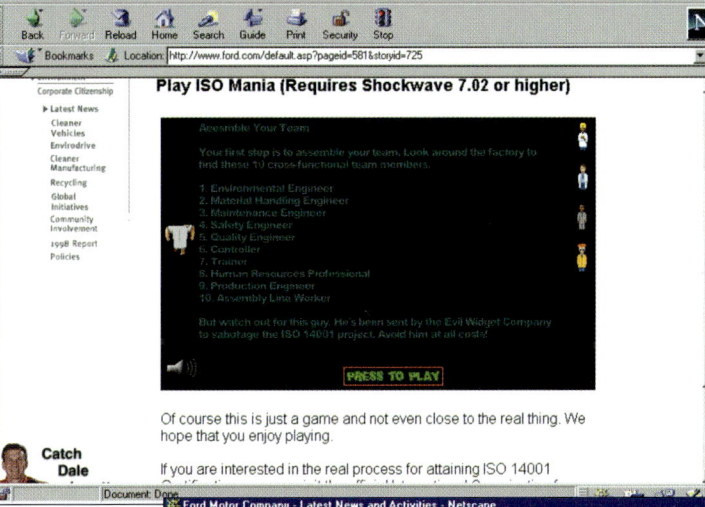

Having assembled your team, you'll navigate another maze, shutting off leaky faucets and unnecessary lights. See for yourself at www.ford.com under the "Environment" section (requires ShockWave 7.02 or higher, available as a free download through the site).

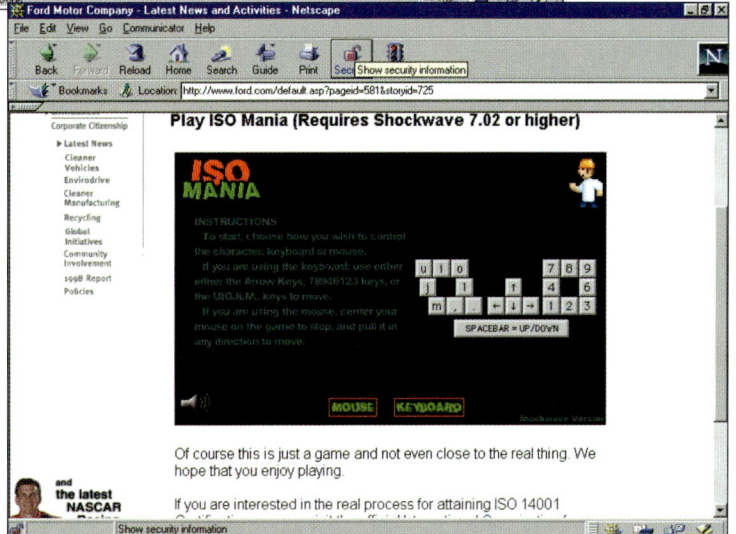

Figure I. Ford's Environmental System

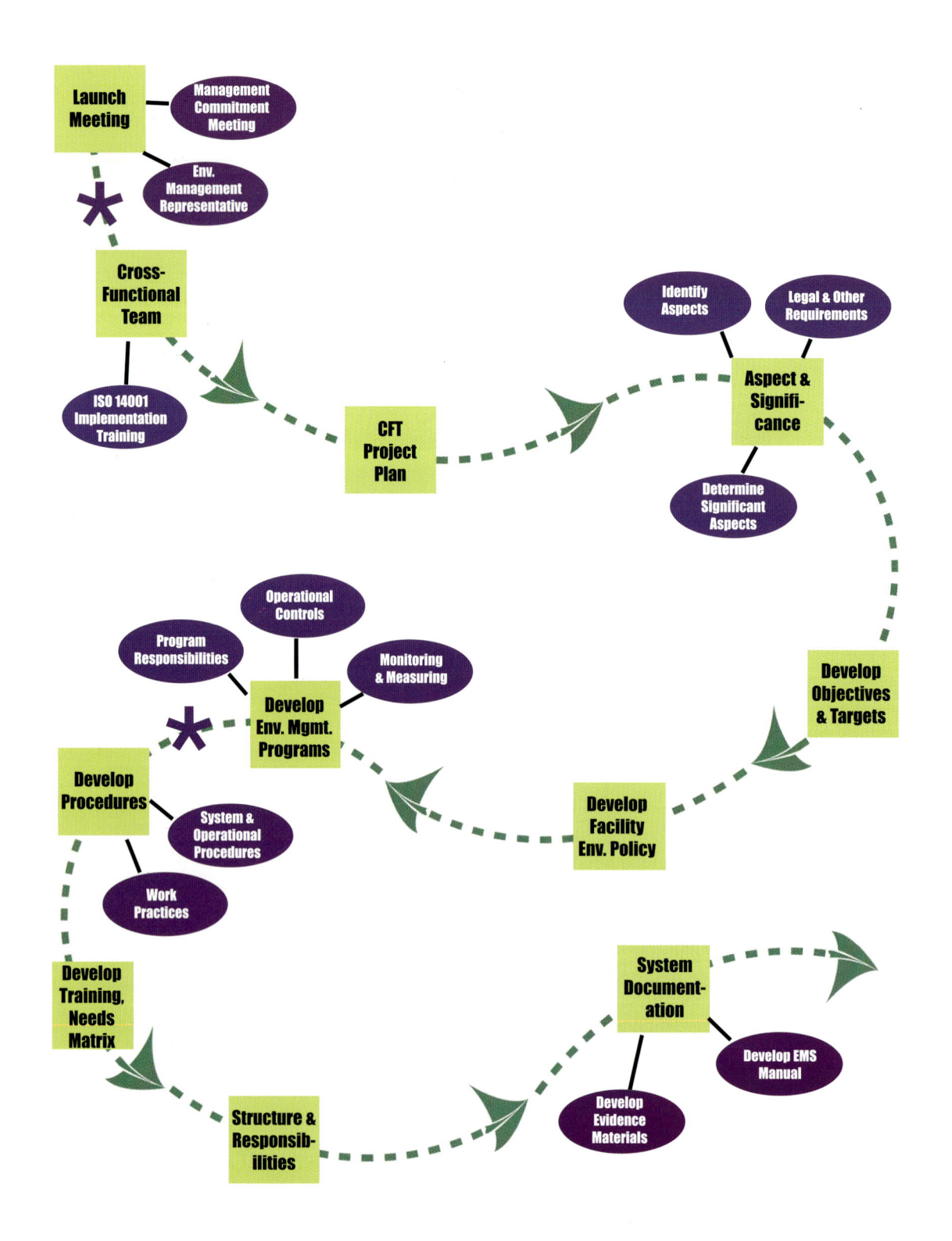

Implementation Flow Chart

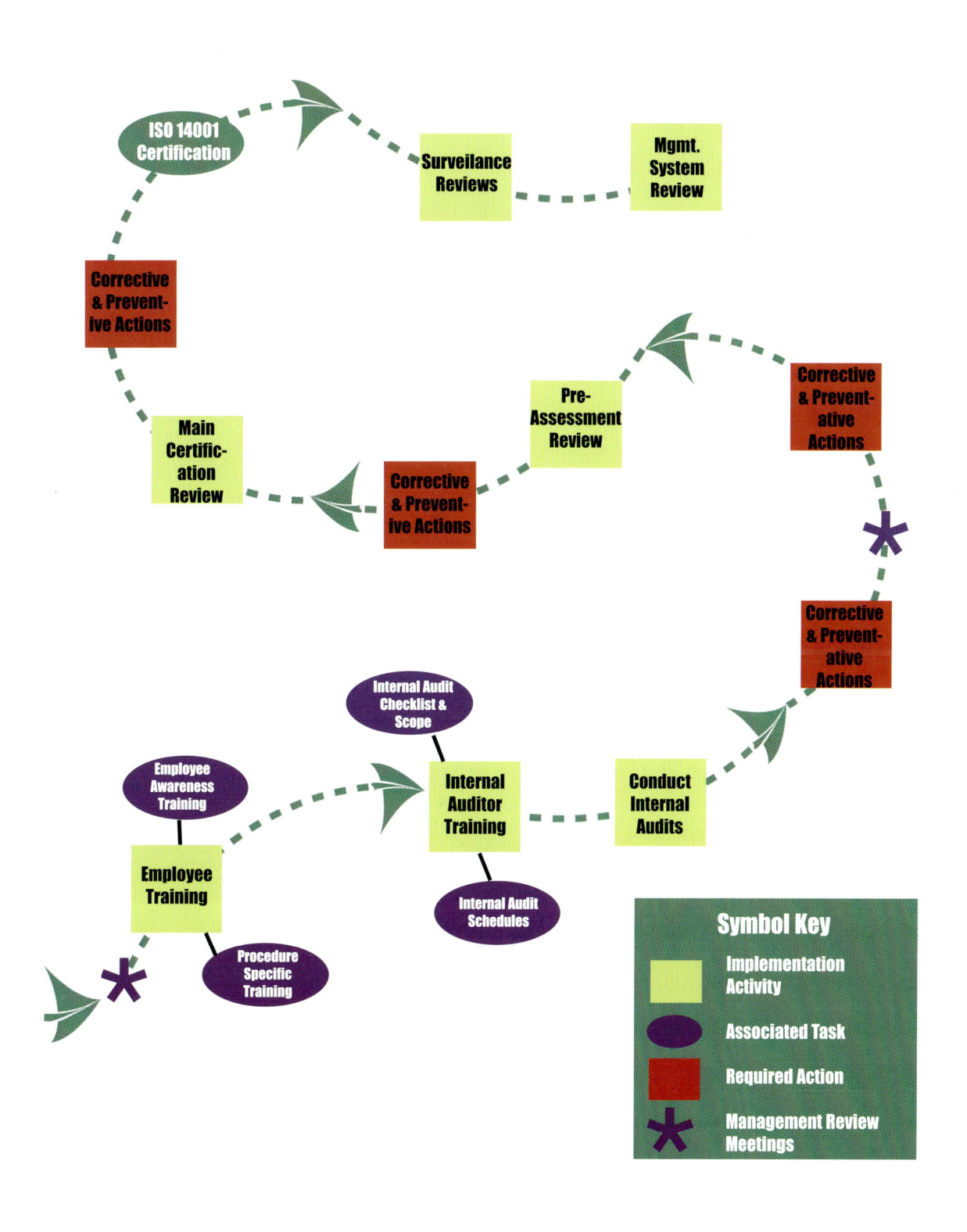

PAINT SLUDGE ELIMINATION — In 1995, a process improvement for the collection and disposal of paint overspray (paint sludge) from the Michigan Truck Plant was initiated. The Philip process recovers paint overspray that is captured in the paint booth (right). An emulsion solution dissolves the paint particulate and the solution is removed and processed off-site (above). A powder and resin material is extracted and sold to produce various products such as telephone pole cross arms. The emulsion is then returned and reused at the plant. This process improvement has eliminated all but a small portion of waste going to landfill (refer to page 87).

4 Ford's Road to Sustainability

Sustainable development is protecting, maintaining and restoring the integrity, functionality and productivity of natural and social life-support services. In the short time since Ford completed implementation of ISO 14001 in all plants worldwide and registration of every facility to the standard, these plants have demonstrated vividly what sustainability means.

Ford's Health and Environmental Policy provides: "Sustainable economic development is important to the welfare of the company, as well as to society. To be sustainable, economic development must provide protection of human health and the world's environmental resource base. It is Ford's policy that its operations, products and services accomplish their functions in a manner that provides responsibly for protection of health and the environment."

We consider sustainable development, or sustainability, to be one of the most significant outcomes of corporate citizenship. A successful company is no longer simply one that survives and prospers, but one that contributes to a healthy planet and its human and other inhabitants. Our company has a long history of corporate citizenship and environmental responsibility, but the stakes have risen tremendously over the last few years. Now we have to view what we're doing through the lens of sustainability, which demands higher standards of performance, higher levels of accountability and more transparency. We have made this an important element of our ISO 14001 program.

One of the things we learned during ISO 14001 implementation was that there are great opportunities for reducing water use, preventing pollution, reducing energy consumption and doing more in the area of recycling. This chapter details some of the benchmark programs throughout our registered manufacturing sites as well as

---

Lessons Learned
Leverage Your EMS

- Build employee awareness
- Reduce energy consumption
- Reduce waste
- Enhance regulatory compliance
- Develop good corporate citizenship
- Aim for continual improvement

---

some of our corporatewide initiatives. They should give you some idea of what might be possible in your organization.

Not all of these programs were the direct result of ISO 14001 implementation. But the degree to which introspective self-assessment and employee involvement are required by the standard can't help but yield environmental success stories like the ones that follow. Even for a company the size of Ford, the savings in resources and waste reduction serve up a powerful lesson in the fruits of sound environmental management.

Pollution and Waste Prevention Strategy

Ford continues to work to integrate pollution prevention, waste prevention and minimization practices into business decision making. The company's manufacturing environmental strategy includes processes for reducing waste/pollution at its source. The goal is to find ways not only to manage wastes, but also to prevent wastes through planning and improved processes.

In July, 1994, Ford advised its suppliers of this environmental strategy and encouraged them to develop similar guidelines. The guidelines focus on three key areas:

- **Materials**
  —Reduce or eliminate use of materials of concern.
  —Reduce, reuse or recycle packaging and shipping materials.
  —Reduce, reuse and recycle other industrial materials.

- **Processes**
  —Consider the environmental impact early in the design of Ford products.

—Consider the environmental impact early in manufacturing planning.
   —Develop ways to conserve and save energy.

- **Facilities**
   —Revitalize sites requiring environmental remediation.
   —Develop contingency plans to handle potential environmental emergencies.
   —Provide protection and enhanced habitats for wildlife at or near Ford facilities.

Ford initiated several projects early in 1995 that were consistent with the elements of the strategy. Projects included research on solvent absorption media, waste minimization/prevention assessments, training for waste minimization teams, energy reduction evaluation at selected plants, evaluation of alternative coating systems and so forth. Substances that were addressed included reportable substances/materials of concern, such as toluene and trichloroethylene and heavy metals, as well as nonhazardous industrial waste materials (oils, fluids, plastics, packaging, etc.).

Evaluations of different processes provide for reducing waste generation at the source. This involves recycling of materials and evaluating improved treatment methodology.

The following are actual case studies from Ford plants around the world. They are presented under logical headings beginning with "Water."

Water

The *Ford Casting Plant in Geelong,* Victoria, Australia, uses more than 200,000 liters of water daily to produce iron and steel engine components (blocks, crankshafts, camshafts, counterweights and brake discs). In 1996, during implementation of the FES at the plant, the site's objectives and targets clearly identified reduction in water and bentonite (clay) usage as a major opportunity. Bentonite is used to hold sand together during the moulding process.

Previously, all process, storm and sewer water runoff was discharged to Corio Bay. In 1998, an AU$1.1 million (approximately $580,668 US) recycling system was designed and built to collect stormwater and process wastewater from the plant for reuse. The recycling system commenced operation in November, 1998.

All stormwater runoff and most process water used on-site is collected. The water is drained to a settling pit where sand, some bentonite and other solids are removed before the water is pumped into a storage lagoon for treatment. The clean water is then pumped through a ring main that feeds recycled water to all wet scrubbers and also to nozzles located in the drains for sand flushing.

Wastewater from the wet scrubbers is collected and fed back to the moulding sand plant. This reclaims bentonite otherwise lost in the process.

The development of water recycling technology for the Ford Casting Plant has been a significant breakthrough for the site. The water recycling system saves 110,000 liters of water per day and minimizes the discharge of process wastewater to the sewer. Calculations show that there is potential to save 660 tons of bentonite annually. Savings in water use alone are estimated to be AU$22,750 (approximately $12,382 US) per year with additional savings from the reused bentonite.

Water recycling is part of a broader program designed to minimize environmental effects on the Geelong community. Another benefit of this project has been the supply of excess water from the plant to the City of Greater Geelong for watering of native plants and shrubs during drought periods.

The *Taubaté Powertrain Operations* in Brazil introduced a water recycling system in which treated wastewater was discharged directly to an internal lake instead of being sent into the public sewer network. Thus, the lake is continuously maintained by treated wastewater and rain water.

The lake is an important ecosystem for migratory birds, fish and other small animals.

Ford Vietnam Limited is a small self-contained operation that was established on what previously were rice fields in an isolated area with no water supply, electricity or sewerage. Ford had to develop its own infrastructure to supply water, generate electricity and treat wastewater and sewage.

The site has two deep groundwater wells. The water they produce requires purification due to high salinity and iron content. This is done using ultrafiltration and reverse osmosis. The water is then supplied to the plant, where it is used in painting, washing, drinking, cooking and cooling towers. All wastes and discharges from these processes go directly to the biological treatment plant. The paint process waste receives primary treatment for metals before going to the biological treatment plant.

The biological treatment plant maintains an active culture of aerobic and anaerobic bacteria that use sewage as a food source. Discharge first undergoes disinfection by ultraviolet light to remove harmful bacteria. It then enters an irrigation channel from which neighboring rice farmers draw water to irrigate their crops. In the dry season, the discharge is the only source of water in the immediate area.

The close proximity of this Ford industrial facility to the community means we must operate it with the utmost care and responsibility. Accordingly, the facility has established the FES as the basis for its environmental management activities.

Ford India Limited covers 356 acres. The site's environmental permit requires 15 acres to be planted with trees and gardens to establish a "green belt." Ford India has gone one step further and committed to planting an additional 47 acres.

The 62 acres of plantings require considerable irrigation, particularly in the dry season. Currently, they need 15 cubic meters (930,000 liters) of water per day. A comparison between the water from the town water supply and the water that was being discharged from the wastewater treatment plant indicated that wastewater reuse was a viable option.

The wastewater treatment plant handles all of the site's processed wastewater as well as sanitary needs. The plant also accepts waste from a neighboring Visteon site. The on-site laboratory monitors the quality of the discharge daily. An extensive network of irrigation pipes has been laid across the site that supplies the plantation drip feed eater from the wastewater treatment plant.

In establishing the "green belt," Ford has planted 13,912 trees, shrubs and ground coverings. Ultimately the program is saving 930,000 liters per day.

There have been other dramatic demonstrations of the benefits of the ISO 14001-based FES on water usage. Altogether, we have reduced our waste stream by 16.3 million pounds in two years — enough to fill 120 football fields waist-high!

Ford's *Windsor Casting Plant* in Windsor, Ontario, Canada, received the Canadian Council of Ministers of the Environment Pollution Prevention Award in 1998 for its outstanding efforts in dramatically reducing organics in wastewater.

The plant's recently upgraded state-of-the-art wastewater treatment uses ozone, generated on-site, to treat organic compounds in a closed-loop process, with all unreacted ozone destroyed on-site as well. This is the first industrial use of advanced ozonation technology in the treatment of casting-plant water, and it is being studied for use at other Ford manufacturing facilities around the world.

Windsor Casting Plant is the largest iron foundry in Ontario and the only automotive iron foundry in Canada. It converts 130,000 tons of recycled steel and iron annually to produce more than one million cast iron engine blocks and 2.5 million crankshafts for new Ford cars and trucks. Built in 1934, the plant employs 1,000 people.

Organic compounds are byproducts of the iron casting process and there has been no proven nonchlorination means for their treatment in wastewater. Following a pretreatment, wastewater is pumped into the ozone building, where it reacts with ozone created by the generators. Ozone consists of molecules of highly reactive oxygen, capable of the chemical destruction of organic compounds.

Ozonation is used in Europe for purification of drinking water, but this is the first technology to treat industrial wastewater use on this scale. Ford invested $3 million in the ozonation facility at the iron foundry's wastewater treatment plant. The concrete block, two-room building contains three computerized ozone generators and a laboratory staffed by four operators. The ozonation facility began operations in June, 1997.

Since 1996, Ford has invested more than $10 million in an aggressive wastewater treatment program that ensures that all water used in processes at Windsor Casting Plant is consistently lower than limits set by the Municipal-Industrial Strategy for Abatement (MISA). Windsor Casting Plant was registered to ISO 14001 in April, 1998.

The *Jaguar Browns Lane Assembly Plant* is a two-model, luxury vehicle manufacturing facility in Coventry, United Kingdom. Each vehicle is given a water test to establish the soundness of the sealing systems as an integral part of the production process.

Jaguar identified usage of water as one of its major opportunities for environmental performance improvement under its ISO 14001 implementation. In early 1997, the water test facility at Browns Lane was identified as a potential significant contributor to this improvement initiative.

A new facility at the site recycles testing water 110 times before discharging it at the end of each shift. Environmental advantages include a greatly reduced risk of accidental contamination of discharged water and a reduction in water usage amounting to 10,000 cubic meters per month, or 120 million liters of water each year — enough to clean one million loads of laundry or fill 800,000 baths.

These efforts earned the site a National Crystal trophy in the Green Apple Awards for Environmental Best Practice among businesses and organizations nominated throughout England, Scotland, Wales and Northern Ireland. Jaguar was praised for having made enormous strides which embrace most areas of its operations, including the paint booth operations, transportation and logistics as well as packaging and energy conservation. With the introduction of the new system facility at Browns Lane, significant modifications were introduced to the layout and operating characteristics of the water test.

The operational advantages gained from the new system are numerous and include improved flow and sequencing of vehicles, improved quality of product and reduced process costs.

In addition to the environmental issues associated with this facility there were also some significant cost and operational issues. Water services were charged at £0.4592 (approximately $0.62 US) per cubic meter and trade effluent was charged at £0.2831 (approximately $0.41 US) per cubic meter resulting in a total cost of £2.14 (approximately $3.03 US) per vehicle.

The operational disadvantages included the following:

- Operator had to remain with the vehicle at all times.
- Severe bottlenecks were experienced.
- Contamination of test equipment occurred after the water test due to inadequate sequencing.
- A further car wash was needed after the external road test as a result of the original sequencing.
- Poor process flow resulted in excessively high stock levels in the system.

The new system combines wastewater with car wash opperations using 4,000 liters of water per minute with a duration of five minutes per test. This results in a more demanding trial of sealing systems. The facility now relies on a recirculating system with the ability to perform overnight leak tests. To facilitate the recirculation, there is a 20-cubic-meter holding tank with twin mesh filters and an oil skimmer. Continuous bromination is used to prevent biological growth through the use of Biotek 785/786 at 0.2-0.5 parts per million (ppm).

There has been a dramatic improvement in water quality, including the ability to monitor and control the pH and the concentration of suspended solids and the Chemical Oxygen Demand.

Operational advantages include:

- A conveyorized system which eliminates the need for operators to remain with vehicles.
- A combined car wash and water test facility which frees up valuable space on the shop floor.

Lessons Learned
Benefits to Ford

- Water reduction of 1.3 billion gallons and annual cost savings of $4.3 millon at 16 identified facilities
- Canadian Engine Plants replaced 3,200 fluorescent lights with energy efficient bulbs and ballasts reduced energy usage by 1.04 million kwh per year and reduced energy costs by $44,000 per year

- An improved filtration system which eliminates contamination of other equipment.
- Reduced vehicle handling and movement which reduces the level of paint damage.
- Greater space which improves the vehicle flow, resulting in reduced stock levels.
- An improved facility for testing and online inspection.
- An optional integrated overnight leak test which is now available.
- More demanding testing due to the greater duration and higher volume of water used.

The project has an estimated 2.5 year payback primarily through:

- Reduction in water usage.
- Reduction in vehicle inventory.
- Reduction in process headcount.
- Reduction in cost associated with the construction of a new sewer.

The *Halewood Body and Assembly Plant* in Liverpool, United Kingdom, installed solenoid valves with timers at its paint booth operations, which allowed demineralized sinks to be shut off when not in use. This initiative saved £40,500 (approximately $57,413 US). The paint booth operations also began recycling water from demin sinks, saving a further 150 to 200 liters per minute of water, resulting in a savings of another £14,340 (approximately $20,330 US) per year.

The *Van Dyke Transmission Plant*, a 1.9 million-square-foot facility in Sterling Heights, Michigan, was one of the first three automotive facilities to be awarded the State's Clean Corporate Citizenship Certificate in 1997, largely based on the work of its employees with regard to maintaining an environmental program (ISO 14001). The plant has been operating since 1968 and produces more than 9 million units annually. Van Dyke products include front and rear suspension, arms, CV joints, half shafts, spindles, knuckles and transaxles for various Ford and Mercury vehicles. The Ford Focus automatic transmission is also produced at the Van Dyke plant.

The prior metal-cleaning process used to wash automotive transmissions after final assembly, "batch cleaning," was similar in nature to water-washing operations used in other domestic and industrial applications (dishwashers, laundering, etc.). Detergent water at 140 degrees F was used to remove transmission oils and suspend them in the cleaning solution until the solution was oil-laden and no longer useful. Twice a week, 2,500 gallons of spent solution was disposed to the Industrial Process Water Treatment Plant. A fresh batch of solution was introduced to the wash after each disposal to continue the cleaning process.

A new washing process was introduced that uses the principle of "self-regeneration" of the cleaning solution. This regeneration process uses an oil-splitting surfactant cleaner that effectively allows the removed oil from the transmissions to float to the top of the solution holding tank vs. suspension of the transmission fluid in the cleaning solution. The floating oil can then be effectively recovered from the cleaning solution. The bath life of the new process was four to six weeks vs. the original bath life of three days. The new process resulted in a treatment reduction of 210,000 gallons of oil-laden wastewater per year.

A new approach of an "oil-splitting" chemistry process was coupled with a requirement that the transmissions be cleaned by chemistry at near ambient solution temperatures. The original bath temperature was reduced from 140 degrees F to 103 degrees F, resulting in energy and water evaporation savings. Water use was reduced by 660,000 gallons a year due to the washing temperature reduction.

This project demonstrated the use of new mechanical equipment for effective separation and recovery of oil from the wash solution. Ten thousand gallons per year of transmission fluid is recovered during the washing process eliminating the oil entering the process waste stream. Recovered oil is stored in a 1,500 gallon tank at the washing site, picked up approximately once a month and delivered to an oil reclaim facility. This recovered oil is consistently above 98 percent oil content.

Engineering analysis demonstrates significant pollution prevention benefits and cost savings related to (1) energy use and cost reduction resulting from near-ambient wash conditions, (2) oil wastestream elimination and oil recovery and (3) water usage reduction. Wastewater treatment decreased by 210,000 gallons a year, use of city water decreased by 870,000 gallons per year, and operational savings were $80,000 per year as a result of this improvement.

The *Valencia Plant* of Ford Motor Company Spain is located in a dry area along the Mediterranean coast. Several initiatives have improved water and wastewater at the facility.

These include:

- Incorporating a reverse osmosis treatment installation (RO) in 1998. As a result, chloride levels in wastewater have been reduced below permissible levels.
- Implementing a continuous process flow treatment in 1999. Heavy metals removal has increased.
- Installing a biological treatment plant in 2000 that uses activated sludge to improve the elimination of organic contaminants.
- Implementing a program in 1987 to determine the feasibility of biological treatment of industrial wastewater.
- Implementing a program in 2000 to treat high concentrate (organics) wastewater using solar energy.

The following initiatives planned for 2001 are intended to reduce water consumption:

- Improving water supply network pressure management. This is expected to save 368,000 m^3/year.
- Installing metering stations. This is expected to save 24,000 m^3/year.
- Automating cooling towers. This is expected to save 94,000 m^3/year.
- Repairing leakage in the fire water network. This is expected to save 35,000 m^3/year.

The *Cologne Estate* in Germany is conducting a study to determine if nickel can be removed from the wastewater stream after the phosphating baths combined with a recycling process for the process chemicals. The study focuses on two processes:

- Niehl (dip phosphate process) — An ion-exchanger removes heavy metals from rinse water after phosphating (currently a partial wastewater stream); regeneration of the ion-exchanger with phosphoric acid (basis of the phosphating chemicals), increases the concentration in different stages of fractionation so that it is economic to use the regenerate (with the content of heavy metal ions (Ni, Mn, Zi) as a raw material for new phosphating chemicals at an off-site location.

- Merkenich (spray phosphate process) — This process is at the final stages of EQO funding approval for using nanofiltration membrane filters to remove heavy metal ions from the rinse water. The filtrate with the active chemicals can be directly recycled into the phosphate bath (on-site), so that chemical mark-up is minimal. The permeate contains only nitrate and can be used as process water in the degreasing zones before phosphating bath. Two experimental trials to investigate the membrane processes are completed. Ford plans to investigate the possibility of treating the whole plant volume.

Other water initiatives include:

- Installation of a closed loop cooling system for laser welders at *Cologne Transmission and Chassis Facility* in 2000. This results in estimated annual water savings of 300,000 m³ and annual energy savings of 340,000 kwh.
- Installed in 2000 a closed loop cooling system for engine test dynos at *Cologne Engine Facility*. This is expected to save approximately 6000 m³ of water per year.

Energy

Energy Use Reductions

Ford continues to search for opportunities to reduce its environmental impact. One method that has gained recent focus is the discovery of more energy-efficient modes of operating pollution control equipment. Assembly plants use pollution control equipment extensively for the abatement of VOC emissions, mainly subsequent to paint booth operations. Approximately 70 percent of the total energy budget at Ford Motor Company's assembly plants is due to painting operations, and a significant amount of this energy requirement is linked specifically to pollution control equipment.

The greatest energy consumption associated with pollution prevention occurs in the large regenerative thermal oxidizers (RTOs) that are used to achieve thermal destruction of VOCs. Ford's corporate Environmental Quality Office completed an independent investigation to determine possible methods to reduce energy consumption by RTOs. Intuitively, if these units are modified to operate at lower temperatures, significant energy consumption reduction and cost savings could be realized. The investigation was focused primarily on the manipulation of the air-to-fuel (AF) ratio in the combustion chambers. Combustion within the RTOs was previously operated in the presence of 10 percent excess oxygen, leading to a cooling effect within the chamber due to the lower temperature of the incoming air. The conclusion was to maintain combustion at 10 percent excess natural gas, thus eliminating the lower temperature air from the process.

Ford & ISO 14001

A secondary objective of the project focused on the maintenance access hatches on each RTO. These hatches are bolted and sealed to prevent too much air from infiltrating, but a gap was purposely left to allow the passage of air around the doors to keep them cool in the event they must be removed. However, it was discovered that the gap did not produce the desired effect. Therefore, as a way to reduce the amount of air infiltrating into the combustion chamber, the gaskets surrounding the hatches were replaced by tighter-fitting models and more bolts were added, leading to a decrease in the amount of natural gas required to maintain operational temperature.

Ford Motor Company recently issued a divisionwide project for all assembly plants to complete these and similar measures to reduce energy consumption by increasing the efficiency of their RTOs. The results show a reduction in natural gas use of 27 percent per unit as well as a reduction in electrical energy use. Capital investment payback times for this project are approximately four months and annual savings in energy costs are $600,000 divisionwide.

ENERGY SAVINGS — In 1998, the Ford Michigan Truck Plant in Wayne initiated a lamp and light bulb replacement project and replaced more than 1,975 higher-energy-use fluorescent lights with more energy-efficient metal halide lamps. This lamp replacement program cut the plant's annual use of electricity by 1.5 million kwh, saving the plant $66,000 a year.

Paint Booth Lighting Retrofit

Ford paint booths use continuous conveyor systems to move units past stationary paint applicator equipment. Each assembly plant has several booths ranging in length from 500 to 1,000 lineal feet. Cars and trucks are primed and painted in controlled conditions of airflow, temperature and humidity.

Most paint booths built in the last 30 years have utilized T-12 Very High Output (VHO) fluorescent lamps enclosed in vapor-proof fixtures. The initial light output for these lamps is very high and the energy consumption also is very high. The lamps have extremely poor efficacy, lamp life, lumen depreciation and color rendering index. Maintenance costs are high due to frequent replacements. Energy costs are high due to the poor efficacy. Quality and operator comfort are affected when lamps burn out.

New fluorescent lighting technology has advanced the development of T-8 lamps to about double the efficacy of T-12 VHO lamps. High-output versions of the T-8 lamps were compared to T-12 VHO lamps for energy consumption, light output, maintained lumen level, life and light quality (color rendering index). A retrofit has been designed and installed in 11 of 21 North American paint shops. Lighting energy costs are reduced by more than 50 percent. Initial light levels are lower, but since there is less, the maintained light level equivalent, the color rendering index is higher and the new lamps will last two to three times longer.

As a result of this improvement, energy usage was reduced 17,500,000 kwh per year. Operational cost savings were $500,000 per year.

Plant Shutdowns to Reduce Energy Use at Halewood

An energy committee meets monthly at the *Halewood Body and Assembly Plant* to identify potential efficiencies. A formal shutdown procedure instituted for each area has resulted in base-load reductions of almost 4,330,000 kwh amounting to a savings of 3,161 tons of carbon dioxide and £200,000 (approximately $283,562 US) in associated energy costs.

Energy surveys have also highlighted further cost savings, including unnecessary energy usage and compressed air leaks. The paint booth operations reduced VOC emissions by 20 percent in 1997 for a savings of £60,000 (approximately $85,068 US) in solvents.

Regulating Compressed Air Usage to Reduce Energy

The *Broadmeadows Assembly Plant* near Melbourne, Australia, was registered to

COSTLY LEAKS — The Michigan Truck Plant in Wayne uses air compressors (right) to power equipment such as vehicle hoists, equipment lifts, power tools and other process equipment. In 1997, the plant added four air surge tanks (above) to eliminate wasted energy from the compressors and equipment. The plant also initiated a maintenance program to repair air leaks. These air compressor improvements have cut energy usage by 7.8 million kwh annually, and are saving the plant $233,000 a year.

ISO 14001 in December, 1997. In implementing the FES, the plant established energy management plans for reduction of gas, electricity and water consumption.

It was recognized that a substantial amount of electricity was consumed to provide compressed air to the plant. This information was presented at EMS management review meetings resulting in incremental improvements in operation and maintenance of the existing system including rudimentary automation of some compressors in November, 1997. Plant management considered the early savings in cost and energy a step in the right direction, but realized that more aggressive action would be necessary to meet voluntary greenhouse gas reduction targets set by Ford of Australia.

Late in 1998, plant management approved a study to evaluate the cost effectiveness of different compressed air system upgrade options. The study, managed by plant engineering staff and performed by a supplier, verified that substantial savings could be made in the areas of automation of compressor control, accurate measurement of system loading, automation of welding cooling tower plants, after-hours pressure reduction and reduction of compressed air leakage. Plant management reviewed the results of the study and approved an AU$85,000 (approximately $46,262 US) project for installation of an advanced energy management system in April, 1999.

The system, which went online in February, 2000, manages the operation of the air compressors using algorithms to determine system loading and provides only the amount and quality of compressed air needed. It also provides real-time monitoring of usage, collection of usage metrics and alarms for high leakage rates.

The project is expected to yield a 20 percent reduction in compressor run-time. The payback period is estimated to be just over one year, when energy and labor savings are combined with equipment lifetime and maintenance savings.

The *Ford Woodhaven Stamping Plant* is a 2.7 million-square-foot facility in Woodhaven, Michigan. The plant has been operating since 1965 and employs approximately 2,700 people. The plant produces body panel doors, fenders, roofs, floor pans, tailgates and steel decklids for Ford vehicles. The plant produced more than 88 million stamped and assembled parts in 1998. Woodhaven applies approximately 25 percent of its electrical energy consumption to produce compressed air for various uses. A high-pressure compressed air system operates the plant equipment.

The plant took several actions to improve compressed air system performance. First, an air leak detection/correction team consisting of two machine repairmen was assigned to identify and correct significant leaks. Leak correction activities occur primarily during the July and December plant shutdowns, lunch breaks and unscheduled downtime. This effort is credited with reducing air consumption by approximately 2,500 standard cubic feet per minute (scfm).

Second, leaking seals on the stamping press die automation valves were replaced, resulting in a reduction of approximately 1,000 scfm. Third, lowering the air header pressure by five pounds per square inch gauge (psig) resulted in electrical savings of 2,300,000 kwh. This effort replaced the existing flow measuring orifice plates with low-loss venturis and replaced the plate in the main system header with an averaging pilot tube. The venturis measure the discharge flow from two of the largest air compressors.

Beginning in June, 1998, the plant reduced its average scfm flow from 25,000 to 20,500 and cut electricity costs. One 800-hp reciprocating compressor was taken completely off-line and the remaining in-service compressors are consuming slightly less energy.

This improvement resulted in a reduction in energy usage of about 7,900,000 kwh. Oxides of Nitrogen (NO_X) emission was reduced by about 60,000 lbs. and Oxides of Sulfur (SO_X) emission was reduced by about 85,000 lbs. Annual operational savings amounted to $400,000.

In a similar activity, the *Michigan Truck Assembly Plant* in Wayne, Michigan, added four air surge tanks to eliminate wasted energy from its compressors and equipment. The compressors were updated to automatically control the amount of air pressure delivered to the equipment. The plant also initiated a maintenance program to repair air leaks. As a result, energy usage was reduced 7,800,000 kwh. Annual operational savings amounted to $233,000.

Landfill Gas Recovery

The *Wayne Stamping and Assembly Plant* integrates stamping and assembly operations. Assembled body units and stamped body components are transferred from the stamping/body area in one building to the paint and assembly area in an adjacent building via an overpass bridge. The assembly process includes welding and sealing of sheet metal body components, metal finishing (sanding and surface preparation), phosphate coating, painting and final assembly.

Three boilers burn natural gas to generate steam used in plant processes and heating the plant. Wayne Stamping and Assembly buildings cover more than 2 million square feet and use approximately 1,000,000 MM Btu of natural gas and 150,000,000 kwh of electricity annually. A long-term agreement between Detroit Edison (which supplies the electricity) and Wayne Stamping and Assembly allows landfill gas from Woodland Meadows Landfill to be collected, compressed and sent through underground piping to the plant. The boilers burn a combination of natural gas and landfill gas to create steam for use in the plant. The landfill gas also powers three engine generators which produce approximately 2.4 megawatts of electricity. The electricity is sent to Detroit Edison's grid system using a step-up transformer.

Flaring of the landfill gas is minimized, which in turn reduces emissions from the landfill. Exhaust from the engines is recycled via ducts to the boilers' fireboxes. The combustion in the boilers acts as a re-burn cycle to further reduce the emissions from the engines.

The 2 MM Btu per hour of recovered heat from the engines means less gas in the boilers, reducing energy consumption and emissions. The partnership of Ford and Detroit Edison gives the utility company an electricity source from garbage that displaces coal-fired power.

As a result of this initiative, use of coal-fired power was reduced by 21,000,000 kwh per year.

Reduce, Reuse, Recycle

Reduce

The *Hermosillo Stamping and Assembly Plant* in Hermosillo, Mexico has successfully worked with its waste management supplier to reduce the amount of waste generated at the plant and to recycle waste that was formerly placed in landfills. This includes grass, Styrofoam, plastic, scrap metal, wood and cardboard. The amount of waste placed in landfills has decreased by 60 percent since the program began.

St. Thomas Assembly Plant received the gold award from the Recycling Council of Ontario, Canada, for its outstanding waste reduction, reuse and recycling efforts. The plant consistently reduced the amount of solid nonhazardous waste it generated over a five-year time period. This, in turn, has led to a 78 percent reduction in the amount sent to landfills, from 5,310 to 1,174 metric tons.

Solvent VOC Reduction

Wayne Stamping and Assembly Plant uses cleaning materials, which typically contain VOC solvents, to clean paint automation equipment and surrounding areas.

Wastestreams relating to these solvents are captured and recycled. The plant has a bulk material/paint applications waste minimization team made up of the paint applications engineer, automation tenders, paint/solvent supplier engineers and an efficiency expert. This team targets solvent reduction as part of an ongoing process to optimize bulk materials and reduce associated VOC emissions.

Four solvent usage areas were identified and targeted for solvent reduction through the use of meters that identified the amount of material used at each area. Usage reductions proceeded and baseline data was shared with operations personnel, enabling the implementation of the necessary changes without impacting product quality.

In one usage area, the Wayne plant team identified maintenance cleaning procedures from the Ford Ohio Assembly Plant. Improved procedures for booth floor cleaning included maximizing the use of water-based cleaning materials. Paint hose sleeves and automation equipment covers were adopted for use, eliminating the need for additional cleaning of equipment in the booths.

In another usage area, clearcoat purge cycles were reprogrammed to allow purging after multiple units instead of after every unit. Clearcoat purge cycles in enamel booths were optimized to emulate ideal settings that were observed at the Ford Twin Cities Assembly Plant.

In a third usage area, improved methods were implemented for handsprayers' cleaning, such as providing daily allotments of cleaning solvent when existing cleaning material became unusable.

Paint Shop Maintenance VOC Reduction

The **Ohio Assembly Plant** is a 3.3 million-square-foot facility on approximately 419 acres in northern Ohio. The plant manufactures and paints bodies for the Econoline van and manufactures, paints and assembles the Mercury Villager.

The plant's paint department and total fluids management supplier undertook a joint venture to implement a low VOC paint shop maintenance program. All cleaning materials that are used to maintain the cleanliness of paint booths are applied to the VOC emission permit report. The plant uses VOC solvents to clean paint hoses, floors, equipment and walls to maintain a clean painting environment and to produce a quality paint finish.

As part of the new program, the paint shop wall coating, which contained VOCs, was replaced with a non-VOC, water-soluble wall coating, thus eliminating the need to wash the walls weekly with a VOC solvent. Also, a water-soluble barrier coating was applied to the paint booth floor grates to eliminate the use of solvents on them. The solvent-based Cleanroom® floor cleaner was changed to a water-based cleaner. The paint hose cleaning procedure was changed from spraying solvent on the hoses until clean to soaking the hoses in a low-VOC cleaner and wiping them clean after each shift.

As a result of these changes, VOC emissions from paint booth maintenance were reduced from 8.6 tons per month when the program began to 1.1 tons monthly. Savings in chemical costs totaled $34,000 annually. The capital/operating investment to bring the changes about was $21,000 in material and equipment plus a one-time labor cost. The Ohio EPA, in recognition of the environmental improvements, nominated the plant for the Governor's Pollution Prevention Award in 1996.

A similar improvement took place at the **Ford Norfolk Assembly Plant** in Norfolk, Virginia. Opened in 1925, the facility manufactures and paints the F-150 and F-250 trucks. The plant, awarded Ford's Total Productive Maintenance Award for checkpoint "C," was the first Ford facility to receive such an award for proactive preventive maintenance.

The facility's total waste management supplier, as part of its contract, is responsible for reducing waste streams at the plant and is paid on a cost-per-unit basis. In the paint facility the solvent supplier captures and recycles waste streams relating to solvents. As part of the plant's ongoing effort to reduce costs, improve quality and fulfill its commitment to reduce VOC emissions, the paint area management asked the solvent supplier to, where possible, review and improve the method of tracking solvent usage and the paint booth preventive maintenance cleaning procedure.

It was determined that solvent was being used on weekends during nonproduction hours. After a series of meetings and employee awareness training programs it was agreed that the solvent supply pumps would be shut off during nonproduction hours. The computer logic for the pumps was programmed to shut off the pumps 15 minutes after production and turn them on 30 minutes before the normal Monday morning production start-up. This arrangement allowed the booth maintenance staff time to obtain small quantities of material to hand-clean equipment before their shift, thereby eliminating unnecessary usage. The existing booth cleanup procedure was updated to reflect the changes made on the computer logic for the solvent supply pumps.

Wastewater Treatment Sludge Reduction

The *Ford Atlanta Assembly Plant* is a 2.3 million-square-foot facility located on 128 acres in the Atlanta, Georgia, metropolitan area. The plant assembles and paints Ford Taurus and Mercury Sable vehicles. The vehicle assembly process at Atlanta generates process waste/rinsewater primarily from the E-coat/phosphate coating area of the paint shop. This process wastewater (along with body shop and other miscellaneous wastewater, excluding sanitary waste) undergoes chemical treatment in an on-site wastewater treatment plant before it is discharged into the municipal sanitary sewer system. Resulting wastewater treatment sludge is dewatered in a filter press and transported off-site for disposal.

In 1996, new municipal pretreatment standards for phosphate (<10 ppm) were established. Additionally, an in-plant process change to reduce vehicle weight by replacing some steel body components with aluminum resulted in a reclassification of the wastewater treatment paint sludge to F019 hazardous waste. This change in classification increased disposal costs and documentation requirements. As a responsible corporate citizen, the Atlanta plant, with its supplier, focused efforts on revising procedures to meet all wastewater discharge requirements and reduce the quantity of hazardous sludge generated.

In coordination with the in-plant total fluids management supplier, an optimization study of current chemical treatment methods was conducted. Representative samples from numerous wastewater batch tanks over a wide range of initial phosphate levels were obtained and bench tests were performed. New batch tank treatment operation charts with revised chemical dosages were developed using data from the bench tests. Additionally, the plant began primarily using calcium chloride for treatment instead of lime. Treatment plant operators successfully began using the new chemicals at revised dosages while carefully monitoring effluent parameters.

As a result of this effort, wastewater discharge requirements were met and hazardous sludge generation and chemical usage amounts decreased. Savings realized were $48,000 annually in hazardous sludge transportation/disposal and $60,000 annually in wastewater treatment chemicals.

Assessment of Magnesium vs. Aluminum for Use as a Lightweight Transmission Case

Ford is performing research on the use of magnesium for lightweight component applications. In one research effort we compared the potential environmental benefits involving magnesium and aluminum.

Magnesium is a lighter-weight substitute for aluminum in vehicle components. Light weighting of vehicle components increases fuel economy and is an important vehicle design metric. Efforts are under way by automakers in Europe and North America to develop a new generation of highly fuel-efficient and lighter-weight cars. For this research study, the 1995 Ford Contour transmission case was chosen.

The production part is currently made of 100 percent secondary die-cast aluminum and weighs 9.435 kg. A weight reduction of approximately 30 percent could be achieved with the magnesium as a substitute.

When comparing the material options of aluminum vs. magnesium for a transmission case, many trade-offs become apparent. For example, energy saved due to increased fuel economy from a lighter part can be overcome by the material production phase for a magnesium case, especially where new magnesium is used. The current and potential future mix of secondary (recycled) magnesium needs to be better understood and may depend on the development of an infrastructure for efficiently acquiring the recycled magnesium.

Actual design changes required for a magnesium component also need further qualification to establish a more accurate weight change between magnesium and other materials. Additionally, sulfur hexafluoride (SF_6) used in the magnesium smelting process has a high global warming potential. Alternatives to it are being researched by magnesium producers.

The findings of this study build a solid foundation for prioritizing areas for environmental improvement and indicate topics for further research in both product design and the manufacturing process.

Prevention First

Ford's **Ohio Assembly Plant** participated in "Ohio Prevention First," a voluntary initiative seeking a reduction in pollution generated throughout Ohio. The plant was recognized in 1997 based on its progress towards achieving its original "Ohio Prevention First" pledge to reduce waste generated.

Among other activities, the plant implemented a program to recycle 55-gallon drums. The drums are cleaned, sent for melting and then reused as raw engine block material. In 1997, 2,327 steel drums were recycled compared to 1,298 in 1996. More than $15,000 was saved in 1997 from the cleaned, shipped and processed drums.

Overall, the plant's off-site shipments of 12,208 tons of manufacturing waste in 1997 represented a 50 percent reduction from the 1993 baseline, significantly greater than its initial 7 percent waste reduction commitment.

The Ohio Assembly Plant occupies 3.3 million square feet on 419 acres. It produces the Mercury Villager/Nissan Quest models and paints the bodies of the Ford Econoline van which are then assembled at the nearby Ford Lorain Assembly Plant. A waste minimization/pollution prevention team identifies opportunities for improvements in those areas at the Ohio Assembly Plant. Many initiatives have resulted in successful waste reduction and were instrumental in the state's recognition of the plant.

One such activity was a reduction in expired materials. Disposal of these materials had the potential of costing the plant more than $10,000 monthly. An inventory tracking system was developed to ensure utilization of materials with approaching expiration dates. For products near the end of their shelf life the supplier is contacted to determine the feasibility of extended shelf life. As a result of this initiative only 250 pounds of expired material were disposed of in 1997.

Total fluids management was another successful initiative. The pollution prevention team worked with the paint and process chemical supplier to maximize efficiencies of all fluids used in specific process applications. Maintenance chemicals (floor cleaners and paint strippers) have been changed to water-based chemicals. Hose cleaners have been modified to use low VOC solvents. Through the fluids management program, solvent usage dropped from 4,000 pounds per week in 1992 to less than 100 pounds weekly in 1997.

The total fluids management program also evaluated the feasibility of recycling paint booth sludge. An attempt to recycle paint solids into concrete aggregate proved unfeasible. However, the effort resulted in discovery of a paint booth sludge water chemistry (already in use at the Ford Michigan Truck Plant) that uses emulsions to solubilize the paint solids in the water system. This allows improved transfer efficiency resulting in decreased paint usage, eliminating sludge in the basin and thus eliminating one more waste stream that would require additional management and disposal.

Solvent Use Reduction

The ***Ford Romeo Engine Plant*** manufactures V-8 engines for midsize and large automobiles including the Ford Mustang, Ford Crown Victoria, Mercury Grand Marquis, Lincoln Continental and Lincoln Town Car as well as the engines for natural gas vehicles. Twenty-two low-volume solvent wash stations were used at the plant in the maintenance and tool set-up areas to clean machine parts and machine tooling. The Romeo Engine waste minimization team identified solvent use as a potential opportunity for preventing/reducing US Resource Conservation Recovery Act (RCRA) characteristic wastes and other targeted or listed substances.

The solvent cleaning stations used recycled mineral spirits containing small quantities of solvents that were included in the company list of substances targeted for voluntary reduction. A solvent recycling company serviced these cleaning stations, collecting the used solvent and replacing it with fresh recycled solvent. The used material was taken off-site to a reclaiming facility where it was cleaned and transformed into a recycled product.

The Romeo waste minimization team adopted a twofold approach to prevent waste: (1) use a product that did not contain listed substances and (2) reduce the quantity of solvent being used. A baseline survey for the cleaning stations was developed and alternatives were evaluated. A 12-week trial of the selected replacement solvent and parts cleaning unit was conducted to verify the performance. The trial demonstrated that the use of petroleum naphtha coupled with a self-filtering and cleaning station greatly improved the service life of the cleaning fluid, does not contain listed substances and has a higher flash point than the recycled material previously used. Based on the trial results, a plantwide conversion to the new material improved cleaning stations.

These changes have produced a 57 percent cost savings and a 47 percent reduction in the volume of waste solvent generated. The changes have brought about elimination of listed solvents in the raw material supplied for this cleaning process, and elimination of four of the 22 cleaning stations.

The waste minimization team submitted the overall project to the Ford Continuous Improvement Recognition System suggestion program and were awarded for their ideas and efforts.

Wastewater Treatment Process Improvement

The **Wayne Stamping and Assembly Plant** processes approximately 877,500 gallons of industrial wastewater per day. The cost-effective removal of heavy metals and suspended solids is the primary process objective. A high percentage of the wastewater and the metals requiring treatment and separation originates at the pre-paint coating operations in the assembly plants. Facilities for waste oil separation, collection and processing are also located at the wastewater treatment operation and used as needed.

The wastewater facility has the capability of using two coagulants for the treatment process. Sample testing procedures compared the quantity of each of the two coagulants that was required to effectively treat the wastewater. Evaluation included the opportunity to reduce the volume of ferric chloride and other commodity chemicals used in the treatment process. A coagulant to optimize treatment efficiency using a broadened evaluation procedure also had to be identified.

Waste treatment operators, plant engineers and an outside consultant benchmarked costs associated with effective treatment of each tank of wastewater. A plan was initiated to conduct a series of comparative cost analyses before treatment to ascertain the most economical procedures and treatments. The primary barrier encountered in the project was gathering and analyzing the data from operators on each treatment tank. For example, data relating to wastewater that was more difficult to treat had to be separated from data relating to wastewater treated under normal conditions.

Through this process, chemical use reductions were achieved and a new concentrated coagulant for treatment was identified. Cost savings were $125,000 from September, 1995, to January, 1997. No capital investment for the project was required.

Reuse

Creating and Preserving Wildlife Habitats

Ford encourages its facilities to provide natural habitats for wildlife within plant boundaries, thereby promoting environmental stewardship.

Ford's Dunton Engineering Centre in Essex, United Kingdom, has received international recognition for its employees' contribution to wildlife habit conservation. It is the first Ford location in Europe and one of only 274 sites worldwide to receive the Wildlife Habitat Council's award. The Council is a nonprofit, nonlobbying organization dedicated to increasing the quality and amount of wildlife habitat on corporate, private and public lands.

At Dunton, the largest automotive design and engineering facility in the United Kingdom, more than 5,000 engineers, designers and support staff design and develop all of Ford's small and medium-size cars and commercial vehicles worldwide. A team of a dozen employees has worked with the Essex Wildlife Trust, Writtle Agricultural College, Chelmsford and the EPA to transform 275 acres of natural grasslands, shrubs, trees and ponds. The group has created nature walks, encouraged re-establishment of wildflowers and grasses by restricting mowing of meadowland and deepened a pond, raising its water level to improve the habitat for plants and wildlife, including 300 fish of various species. More than 22,000 trees and shrubs and 17,000 wildflowers and grasses have been planted across the site.

The ***Essex Engine Plant***, near the Detroit River in Windsor, Ontario, Canada, was also certified as a "Corporate Wildlife Habitat Location" by the Wildlife Habitat Council.

To achieve certification the facility created a wildflower meadow, planted seedlings

Benefits & Examples

Wildlife at Work:

Essex Engine Plant was certified as a "Corporate Wildlife Habitat Location" by the National Wildlife Habitat Council.

For other examples see Michigan Auto Project web site at: www.deq.state.mi.us/ead/p2sect/auto/

---

and built nesting boxes for songbirds. The plant formed a wildlife committee to monitor nesting boxes, created education and awareness programs and increased the volunteer ranks. A majority of the volunteers are plant employees. It helps Boy Scout troops and local schools learn about nature while helping to bring back the natural habitat surrounding the plant.

The plant also has launched a site restoration program to convert 33 acres of property back to forest, complete with prairie grasses, shrubs and trees native to southwestern Ontario. What once was mowed turf grass is being restored as an oak hickory forest with hundreds of seedlings.

As a result of this effort about 70 acres of wildlife habitat were restored with 60 songbird nesting boxes and the planting of 600 tree seedlings.

Coolant Recycling

The ***Automatic Transmission New Product Center*** (ATNPC) is a 550,000-square-foot facility in Livonia, Michigan, that employs 980 people. Operating since 1990, it manufactures, assembles and tests prototype automatic transmissions and transmission components. The ATNPC contains a machine shop, converter lab, gear lab and flexible machining shop (FMS) where various machining operations are conducted. The facility includes a garage and build up area where transmissions are torn down, built up or repaired. Transmissions and their components are tested in the drivetrain analysis, hydraulic and mechanical systems and the dynamometer laboratories.

Coolants are used within machining operations to flush oil and chips away from the tooling and part being machined. During machining, coolants become contaminated with dirt, oils and metal chips. This contamination results in the need for frequent coolant changes in the machining operation. Coolant must be disposed of through appropriate, permitted waste treatment facilities. At ATNPC each coolant sump was being pumped down, cleaned and recharged every month and a half.

The ATNPC now uses a portable coolant reconditioning unit on six machines in the FMS. These machines have an aggregate coolant capacity of 1,850 gallons. Using the Coolant Wizard®, a hose draws the coolant out of the equipment and into the reconditioning unit.

The coolant passes through a reusable screen filter to remove debris and is then exposed to dissolved ozone, which kills bacteria. A coalescer skims tramp oil from the coolant, and the coolant is returned to the machining operation after final filtration. A pressure gauge on each of the two filters indicates when the filters need to be replaced. As a result of this improvement, the amount of water coolant was reduced by 900 gallons a year, and the amount of wastewater was reduced by 10,200 gallons.

Conversion of Regenerative Thermal Oxidizers to Regenerative Catalytic Oxidizers

The *Ford Wixom Assembly Plant* is a 4.7 million-square-foot facility in Wixom, Michigan. The plant, operating since 1957, produces the Lincoln Town Car and the Lincoln Continental. It also houses the pilot plant for the Low Emission Paint Consortium, a project of the United States Council for Automotive Research.

RTOs were used to destroy VOC emissions from the prime paint booth, the base coat paint booth and the clear paint booth. The RTOs operated at 1,400 degrees F and consumed both natural gas and electrical energy. The paint booth RTOs were converted to regenerative catalytic oxidizers (RCOs), which use metal catalysts enabling them to operate at 800 degrees, a lower temperature than the RTOs, but with the same level of destruction efficiency.

In addition to a lower temperature, the change resulted in lower energy consumption, a 66 percent reduction in carbon dioxide emissions, up to 50 percent longer life due to lower thermal stress, a shorter time required to reach the operating temperature and increased capacity due to better system flow characteristics, which allows for increased production without installation of a new RCO. There was an operational savings of $150,000 annually.

Recycle

Elimination of Paint Sludge Landfill Disposal

Nine Ford Motor Company assembly plants worldwide and one engine and fuel tank plant have incorporated new technology in their paint departments. Each facility employs from 1,000 to 4,000 persons depending on its size and production output. Cars and trucks assembled at these plants include the Ford Focus, Lincoln LS, Econoline van and European Transit van. Total production for 1998 at the 10 facilities was approximately 1.9 million vehicles and 3 million fuel tanks and engines.

Typically, the paint booth waterwash systems in automotive assembly plants are chemically treated to produce a conditioned (detackified) paint sludge, which settles in the sludge basin. Periodically, the sludge basin is drained and the deposited sludge removed for solidification and landfill disposal. A full-scale assembly plant generates about 1,000 cubic yards of paint sludge each year (see page 60).

Since 1995, a number of Ford assembly plants have used a patented solvent-in-water emulsion to replace conventional chemically treated water as the scrubbing medium in the paint booth system. This unique chemistry enhances many aspects of paint booth system operation and serves as the basis for a recycling process that eliminates the need to send paint sludge to landfills.

The recycling program, called EPOC II™ (Emulsion Program for Overspray Capture), is a service provided by Philip Services Corporation's Automotive Paint Services Group. The emulsion solubilizes the resin (organic) portion of the paint overspray and disperses the pigment and other inorganic ingredients. Paint sludge in the conventional sense is no longer generated. Rather, the emulsion accumulates paint components that are removed periodically by replacing all or part of the recirculating emulsion with fresh emulsion. The saturated emulsion is transported for processing to Philip's dedicated processing facility in Detroit, Michigan, where the paint solids are incorporated into useful products and the active chemical ingredient is recycled for use back into fresh emulsion.

As a result of this improvement, landfill disposal of paint sludge was reduced more than 90 percent. The capital/operations investment was $1 million per facility.

Packaging Waste Reduction

The ***Dearborn Assembly Plant***, one of Henry Ford's first assembly operations, is located at the historic Rouge Manufacturing Complex in Dearborn, Michigan. Construction of the 2.6 million-square-foot facility began in 1918, and over the following 82 years the plant's seven miles of assembly line have produced such products as Fordson tractors, wooden components for the Model T and Model A, Ford and Mercury station wagons and Ford Thunderbirds. Today more than 1,700 employees produce nearly 600 Ford Mustangs each day, enough to distinguish the plant as the most productive sports car manufacturing plant in North America. Since 1964 when production of the Mustang began, more than 7.5 million have rolled off Dearborn's assembly line.

Each Ford Mustang assembled at the plant is composed of more than 3,000 parts delivered by truck and rail. An average of 150 truckloads of parts are unloaded each day. Since demand for the newly redesigned Mustang has increased, production has been stepped up accordingly, resulting in an increased flow of parts to the plant. Typically, these parts arrive in cardboard packaging. Once the parts are unpacked the empty cardboard containers are sorted and consolidated, producing well more than 100 tons of cardboard per month.

With the unprecedented effort to establish the Rouge Complex as an icon of environmentally responsible manufacturing, several environmental programs have been developed at Dearborn Assembly. Although the plant has been recycling old corrugated cardboard for years, process improvements have recently been identified and implemented to streamline the recycling process and increase the volume of cardboard being recycled. Simultaneously, the plant has instituted a greening project to identify which packaging material has the potential to be replaced by returnable metal or plastic dunnage to reduce the volume of solid waste it generates. The goal is to eliminate cardboard packaging altogether and move towards totally returnable/reusable dunnage.

The cardboard recycling process is divided into two phases: collection and compaction. Initially, as much loose cardboard as possible is recovered to reduce the amount disposed of in general trash. The cardboard packaging waste that is recovered along the assembly line is aggregated before being loaded into a main compactor in which the cardboard is baled. Satellite balers located strategically throughout the plant facilitate this process and currently generate cardboard bales that weigh 700-900 pounds. Bales throughout the plant are accumulated and transported from the Rouge complex to vendor facilities for processing and consolidation to increase the weight per bale to 3-4 tons.

The cardboard bales are primarily sold to paper mills, where the cardboard is

CONTAINER SAVINGS — In 1997, the Michigan Truck Plant in Wayne instituted a returnable container program for most incoming parts delivered to the facility. Thus far, Michigan Truck has achieved 60 percent use of returnable containers. By 2001, the plant will be using 90 percent returnables. The facility has installed 24 cardboard compactors to help recycle most of the remaining cardboard. A wooden pallet recycling program has kept pallets from being diverted to landfills. The plant is now recycling 9,033 tons of cardboard annually and 4,032 tons of wooden pallets, saving $2.7 million a year.

broken down and recycled into paper products. To streamline the process, the plant is undergoing an effort to increase the weight of the bales that it produces to more than 1,000 pounds, which would allow the plant to sell the bales directly to the paper mills and other major purchasers. Currently, the recycling rate of approximately 150 tons per month produces cost savings of approximately $11,000 monthly.

Environmental Leadership at the Ford Romeo Engine Plant

With a strong EMS, a facility-specific pollution prevention program and consistent compliance with environmental requirements, the **Romeo Engine Plant** became one of the first Ford powertrain facilities in North America to be independently registered to ISO 14001. In recognition of its environmental stewardship, it also was one of the first Ford facilities to be honored as a Michigan Clean Corporate Citizen. Further, it is one of the Wildlife Habitat Council's "Wildlife at Work" sites.

The Romeo Engine Plant, in Romeo, Michigan, manufactures 4.6 liter car and truck engines. The plant departments include engine assembly and machining as well as all necessary support groups, including coolant, wastewater, central maintenance and engine testing. In 1999, the plant produced 640,000 units and was recognized in 2000 as North America's most productive V-8 engine plant.

Every engine produced at the plant undergoes a process called "hot testing" to verify proper engine assembly, including compulsory electrical connections and the absence of leaks. The engines currently are tested on a rotating carousel system. However, this system has many drawbacks. The existing procedures are not adequate to detect engine defects such as missing gaskets, cross-threaded drain plugs and low compression ratios. These problems are discovered at vehicle assembly facilities and perhaps later by consumers.

In addition to being expensive, these hot tests also present major safety and environmental concerns. When completing a hot test, workers are exposed to moving parts in extremely close proximity, highly combustible fluids and high noise levels. From an environmental standpoint, the execution of these tests also results in the emission of VOCs, carbon monoxide and nitrogen dioxide.

Areas of current focus at the Romeo Engine Plant are camshaft grinding and machining operations. When engine camshafts are machined, coolant oil is applied to the parts, which also carries away steel shavings as well as grinding wheel dust. The process results in the formation of a pulpy sludge, called swarf. Presently, the camshaft machining sludge is removed from machining operations by conveyors, aggregated and picked up by an outside contractor who solidifies it and transports it to a landfill. With the existing process, camshaft machining loses an estimated 8,200 gallons of the reusable coolant oil associated with the sludge per year. The process also leads to an estimated 690 tons of sludge being sent to landfills each year.

Engine hot testing process improvements are being developed and implemented at the plant. Planned changes include replacement of the 100 percent final assembly hot test with an in-process test system and an audit test system which would test only 5 percent of the assembled engines. The new process consists of nine test stations that will test the engines at various stages of assembly. This modification will greatly increase the plant's overall quality assurance, reduce annual operating costs, improve customer satisfaction and eliminate safety and environmental concerns.

Since April, 2000, investigation has been under way to discover environmentally friendly treatment alternatives to current grinding swarf disposal methods. The Romeo Engine Plant is taking part in a pilot study with the oxidation facilities at the Rouge manufacturing complex to use a treated form of its grinding swarf as a supplemental fuel in prereduction shaft furnaces. During this study, the grinding swarf waste stream from select machining operations has been diverted from landfill disposal. This process alternative includes treating the sludge with a procedure called briquetting, which dewaters the sludge, densifies it and conglomerates it into small masses called briquettes. This process not only separates a large portion of the coolant from the sludge solids to be reused, but will also facilitate the recycling of the swarf by creating an efficient fuel source.

Future Vision of Sustainability: Restoration of the Rouge

While the case studies demonstrate our commitment to sustainability, they are largely things that we have already done. No project demonstrates our future direction more than Ford's Rouge Center. At one time, the Center employed more than 100,000 people at 29 factories over a sprawling 1,100 acre complex built along Michigan's Rouge River. In its heyday one new car rolled off a Rouge assembly line about every 49 seconds.

Built under the watchful eye of founder Henry Ford between 1917 and 1925, the complex serves as a monument to 20th century manufacturing. Today, the complex is on the verge of being reborn as a symbol of Ford's 21st century commitment to sustainable manufacturing under the direction of renowned environmental architect William A. McDonough.

"Today we are laying the groundwork to transform a 20th century industrial icon into a model of 21st century sustainable manufacturing," William Clay Ford, Jr. said at the start of construction on November 14, 2000.

"This is a testament to Ford's corporate citizenship and commitment to its hometown community," he added. "While most companies would rather move than invest in a 83-year-old site, we view this as a reinvestment in our employees, our hometown and an American icon of the 20th century."

Our plans for the Ford Rouge Center encompass testing numerous advanced environmental concepts and planting 1,500 trees. The Rouge of the future will include the country's largest "living roof" covered with sedum — a succulent groundcover — and other plants that will reduce water runoff and reduce energy consumption at the state-of-the-art manufacturing facility. Project planners are designing a system, which, over time, "will use ecologically advanced methods for stormwater management, water and energy usage, air quality and soil restoration."

The living roof reduces stormwater runoff by holding an hour's worth of rainfall. The net area of the roof will be 454,000 square feet. It will not only slow down stormwater runoff, but living plants will absorb carbon dioxide as part of photosynthesis, so oxygen is emitted and greenhouse gases are reduced.

Outside, mustard seed and other plants will help rid the soil of contaminants through a process called phyto-remediation, which uses natural plants to clean soil. Michigan State University is partnering with Ford on this project — believed to be

A computer rendering of the future Rouge Assembly Plant, with skylights above the mezzanine-level walkways.

A computer rendering of the enclosed bridge linking the assembly plant and paint shop at the future Ford Rouge Center, seen on the front cover.

the first experiment of its kind on an active manufacturing site. Phyto-remediation is a natural alternative to incineration or landfills.

Better stormwater management on the site will be achieved through the use of swales, or shallow green ditches, seeded with indigenous plants. Retention ponds in combination with the swales will help regulate water flow and evaporation near the new assembly plant.

Porous paving, a surface that filters water through retention beds with two to three feet of compacted stones, will also be employed at the site. Another pilot involves the use of "green screens" on both sides of the Rouge Office Building. Nylon netting or wire mesh will serve as the base for vines and other climbing plants that absorb heat and help cool the building. If the screens prove successful on the Rouge Office Building, they will be used on the new plant. Fuel cells also are being tested as backup power for some computer platforms.

From a business standpoint, the facility will dramatically reduce the space normally needed for both component and finished vehicle storage. Eventually replacing the Dearborn Assembly Plant, finished vehicle storage space at the new facility will be reduced by 50 percent inside and outside the plant. This means 90 percent of the vehicles produced will be shipped the same day. Its assembly lines will be capable of handling three vehicle platforms and nine different models starting with the Ford Ranger pickup and other trucks.

"We think the new assembly plant will provide a terrific opportunity to begin transforming one of the enduring symbols of the industrial age," declared Mr. Nasser. "This will be a facility designed to expand our manufacturing vision, test advanced environmental concepts and over time become a new model for future Ford facilities." The project also reflects the speed in which 21st century business operates. We started with no specific plan, just a well thought-out instinct by top management that this could be done.

A founding member of the American Institute of Architects Committee on the Environment, Mr. McDonough serves as an advisor to President Clinton's Council on Sustainable Development. He was the lead designer on the "Greening of the White House" project that made environmental recommendations about parts of the White House buildings and grounds complex. In 1992, his firm, William McDonough + Partners, wrote the *Hannover Principles* — a manifesto for environmentally conscious building and design commissioned by the City of Hannover, Germany — as the official guide for the design of the World's Fair in 2000. In 1996 he became the only individual to receive the nation's highest environmental award, The Presidential Award for Sustainable Development.

Thanks to the insightful design of Mr. McDonough and Ford's environmental commitment, this project will implement a combination of water and energy savings and waste reduction.

Global Water Management Initiative

Our future commitment to sustainability was also outlined in a June 29, 2000, speech by Ford Motor Company Chairman William Clay Ford, Jr. at the opening of "Viva el Agua," a water exhibit at the Papalote Children's Museum in Mexico City. Ford Motor Company and its dealers cosponsored the exhibit with the Mexican Ministry of Environment, Natural Resources and Fisheries and the National Water Commission. Mr. Ford said:

> *Life on Earth is sustained by water. Seventy percent of the planet's surface is covered with water. But the water supply is still limited and fragile. Only three percent of the Earth's water is fresh, and three-fourths of that is frozen in glaciers and ice caps. Pollution and increasing demand threaten this vital resource. For anyone concerned about the environment, an understanding of the role water plays in nature and mankind's impact on that role is essential.*

In his speech, Mr. Ford announced the launch by Ford Motor Company of a major Global Water Management initiative covering not only water conservation but also reuse of storm and process water and management of water quality. Under this initiative the company will set internal targets for reduction of water use and work with our suppliers to encourage them to do the same.

Over the previous three-year period Ford had already reduced its worldwide water consumption by an amount equivalent to what 162,000 people drink in a lifetime! In doing so, we reduced our costs by more than $6 million.

5 Supplier Program

Early in our implementation of ISO 14001, we were inundated with questions from Ford suppliers, along the lines of, "You guys have made this crazy decision to do this environmental program, but you're not going to make me do it, are you?" And early in the process, we decided that the answer was "No." We were not going to make anybody do it, because we weren't convinced ourselves that it was the right thing to do. As stated earlier, it was an intuitive decision in the first place.

But as we completed implementation in our plants worldwide and began to recognize the operational benefits, including improved operating efficiency and reduced costs, the Ford purchasing department suggested that we should require implementation of ISO 14001 for our suppliers as well.

To an environmental professional, that's the ultimate success. When the business people begin supporting environmental programs for their business benefits, not just the environmental advantages, then you know you have it made.

We had been asking our suppliers for a long time to do everything they could to drive down costs, because that drives down costs to our ultimate customers. Now, with ISO 14001, we had a program that would actually help suppliers do that. Instead of just requiring them to lower their costs, we could show them how to do it.

Suppliers of production materials, equipment, services and goods — our Tier 1 suppliers — play an especially important role in the development and production of our products. In fact, purchased parts and materials account for more than 60 percent of the total value of a vehicle Ford produces.

We also view our suppliers as an extension of Ford Motor Company. They extend

Why ISO 14001 for suppliers?

- Purchased parts and materials account for over 60 percent of total vehicle value!

- Suppliers are viewed as an extension of Ford Motor Company — extended leadership on facility environmental matters through a value chain

- Protecting the environment is everyone's job

our leadership on facility environmental matters through the value chain. And, of course, we believe that protecting the environment is everyone's job.

In February, 1999, we sent this letter to our top 200 production and top 90 non-production suppliers in North America:

> Ford recently celebrated a major environmental milestone, becoming the first and only automotive company to obtain certification for all of its plants around the world to the ISO 14001 international environmental management standard. We view this accomplishment not only as doing the right thing for our environment but also as a competitive advantage.
>
> An important element of being an environmentally responsible ISO 14001 organization is to ensure that you, as our partners, are clear on your roles and responsibilities as a supplier to Ford. As such, we are encouraging all of our suppliers to pursue certification to ISO 14001, recognizing its benefits to the environment, opportunity for cost savings through the elimination of waste, and its importance to your future competitiveness as a world class supplier.
>
> As a first step, we are asking that you complete the enclosed survey. Your responses will help us to better assess the present state of our supply base and to identify barriers and enablers to extend ISO 14001 throughout the value chain.

The point of the letter essentially was to encourage our suppliers to voluntarily pursue registration to ISO 14001. At the same time, we wanted to determine where our suppliers were at that time in terms of their registration status or plans. That was the purpose of the survey. Survey results indicated that there were no serious

Chapter 5

objections. Many of our top suppliers — certainly the major ones — were already registered to the standard or moving toward registration. A few suppliers were encouraging their own suppliers to do the same thing. Many suppliers responded along the lines of, "We wish you would require it, because then we'd all be doing it."

So that's what we decided to do. In September, 1999, we sent this letter to our Tier 1 suppliers:

> *Earlier this year, we encouraged our supply base to pursue registration to the ISO 14001 international environmental management standard. We also conducted a survey to assess supplier readiness towards ISO 14001. The feedback from suppliers was very encouraging. Several suppliers responded that they have already registered some of their facilities to ISO 14001. The majority indicated that they plan to register their plants to ISO 14001, recognizing its benefits to the environment and potential for cost savings through waste reduction.*
>
> *Ford Motor Company led the automotive industry by becoming the first automotive manufacturer to certify all of its manufacturing facilities around the world to the ISO 14001 standard. As our suppliers share a key role in our environmental commitment and efforts towards continuous improvement:*
>
> - *Ford will require all production and nonproduction suppliers with manufacturing facilities to certify a minimum of one manufacturing site to ISO 14001 by December 31, 2001.*

Percent of Suppliers With a Corporate Environmental Policy

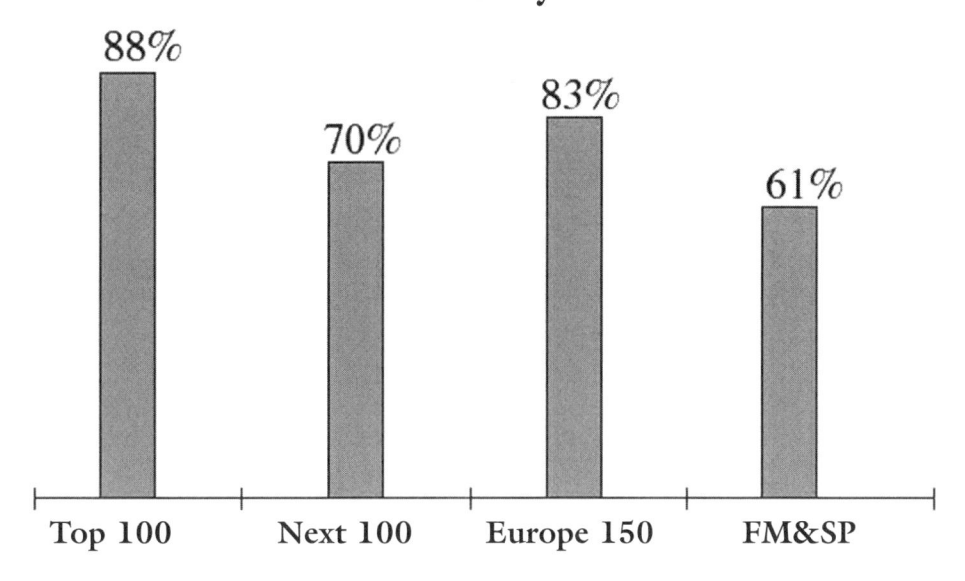

Top 100	Next 100	Europe 150	FM&SP
88%	70%	83%	61%

- *Ford will require all supplier manufacturing sites to be certified to the ISO 14001 standard by July 1, 2003.*

Suppliers were encouraged to take similar actions with their subtier suppliers. The time schedule we laid out was somewhat arbitrary, guided by our internal implementation experience. We determined that the journey from initial application through full implementation was about three years. That, coupled with the encouraging responses we had received from suppliers, gave us confidence that this was a reasonable time frame.

The registration requirement affected about 5,000 manufacturing-oriented suppliers. About 1,600 of them provide all the parts that go into an automobile in our production facilities. The rest of them are "nonproduction" suppliers of everything from work gloves, safety glasses, oils and lubricants to bricks and mortar, major presses and assembly line machinery.

To assist these suppliers in accelerating their ISO 14001 efforts, we offered Supplier Awareness Training on a voluntary basis. We scheduled an introductory session for November 18, 1999, and another one for December 2, 1999, at the Total Cost Management (TCM) center in Dearborn. We enclosed information on the sessions and a registration form with the letter to suppliers. We also scheduled sessions for Europe, Mexico, Latin America and Asia Pacific.

ISO 14001 Compliant Suppliers*

- A total of 35 European suppliers had plants registered to ISO 14001 or EMAS (Europe 150 Production)

- A total of 38 North American suppliers had plants registered to ISO 14001 (Top 100 & Next 100)

- Among nonproduction suppliers, seven reported registration to ISO 14001

* Suppliers currently shipping to Ford reporting minimum of one plant registered to ISO 14001 or EMAS as of July, 1999.

We suggested that environmental or production managers with responsibility for implementation of an EMS should attend, but we limited participation to two representatives per supplier and gave priority to suppliers who had not achieved ISO 14001 registration at any of their facilities. The purpose of the training sessions was to provide an overview of ISO 14001 and an introduction to the development and implementation of an EMS. The 8 a.m. to 5 p.m. program covered these topics:

- ISO 14001 — What it is/What it is not.
- Ford Plant Perspectives — Lessons Learned/Case Studies.
- Overview of Environmental System Design.
- Linking ISO 14001 to QS-9000/ISO 9001 Quality Systems.
- Developing an Implementation and Roll-out Plan.
- Leveraging Resources.

The response to the training invitations was so overwhelming that we had to move the sessions in Dearborn to a larger facility. In a *Supplier Environmental Requirements Manual* that we developed for suppliers to guide and assist them in the ISO 14001 process, we stated: "Suppliers should recognize ISO 14001 certification as not only a customer requirement, but as the right thing to do from an environmental standpoint. And they should understand that it is a driver for improved efficiency, waste reduction, long-term cost savings and important to future global competitiveness."

Survey Results Indicate...

- A high percentage of our top suppliers had corporate environmental policies
- Supplier plans towards ISO 14001 varied to some degree by region and commodity
- Most suppliers had general awareness regarding ISO 14001, several reported certified facilities (timing, gaps and opportunities identified)
- A few suppliers encouraged ISO 14001 to their suppliers or planned to do so when certified

Ford & ISO 14001

The *Supplier Environmental Requirements Manual* spelled out in detail Ford's policies, strategies and requirements pertaining to recycling, restricted materials such as chemical substances and other materials of concern. It broke down requirements and specifications for Ford, Jaguar and Volvo products. The manual listed nonproduction environmental requirement guidelines by these supplier/contractor categories (see *Supplier Environmental Requirements Manual*, Figure VII, pages 103-104):

- Industrial Materials
- Machinery and Tooling
- Contractors Working On-site at Ford Motor Company Facilities
- Waste Management Suppliers and Environmental Testing Suppliers
- Engineering Contractors
- Subcontractors
- Transport Contractors

We also created a special Environmental Award to recognize suppliers for outstanding environmental achievement and innovation. Examples of environmental excellence include:

- Implementation of new technology that reduced the environmental impact of Ford, Jaguar and/or Volvo products.
- Significant improvement in the use of post-consumer recycled content materials in products shipped to Ford, Jaguar or Volvo.
- Innovation in materials and/or substitution for "Restricted" or "Grey" substances in components or materials implemented in Ford, Jaguar or Volvo programs. Preference given to cost-effective, performance-enhancing solutions.
- Significant reduction in the use of energy or waste produced in the supplier production process.

We have not extended the registration requirement down the supplier chain beyond Tier 1. We believe that as more suppliers learn more about ISO 14001, and recognize the business as well as environmental benefits that can be achieved, they will become as enthusiastic about it as we are. We would like them to feel that they "want to" do it instead of feeling that they "must" do it.

Figure VII. Nonproduction Environmental Requirement Guidelines by Supplier Categories

Supplier/Contractor Category	Environmental Requirements	Date
Contractors Working On-Site at Ford Motor Company Facilities	Established environmental work plan including legal requirement follow-up.	*Ongoing*
	Select suppliers to Volvo required to implement ISO 14001 environmental management system.	*12/31/2000*
	Fulfillment of local procedures for handling of waste, chemicals, emergencies, etc.	*Ongoing*
	Materials used by the contractor must meet restricted material requirements, and specifications of materials used on premises must be available.	
Waste Management Suppliers & Environmental Testing Suppliers	ISO 14001 environmental management system recommended.	*Ongoing*
	Select suppliers to Volvo required to implement ISO 14001 environmental management system.	*12/31/2000*
	Environmental training for workers.	*Ongoing*
	Fulfillment of the local procedures for handling of waste, chemicals, emergencies, etc.	
Engineering Contractors	Design for environment training for engineers recommended.	*Ongoing*
	Select suppliers to Volvo required to implement ISO 14001 environmental management system.	*12/31/2000*
Subcontractors	First-tier contractor responsible.	*Ongoing*
	Subcontractors working on premises must be informed and agree with local procedures.	
Transport Contractors	ISO 14001 environmental management system recommended.	*Ongoing*
	Select suppliers to Volvo required to implement ISO 14001 environmental management system.	*12/31/2000*
	Established environmental work plan, including legal requirement follow-up, improvement plans.	*Ongoing*
	Environmental training for drivers.	
	Declaration of vehicle fleet (vehicle types, age, fuel consumption, etc.)	

All Environmental Requirements apply to Ford, Jaguar and Volvo, unless otherwise noted.

Figure VII. Nonproduction Environmental Requirement Guidelines by Supplier Categories (continued)

Supplier/Contractor Category	Environmental Requirements	Date
Industrial Materials	ISO 14001 environmental management system.	
	One manufacturing or processing facility shipping product to Ford or Jaguar.	*12/31/2001*
	One manufacturing facility shipping product to Volvo for select suppliers.	*12/31/2000*
	All facilities shipping product to Ford or Jaguar.	*7/1/2003*
	All manufacturing facilities shipping product to Volvo for select suppliers.	*12/31/2002*
	Compliance with restricted materials specifications. 　Ford/Jaguar – WSS-M99P9999-A1 　Volvo – STD 1009,1 and 1009,11	*Ongoing*
	Product-specific requirements (as specified by requester).	*Ongoing*
Machinery and Tooling	ISO 14001 environmental management system.	
	One manufacturing or processing facility shipping product to Ford or Jaguar.	*12/31/2001*
	One manufacturing facility shipping product to Volvo for select suppliers.	*12/31/2000*
	All facilities shipping product to Ford or Jaguar.	*7/1/2003*
	All manufacturing facilities shipping product to Volvo for select suppliers.	*12/31/2002*
	Compliance with restricted materials specifications. 　Ford/Jaguar – WSS-M99P9999-A1 　Volvo – STD 1009,1 and 1009,11 Product-specific requirements (as specified). For example: *Low total energy consumption (start-up, use, and stop).* *Low noise levels.* *Low consumption of chemicals, use of standard chemicals with low environmental impact.*	*Ongoing*

All Environmental Requirements apply to Ford, Jaguar and Volvo, unless otherwise noted.

6 The Ford Retail Program

Dealerships are the face of Ford Motor Company to the buying public. They also are independent businesses and cannot be made to do something they do not want to do.

Furthermore, this is a time of great change in the auto industry's retail distribution system. With new elements like the Internet and national sales organizations impacting the way cars are sold and bought, it is a dynamic time in the industry.

For both of these reasons, we do not think this is the right time to require our dealers to adopt, implement and register to ISO 14001.

Still, we think it is important that they seriously consider the benefits of ISO 14001. It would be helpful to them as independent businesses and to Ford Motor Company, because the general public associates these businesses with us. When consumers see a Ford dealership, it signifies Ford Motor Company to them. And if they see a Ford dealership with a leak in an underground storage tank that impacts a community's groundwater, they could associate it with Ford Motor Company.

We have piloted an ISO 14001 program at selected dealerships in the United States and Canada to demonstrate our intuition that adopting the program is good for them from both business and environmental standpoints. Discovery Ford — a dealership located in Burlington, Ontario, Canada — was certified in November, 2000. We believe it is the first dealership in North America to do so. Based largely on its experience we have developed a *Ford Dealership EMS Workbook* to assist other dealerships with implementation.

We plan to communicate the results of those activities to all Ford dealers with the hope that they will recognize the advantages of implementing an EMS in their own facilities and will proceed to do so. We hope they will recognize that it is the logical thing to do as ISO 14001 takes root in the automotive industry supply chain from suppliers to building the components through the assembly process and ultimately into retail distribution. We believe that we haven't fully done our job if the environmental aspects are not considered at every step of the process.

There is another aspect to the Ford retail system — businesses that consumers use after they purchase a car. These include muffler and tire facilities, auto recycling centers and the like. Most of these, like dealerships, are independent businesses. However, Ford Motor Company has purchased some of these businesses and has organized them under the Automotive Consumer Services Group.

We are now discussing developinging an environmental strategy with them. One area of sensitivity is that these are small businesses with slim profit margins; implementing ISO 14001 might be costly to them and require more than they are able to do. However, we believe we can proceed in two significant ways. One is to develop a compliance program for them to ensure that they are complying with applicable environmental laws and regulations. The second is that they would strongly consider achieving registration to ISO 14001.

GreenZone

On June 16, 2000, the newest Ford dealership in Europe, and what is believed to be the world's first purposely built green dealer facility, was opened at Umea in northern Sweden. It is expected to provide valuable knowledge for possible future applications to Ford dealerships globally.

Called *GreenZone*, the project includes three separate buildings — a car dealership, a restaurant and a fuel station. It demonstrates that by applying a combination of different environmental technologies energy requirements can be reduced 60 to 70 percent.

The car showroom building is equipped with a geothermal system and thermal solar collectors which regulate the heating of the building. The dealership, restaurant and fuel station are linked by culverts which serve as conduits for excess heat between the buildings. For example, excess heat from the restaurant kitchens can be used for heating the car showroom.

Lantern skylights have been installed to provide better light and reduce energy consumption. Remaining energy demands are met by renewable energy provided by the national grid. In the fall of 2000, a wind generator went into operation to satisfy the entire facility's energy demand.

The GreenZone turned a restaurant, car dealership and fuel station into a combined eco-friendly enterprise.

In addition to its innovative handling of energy demands, the *GreenZone* project applies other environmental technologies. The three buildings have green sedum tile roofs as an integral part of the climate control and water circulation system including the use of rainwater. The demand on public water supplies is reduced by 90 percent, mainly through the recirculation of used water and its regeneration through an internal wastewater treatment system.

Air within the facility is purified by living plants, known as green filters, and all building materials that were used in construction can be reused or recycled. The facility will be registered to ISO 14001. The environmentally friendly dealership marks a new step and emphasizes Ford's holistic approach to environmental matters, from our plants to our products and through to our dealers. Twenty thousand Ford dealerships all over the world will benefit from the experiences gained from the *GreenZone* project.

7 Reflections of Senior Management

Launching a new program that you don't know much about but feel is the right thing to do is not a traditional way to do business. That's how ISO 14001 began in the Ford Motor Company. When Mr. Hagenlocker signed the letter committing the second largest automotive company in the world to implement the FES at all of its facilities worldwide, he knew it was an environmental program, but that's all he knew about it. He signed the letter because a lot of other people in the company whom he trusted said it was the right thing to do.

You can view that as a negative. Looking back on it, we view it as a positive. ISO 14001 became a major milestone in the management of the company, helping Ford move from a deliberative analytical approach to environmental management into a true leadership position. Ford not only moved ahead of the curve on environmental management, it set the curve.

One of the most important aspects of ISO 14001 implementation is getting senior management commitment. Three key members of the Ford corporate leadership team look back on the experience; their candid observations providing valuable insight into the process of Ford's implementation.

Helen Petrauskas, Vice President, Environmental and Safety

It turned out better than I thought it would. We completed implementation and registration sooner than we thought we would, and we're getting more out of it than I thought we would.

We anticipated some things and others we didn't. We anticipated that if we went to the senior management of the company and got their support, it would be real support. My view of our management is that they wouldn't say "yes" without really meaning it. When they said "Yes, this is something we ought to do," I knew we had their strong support.

What I didn't expect — and maybe I should have because of our ISO 9000 experience — was the huge support, interest and energy that we got from our entire workforce. My experience on environmental issues is that it's easy to get senior management's support for programs of this nature. That's not the challenge. The challenge is getting the support of the people who really make things happen. Senior management can certainly preclude something from happening by not supporting it. But their support in and of itself, if that's all you have, is not enough. That's why building the operating committee in each plant and developing the support locally was critical.

ISO 14001 is the best example of a broad, consistent framework that has enough flexibility for local situations. It's sufficiently flexible so that it permitted a lot of innovation, things we may not have expected. By the same token, it doesn't arbitrarily assume something.

The whole notion of third-party registration was something we worried about. We worried that registrars weren't going to understand our business, our manufacturing processes, and we were going to get a bunch of suggestions we wouldn't know how to deal with. But that turned out not to be a big issue.

One of the benefits of the ISO 9000 experience that spilled over was just the way you organize yourself to do it and do a pilot. But don't take forever doing the pilot; you don't have to do the pilot perfectly. Don't make a big year-and-a-half-long production out of a pilot and a big study. Just make sure you put enough resources in there at the outset and then just do it. Quickly capture what you have learned and go off to do the next one.

We did a number of pilot plants when we started. We asked plants to pilot it and we gave them a lot of support. One of the things we really did right was to put a high level of resources into the first several plants. We brought some additional funding so the first plants could provide learning experiences, and that paid off for us. Because once you've done one assembly plant, you have a pretty good idea of how to get the next assembly plant started. The same goes with a stamping plant, and so on down the line.

We found a significant number of instances where, by doing something good environmentally, we also could reduce operating costs. We could look at the pattern of those kinds of things and then replicate those good experiences in other plants.

One part of it is education. One of the unrecognized benefits of all of this is that by participating people learn by doing and, in my book, learning by doing is a thousand times better than learning by listening. We started out by sensitizing and educating people on what potential environmental impacts are and what one can do about them. That allowed people who know every nook and cranny in a plant to take that knowledge and adapt it.

Another part of it is that sometimes we tend to forget that our employees are interested in the broader society in which they live. We think of them as Ford employees, but they have the same views, aspirations and hopes as the population at large. When we look at public opinion polls that say the vast majority of Americans care deeply about the environment and protecting the environment, that's a view our employees share.

So being able to do something about it at your place of work is a source of much pride. We are becoming, in our operations, the beneficiary of people's views about the kind of world they want to live in, the kinds of things they want to work on, and what they want to be part of. It makes people feel really good about what they're doing. It gives them a tremendous feeling of satisfaction.

The fantastic thing about ISO is that it provides a baseline; it tells you where you are. That's extremely important. So the fact that it gives a systematic picture of where you are today and then an ongoing picture of where you are headed supplies a high level of confidence that you have a process in place that assures you are taking on environmental responsibilities.

There are two ways you can assure yourself that you're doing the right things, whether with your plants or products. You could have an army of auditors, or you could put a system in place that organically grows and stays alive and gives that information. I'll take the latter any day, not just from an efficiency standpoint, but also from the standpoint of allowing us to do something without having a lot of people running around checking off boxes on a clipboard.

I have been in this business 30 years, and I have had the privilege of watching a migration from, "Tell us what the rules are, they're probably silly, but we'll go ahead and do them if that's what you want," to an attitude of really trying to understand both the real and perceived environmental rules of a community, a country, a planet. That transition is true not just for our company, but for our industry. I think you would find individual companies in various places on that spectrum.

If there had not been an ISO 14001 EMS, I think we would have tried to develop our own, but it would have been a lot more difficult and it would have been harder to get others to recognize it. There still is less recognition in the United States than outside. It isn't that somebody went off and wrote a bunch of rules. In a general way, it really does represent the consensus of people who are smart and knowledgeable on this subject.

We would have headed down the path, but what we would have done, because it's our nature, is start out with a bunch of top-down initiatives. We would sit around at the corporate level and decide it's important to do this, that and the other thing; to reduce this by 12 percent, that by 20 percent.

We have a demonstrated history that is less successful than we would like it to be. But it's our first reaction, we'll eyeball this and give everybody tasks and they'll go off and do them.

Without our knowing it, or fully appreciating it at the time, ISO changed that paradigm for us. I'm extremely happy that we did it. The discipline it introduces is going to continue to pay off for us. It's a way of life for us now and will continue to be a way of life.

Roman Krygier, Vice President, Powertrain Operations

One of the key benefits that came out of ISO 14001 was the company's leadership role in corporate citizenship. It entails many aspects of our business, not only in the safety of our vehicles but also the environment in which our people work and the environmental aspects of the materials we use in our plants to build our products.

When we heard about ISO 14001 we were developing our Ford Production System, a way to manage our business from raw material to the factory and through the factory to the customer. One of the key aspects of the Ford Production System was our environmental responsibility, our safety leadership initiative. We thought ISO 14001 would be a way to put a process in place that leveraged best practices — the best of what was happening around the world. Our corporate citizenship focus told us we needed to do this. It has become a base requirement of the Ford Production System.

ISO 14001 brought the whole aspect of environmental responsibility into the everyday workings of how we run our business. We looked at our hazardous materials, at how we managed our effluents, from the paint shops and throughout the manufacturing process. We have used the standard to make us think more up-front about how we design our manufacturing processes, how we design our product, so that they become positives for us.

It also has contributed to our operational efficiency. We have reduced hazardous waste and water usage. We have found substitute materials that are more cost-effective. Polychlorinated biphenyl (PCB) has to be eliminated in our older facilities, and we have accelerated that.

Obviously, environmental requirements are going to be different in the United States than in India, Mexico or many of the other countries among the 26 where we operate our plants. But we are saying that there are some fundamentals to which we will always pay attention when it comes to the health and safety of our employees. That rolls through our best practices and approaches on a worldwide basis.

ISO 14001 has also helped us develop a proactive relationship with government agencies. Too many times in the past we have been at odds with government on various matters. Now the interface with government agencies becomes more friendly and interactive instead of adversarial. It's not that we didn't pay attention to our regulatory requirements in the past, of course we did. Now ISO 14001 has given us a more robust process to deal with those issues early on. It provides a means to bring government agencies and corporations like Ford together early to preclude many of the types of issues that might have developed in the past. As a result, we have a more robust, friendly environment for our workers and for the communities in which our plants are located.

Having an ISO 14001-based EMS really sends a signal to people that we care about them. If you don't manage hazardous materials and effluents that go into communities, you're going to have problems with those communities. ISO is a positive in terms of how people view the company's commitment to them.

One lesson we learned from the ISO experience is the importance of thinking about processes first; having people understand what this is all about and bringing them into the process early. You can't just dump ISO into a plant and expect them to make it happen. We laid out a process. We brought the plants in, had understanding, gained leadership commitment at the plant level. We had people in place in the plants who were sort of coaches; they took a leadership role. Having champions in your facilities and having buy-in before you roll it out is critical.

This may sound like commonsense. But too many times, expediency takes over. You say, "Let's put this in place, what's so difficult about it? There's a process and let the system take it." We didn't do it that way. We put a lot of thought into the implementation process, and, as a result, the plants took off with it. We also make it a big deal to get certified. We put some recognition behind it. We publicized it.

ISO 14001 is the environmental element in a comprehensive manufacturing process. Consider machining, for instance. We use coolants to cool spindles and machine tools, and we don't want that to become a mist that creates an environmental hazard to our employees. So we have come up with different materials and ways to reduce that mist.

It all becomes part of the metrics in terms of understanding the ISO requirements and what we have to do — keeping noise levels in plants below a threshhold level, for another example. The metrics of ISO 14001 drive us to think about how to design the manufacturing process. Sometimes it even gets into the design; maybe we can eliminate some machining operations if we rethink the manufacturing and design requirements.

How do we keep this up? It's built into our work. It's ingrained in the whole way we do our business. Our manufacturing engineers have an obligation to design processes, types of materials from those processes, to be robust and meet the guidelines for ISO 14001. The audits will provide checks and balances over time so things don't slip away.

I think this is all about the commitment of a corporation to its people and its customers. Our plants are in communities that are going to form perceptions of Ford Motor Company. Corporate citizenship is all about the views of people on what a company stands for, where we put our emphasis. If companies don't have a strong commitment to their people and their safety, as well as to the community, people are going to see that, and it's going to be negative for the companies.

Jim Padilla, Group Vice President, Global Manufacturing

The ISO challenge, both for quality management with ISO 9000 and environmental management with ISO 14001, has become a major driver in our business from the standpoint that they provide two things. They provide us with a framework to deploy best practices across all of our manufacturing plants, and consistency is important. They also provide us the opportunity, particularly ISO 14001, to improve our business situation through conservation of resources.

So it has tremendous leverage in our system in terms of setting standards and expectations, and by developing defined processes and best practices, it also serves as a major training tool for people. So it's a tremendous framework for how we want to move forward.

In the area of quality, we have seen the effectiveness of the procedural approach in ensuring that we get consistency in the way we do our business — consistency that delivers better results for the customer. In the area of the environment, we see this dovetailing into our other manufacturing process initiatives. The Ford Production System (FPS) is about everything we do in a manufacturing environment relative to how we build the product, process the product and the activities of individuals around that, safety aspects in terms of hazards, prevention and the like, maintenance, upkeep, throughput, quality and utilization of any type of material. It all plays together.

ISO is not a stand-alone proposition. We work really hard to integrate it into the fabric of the way we do business and to bring our people skills up to another level. We have found that it is tremendously beneficial.

The EQO in this or any other company is never going to move the needle of environmental performance significantly. The only way to do that is if the people running the business, running the plants, running the equipment in the plants, have that as part of their job — not as the environmental piece you do after you do everything else, but as a natural component of their job.

The ability to do well environmentally, and to do well in more traditional business terms, can probably be summarized as harmonized or aligned objectives. The way to get things done is not to give people programs that compete with each other for their time and attention and resources, but give them programs that are complementary to one another. And to do that, you need to let people have some influence over what the program is and what they are trying to achieve. If we come up with different programs, different objectives, the likelihood is that they are not going to be in harmony with one another.

When we started out, I was concerned that some of the places where we were doing business, like South America, had difficult business and economic conditions, and that they would just say, "Gee, we can't take on another program at this time." What we actually found was that those were the most receptive locations, because they immediately recognized this point of harmonization; that this could help, not compete, with what they needed to do as a business.

We find that, irrespective of the economic environment, the enthusiasm of our employees to do the right thing — to achieve improvements in their overall operations to reduce waste — is significant. We found that our South American team, for example, was very enthusiastic about making a difference in these areas. They were very conscious of their environment and desired to make a difference, and they did. They picked up the challenge that we gave them. We didn't give them much of an option; we said this wasn't a voluntary trip. But we did it in a fashion so that they recognized the value added. They came away believing that it was the right thing to do, and that it produced the right results for the company in terms of the bottom line. It was a win-win proposition.

In other parts of the world, people haven't yet mentally distanced themselves from ecological and natural resource issues as we sometimes have here in the United States. I think that sometimes we forget that water comes from somewhere other than just out of the tap. We assume it is essentially free and pure. In other parts of the world, people live with conditions like availability of clean water as a basic day-to-day human situation. They appreciate more than we do here the importance of performing in all these respects.

So in many ways, although I was expecting more difficulty internationally than in the United States, it was just the opposite. There was a much more enthusiastic and effective implementation of the program outside the United States.

I think that often people assume that when you go after ISO registration it's going to cost a huge amount of money. You find that yes, it does require a good degree of organization and focus, but in terms of capital spending, there are easy steps you can take quickly that provide quick paybacks and don't have to cost a huge amount. Once you get the processes in place and the people trained, they become self-sustaining. So it's a modest investment that you make over time.

It also sensitizes the organization to make sure you are continuously driving for improvement. The fundamental element of the FPS is to eliminate waste; to think about eliminating excess effluent from your plant, to recycle that water. We need coolant in our body shops for welding, but can we recycle it? How? These types of things pay huge benefits, and you don't have to spend a lot of money on them. If you think your way through some clever, simple solutions, you get good results and do a lot of benefit for the environment.

I believe a lot of those processes were there, but they weren't necessarily prioritized. ISO provided the catalyst to get people to say, "Well, we know about that, why don't we try this." It isn't so much that ISO causes invention, but it certainly causes you to accelerate adaptation. It isn't rocket science, but it is paying attention to details, and getting people sensitized and recognizing that they can make a difference. It's like safety. You don't have to invent a lot of stuff to have a safe workplace or produce high-quality products; you just need to be attentive to the issues.

The ISO registration process provides a discipline for careful formulation of a strategy and specific laying out of the steps of implementation, as well as a follow-up mechanism in terms of the progress you are making. It requires an organization's focus and attention. It provides the organization with a route map to get things done and with a training formula to get people involved.

We found that through many of our programs, including ISO 14001 and many of our other shop floor programs, the strongest tool we have, our best resource, is our people. And by asking them, involving them, they become the most important drivers. Because they are at the source. They know where the waste might be, where opportunities are for improvement and how to make it happen. It's a good mobilizing tool to get people involved to do what's right. And people want to do what's right.

One of the effects of the ISO 14001 system at Ford is that commitments people have made to achieve specific results are an element of their job evaluation. It cascades down through the system and is part of the performance evaluation and compensation decisions of everybody in the system.

Before ISO, we didn't have the mechanism to identify the objectives and metrics with the degree and fairness that you need to have that kind of link to compensation. Now, we do. We know that if we want to save this much, reduce this by x, improve here by y, and write it down, so that we can go back and see how we're doing. ISO facilitates that; it keeps you focused on what you said you were going to do and how you do it.

Recycling — of effluents, waste oils, packaging — is an example of the positive type of approach that ISO provides. For many years in our operations, we have used cardboard and other types of packaging to ship in components. That cardboard could build mountains of waste and it's not reusable.

So one area of attention was trying to eliminate that cardboard. Our vision of the perfect process in an assembly plant is one that has all-returnable containers; small containers that people can easily move around so they are ergonomically friendly too. You don't have to take them to the incinerator or dump; you just recycle them back through the system.

We're trying to move that forward as rapidly as we can throughout our plants. It aligns very well with what we're trying to do with the ISO compliance procedures and comes back to integrating into the FPS. If you just did it as an environmental program, you wouldn't think about the ergonomic benefits of whatever other implications there might be. If you're integrated into the FPS, it forces you to think in a multidimensional sense about what you're doing and why you're doing it.

Ford & ISO 14001

Macroeconomists have calculated that it takes about 50,000 pounds of raw materials to produce a 3,000 pound automobile. About half of that is recyclable, and about half of that is recycled. That's not a pretty picture. In traditional business terms, waste is anything that goes out of the plant that's not on the product. If we drive down waste from a traditional business perspective, we're also driving down the cost and the environmental impact of what we're doing, because that waste goes somewhere — to a dump or incinerator or into the air or water — and it takes energy to produce that waste.

The whole element in terms of our environmental focus, in terms of utilizing ISO 14001 as a tool to drive that into our system, is a reflection of a vision that Mr. Ford sets forth in very eloquent terms. Our intent here is to walk the talk. What you see through our compliance procedures, through the waste elimination elements we have, through our production systems, aided by ISO, is very consistent.

The other thing that is astounding is that the opportunities are huge. Every time you look, there is more opportunity. That's part of the continuous improvement process we're trying to stimulate, and why the involvement of all of our people is key. Because we need all those different sets of eyes looking for those opportunities.

8 The Future of ISO 14001 at Ford

Continuous improvement is the engine that drives the FES. It also is the foundation of ISO 14001 registration. To remain certified, each Ford Motor Company facility must undergo yearly audits to ensure adherence to ISO guidelines and to measure progress against targets for improvement.

This discipline of setting metrics for improvement is becoming a way of doing business. Indeed, even the culture of the FES, which is driven by the methodology and reporting structure of ISO 14001, is becoming the mind-set at Ford. The spirit at Ford is to document our efforts at continuous improvement clearly and consistently. This includes documenting not only our successes, but also instances in which we fall short of our goals.

ISO 14001 is built into our work. Ford's manufacturing engineers have an obligation to design processes and materials from those processes that are robust and meet the ISO guidelines. And over time, the audit process of ISO provides a checks-and-balances mechanism to make sure we do that and do not slip.

As a constant effort to strive for improvement, we plan to register facilities that came aboard after the initiation of the FES, as well as other nonmanufacturing facilities, globally. Ford Customer Services Division and Global Testing Operations as well as Ford Land Development and Product Development Centers have either begun the process to implement the FES or are making plans to begin implementing it in the near future.

Implementation of ISO 14001 in manufacturing has been such a success that all other elements of the company down to operation of our World Headquarters Building in Dearborn, Michigan, will be registered to the standard. The awareness is sweeping through the company that we all have a part to play in Ford's being a "Good Corporate Citizen."

We believe that ultimately many companies will report similar success. People will find that even if ISO 14001 provides no reputational benefit or regulatory relief, even if they don't sell another car or truck or whatever their product is, it will help them operate better. Perhaps they will turn off the lights sooner, or recycle paper more efficiently or use automatic flushing units on toilets. Any number of environmentally important elements will be institutionalized.

Extending the ISO program into product development might be harder to do than it was in manufacturing because it will be more difficult to identify a pilot. Product development is also a longer process than manufacturing. The time from a twinkle of an idea in somebody's eye to a product going out the door usually is measured in years. We will have to apply what we have learned from ISO 14001 to what can be done relatively quickly and recognize that some of it will take a longer time.

On the positive side, our product development engineers have a better understanding of environmental impacts overall. The automotive business has been so heavily regulated that thinking about environmental issues has become second-nature to them. That affords optimism that we will be able to achieve something here, do it well and gain some early payoff.

Product development also offers a real opportunity to connect with Ford customers. To say to a customer, "You really ought to buy this product because it was manufactured in an ISO 14001-registered facility," may not mean much. But if, as a result of an ISO 14001 discipline, we do something to a product that makes it more environmentally benign, that will mean something to customers.

We don't have to tell people that ISO 14001 had anything to do with it. But, we can talk about features of a product that came about because of the ISO 14001 process. Product features mean more to a customer. It's like air bags in a car; few care about the standard that mandated air bags, but people inherently appreciate the feature itself.

Ford's reputation as a company on the environmental front is largely measured by our products not our facilities. It's the products that are visible to customers, and the opportunity to make significant changes is in the product development process. So, if an employee gets a twinkle in his eye thinking about the environmental performance of a product, we can act upon it quickly and produce it at less cost than if we decided to do something a year before going into production.

There is considerable debate about the future direction of ISO 14001 itself. As this goes to press, the first revision to the standard is getting under way and should be completed in June, 2003 or 2004. At this time, however, a decision has been made to introduce no new requirements.

Among the factors likely to boost ISO 14001 popularity is the ground swell of pressure on corporations to buy into global standardization systems for social responsibility and accountability — right along the supply chain.

There is clearly a connection between ISO 14001 and social and environmental accountability. More and more businesses want to put together a socially responsible record to which they can point with pride. System registration is one well-proven route to doing that.

Ultimately, companies get out of management systems what they put into them. Roger Strelow — a former US EPA official and environmental management consultant now associate general counsel and director of environment, health and safety at Federal-Mogul Corporation — sees substantive business value in ISO 14001. As with ISO 9000 quality management, he says that if companies commit to it for the wrong reasons, they may get little benefit and indeed find their devotion of resources is a waste. But, if they adopt ISO 14001 in order to more methodically and cost-effectively manage important activities, they can expect significant benefits.

Environmental management processes used by many companies today are inadequate to examine emerging issues that may have a profound impact on long-term profitability. The challenge is to make these processes more robust. If application of ISO 14001 can help achieve this goal, then it is quite worthwhile.

Two criticisms heard regularly are that the standard fails to focus on environmental compliance and that it fails to engage external stakeholders.

The first criticism is wrong. An organization or facility cannot be registered to the standard without identifying its compliance obligations as significant environmental aspects. You also cannot be registered unless you have a continual improvement objective in place against your significant environmental aspects.

The standard does not guarantee 100 percent compliance 24 hours a day, 365 days a year. It does, however, suggest that you have a disciplined process in place for either being in compliance or knowing that you are not, in which case the system would prescribe a means to do something about it — quickly.

It may be true that ISO 14001 doesn't sufficiently engage external stakeholders, but the more important point is that the standard does not preclude such engagement. You don't have to include external stakeholders to be registered. Ford, either formally or informally, does it anyway.

We believe that in the future we will see regular stakeholder engagement in local communities. That makes sense. It provides a broader, more enriched view of what should be a facility's focus. It also enhances the credibility of a plant's environmental program, which is a key reason to have the program in the first place.

Ford's Broadmeadows facility in Melbourne, Australia, provides an example. The plant has engaged a body of external stakeholders who review Broadmeadows' environmental programs and endorse or acknowledge them. I believe we will see that type of practice globally over time. It certainly will be the case at Ford Motor Company.

Another issue developing, particularly in the United States, is the view of some people that regulatory agencies will want to modify ISO 14001 to conform to regulatory programs. The thinking is that organizations adopting ISO 14001 would seek regulatory relief for taking that step.

This would be a huge mistake, and totally unnecessary. It never was and never will be the premise at Ford. We pursued ISO 14001 because we thought it was a good operational decision, and it turns out to have been a good cost savings decision as well. We are not asking anything of the regulatory agencies.

The "Clean Corporate Citizen" program in Michigan provides an example of the right way to do it. Under this program, a company with an EMS — and the program doesn't favor ISO 14001 as such — and a good compliance record will receive certain regulatory benefits, primarily in expedited permit reviews and approvals. A certain amount of favorable publicity also accrues; the company receives a nice plaque from the governor.

An independently registered ISO 14001 EMS is a de facto acceptable system under the program. If a company has not received such certification, it at least must demonstrate that it has the elements of the system in place. This approach offers incentives to move beyond compliance and implement systems like an ISO 14001 EMS instead of trying to turn in into a command-and-control regulatory system.

No regulatory agency tells us how much water we can or cannot use, how much solid waste or packaging waste we can send to landfills or how much compressed air we can use. There are market dynamics, but no controls. At Ford, we have found cost savings in areas where there has not been a traditional body of regulation.

One of the great benefits of ISO 14001 is that it provides the ability to identify best practices operationally and environmentally. There are more than 100 Ford plants around the world thinking about what they can do better. Chances are, somebody will come up with a good idea. Then, all we have to do is recognize it and communicate it to the other plants, which will decide if it applies to them.

9 Ford's Approach to Implementation

As defined by ISO 14001, an EMS is the part of the overall management system that includes organizational structure, planning activities, responsibilities, practices, procedures, processes and resources for developing, implementing, achieving, reviewing and maintaining the environmental policy.

The standard itself is based on a "Plan-Do-Check-Act" cycle that drives continual improvement of the management system. It has been drafted around the following principles:

- An organization should improve its environmental performance by controlling the environmental impact of its activities, products and/or services.
- An EMS should be capable of being merged into other management systems.
- An EMS should help an organization meet its economic and environmental goals concurrently.
- An EMS should be applicable to all types and sizes of organization.
- An EMS should involve all parts of an organization, including top management.

An organization is defined as a company, corporation, firm, enterprise, authority or institution, or part or combination thereof, whether incorporated or not, public or private, that has its own functions and administration.

The heart of ISO 14001 is contained in Section 4 of the standard, which specifies the core requirements that companies will be audited against. Each requirement can be identified by the word "shall" within the elements. This is consistent with the approach taken in the more widely known ISO 9000 standards on quality management systems.

ISO has created a companion guidance document for ISO 14001, which is also extremely helpful. This document is *ISO 14004, Environmental Management Systems — General Guidelines on Principles, Systems and Supporting Documents*. It is not itself an auditable standard.

ISO 14001 consists of four main sections and three annexes as follows:

1. Scope	This section specifies that the standard applies only to those environmental aspects of the organization that it can control and influence.
2. References	This section is intended to reference other environmental standards and requirements that become part of this standard. There are none for ISO 14001 because it is the main specification standard in the ISO 14000 series.
3. Definitions	The definitions in this section reflect an effort by ISO technical experts to use words that accommodate translation into multiple languages to the extent possible.
4. EMS Requirements	Only three pages long, this section specifies all of the auditable requirements for the purposes of ISO 14001 certification. The requirements are meant to be generic and flexible in nature.
• Annex A	This section provides interpretations and suggestions, explaining many of the key elements of the standard. It is a good place to go to if you have questions about ISO 14001.
• Annex B	This section contains correspondence charts of the relationship between ISO 14001 and ISO 9001. This annex is particularly useful if you plan to integrate your environmental and quality management systems.
• Annex C	This is a bibliography.

Copies of the standards may be purchased directly from the ISO in Geneva, from your country's member body to ISO (ANSI in the case of the United States), or from other authorized organizations.

Here is a brief overview of the core elements of Section 4. Each element is explained in greater detail later in this chapter:

4.1 General Requirements — Sets the scope of an EMS for an organization by specifying the requirements defined in all the 14001 elements listed in Section 4.

4.2 Environmental Policy — Defines the organization's intentions, principles and commitments in relation to its EMS, and provides a framework for the establishment of environmental objectives and targets.

4.3   Planning — Encompasses the elements that go into putting your environmental policy into practice: environmental aspects, legal and other requirements, and objectives and targets.

    4.3.1   Environmental Aspects — Requires that the organization identify ways in which its products, activities or services interact with the environment, and those whose interactions could have a significant impact on the environment.

    4.3.2   Legal and Other Requirements — Requires that the organization identify all environmental regulatory and other requirements that apply to it, and ensure that it has access to those requirements as needed.

    4.3.3   Objectives and Targets — Requires that the organization establish environmental objectives and targets in line with its significant environmental aspects and environmental policy.

    4.3.4   Environmental Management Program(s) — Requires that the organization establish programs to achieve environmental objectives and targets.

4.4   Implementation and Operation – The seven elements under this heading form the "Do" part in a "Plan-Do-Check-Act" cycle.

    4.4.1   Structure and Responsibility — Requires the organization to specify roles and responsibilities relating to the EMS and provide the resources needed to sustain the EMS.

    4.4.2   Training, Awareness and Competence — Requires that the organization provide training to all personnel involved in the operation of the EMS or whose work could have a significant environmental impact.

    4.4.3   Communication — Requires that the organization establish both internal and external communication procedures to provide information about its EMS.

    4.4.4   EMS Documentation — Requires that the organization provide documentation about its EMS.

    4.4.5   Document Control — Requires that the organization control its environmental documentation to ensure its accuracy and availability.

    4.4.6   Operational Control — Requires that the organization establish control over those activities that could have a significant impact on the environment.

    4.4.7   Emergency Preparedness and Response — Requires that the organization establish and test emergency preparedness plans where needed.

4.5   Checking and Corrective Action — Encompasses elements that form the

"Check" and part of the "Act" in a "Plan-Do-Check-Act" cycle. The intent of these elements is to find out if you are getting the intended outcome of your EMS and if not, to take the necessary action to address weaknesses and opportunities for improvement.

- 4.5.1 Monitoring and Measurement — Requires that the organization establish monitoring procedures to ensure it is meeting its regulatory requirements and its environmental objectives and targets.
- 4.5.2 Nonconformance and Corrective and Preventive Action — Requires that the organization establish procedures to allow appropriate response to nonconformities associated with its EMS requirements.
- 4.5.3 Records — Requires that the organization maintain environmental records that demonstrate conformance to the EMS.
- 4.5.4 EMS Audit — Requires that the organization establish procedures to periodically examine its EMS.

4.6 Management Review — Requires that the organization perform periodic top management reviews of the EMS to identify improvement opportunities and to address any weaknesses in the system.

Steps to Implementation

The following clause-by-clause guidance to ISO 14001 implementation represents Ford's interpretation of the standard. Some registrars or auditors may disagree with our interpretation of a particular clause. Consult your own expert in adapting the system to your organization.

4.1 General Requirements

This section merely outlines the general requirements that must be met to comply with the standard.

4.2 Environmental Policy

Your environmental policy is the centerpiece of your EMS and serves to align your environmental objectives and targets with your corporate values and goals. An environmental policy is defined as a statement by the organization of its intentions and principles in relation to its overall environmental performance which provides a framework for action and for the setting of environmental objectives and targets. This element requires that top (senior) management develop and communicate an environmental policy for the organization. In the policy, you must identify specific environmental commitments. Since the entire system will be built around the commitments in this policy, it should be considered a critical element of your ISO

14001 EMS. The policy, at minimum, must include commitments to:

- Prevent pollution.
- Comply with all regulatory requirements and any additional requirements by the organization.
- Continual improvement.

Other commitments with respect to environmental improvement may be added as appropriate, given the nature of your product, service or activities. Management must communicate this policy to all employees throughout the organization and make it available to the public. ISO 14001 defines "continual improvement" as the process of enhancing the EMS to achieve improvements in overall environmental performance in line with the organization's environmental policy.

Continual improvement is where real, long-term progress is made. Although some immediate payback is usually realized as a result of implementation of a properly designed EMS, the most significant economic and environmental returns are usually realized through ongoing improvement activities.

4.3 Planning

In planning your EMS this element requires you to:

- Identify the environmental aspects of the organization's products, services or activities and evaluate these aspects to determine which could result in a significant impact to the environment.
- Identify regulatory and other requirements that apply to the organization.
- Set environmental objectives and targets based on your regulatory, business and other requirements, significant aspects, environmental policy and available financial and technological resources. You should also consider the views of other interested parties.
- Develop EMPs that outline responsibilities, means and time frames for the accomplishment of your objectives and targets.

4.3.1 Environmental Aspects

This element describes a critical step in the ISO 14001 implementation process — identifying and evaluating your environmental aspects. The results of your significant environmental aspects review are referenced in several elements and form the basis for:

- Setting objectives and targets as required in Element 4.3.3. Those aspects that have, or potentially could have, a significant impact must be con-

sidered during the establishment of your environmental objectives.
- Training employees as required by Element 4.4.2. Employees with work activities that have, or could have, a significant environmental impact must be made aware of these impacts, must receive appropriate training and must also be competent.
- Communication as described in Element 4.4.3. Procedures for communicating information related to significant environmental aspects to external interested parties must be considered by the organization, and the decision must be recorded.
- Operational control as outlined in Element 4.4.6. Operations and activities associated with significant environmental aspects must be identified and planned to ensure their control. Identifiable significant environmental aspects of goods and services used by the organization must also be planned and controlled, with relevant procedures communicated to suppliers.
- Monitoring and measuring as required by Element 4.5.1. Key characteristics of those operations and activities that have, or could have, significant environmental impact as required to be identified in Element 4.4.6, must be monitored and measured according to documented procedures.

An "environmental aspect" is anything about your facility that can interact with the environment. It can be related to your products, services, processes or activities. The term environment is defined as, "surroundings in which an organization operates, including air, water, land, natural resources, flora, fauna, humans and their interrelation." Natural resources include raw materials, oil and mineral reserves. Air is nothing more than the atmosphere. Flora includes plants and vegetation. Fauna refers to animals. Humans refers to people. Land refers to soil and the earth. Water includes rivers, lakes and oceans.

You must develop documents for identifying environmental aspects associated with your products, services or activities. This is done in order to determine related impacts to the environment. Please note that only aspects you can control or influence need be considered but whatever environmental aspects you do list must be kept up to date after you become registered.

In essence, you will need to develop a systematic process to first determine what your environmental aspects are, and then to determine which of these are "significant." Try thinking of aspects as those inputs and outputs of your facility that interact with the environment.

An examination of the environmental aspects related to a steel automobile frame, for example, might begin with the question: How might this part interact with the environment? Of course, raw materials and other substances must be consumed to produce it, energy is needed both in the manufacturing and use of the product, and the steel frame will eventually have to be disposed of or recycled.

You must also consider activities or processes such as a painting process for example. How might this process interact with the environment? Certain types of paints and solvents may contain substances that can significantly impact the environment.

The painting process also generates airborne emissions. Painting typically involves

ISO 14001 STANDARDS

ISO 14001 is a series of environmental management system standards developed by the International Organisation for Standardisation. These generic standards provide a framework for integrating environmental responsibility into everyday business operations. ISO 14001 also provides a benchmark for third-party certification.

1. Environmental Policy

Top management defines environmental policy and ensures it is appropriate to the nature, scale and environmental impacts of its activities, products or services. The policy:

- Includes a commitment to continual improvement, prevention of pollution and compliance with relevant environmental legislation and regulations, and with other requirements to which the organisation subscribes
- Provides the framework for setting and reviewing environmental objectives and targets

Management will document, implement and maintain policy, and communicate it to all employees, and make the policy available to the public.

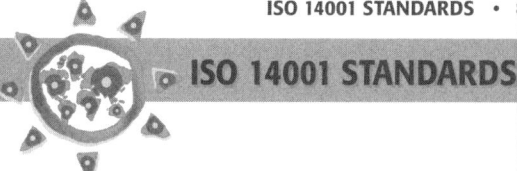

2. Environmental Aspects

- Establish and maintain a procedure to identify the environmental aspects of activities, products, or services that you can control and influence to determine those which have or can have significant impacts on the environment
- Ensure that the aspects related to these significant impacts are considered in setting environmental objectives
- Keep this information up to date

3. Legal and Other Requirements

- Establish and maintain a procedure to identify and have access to legal and other requirements to which the organisation subscribes directly applicable to the aspects of its activities, products or services

4. Objectives and Targets

- Establish and maintain documented environmental objectives and targets at each relevant function and level within the organisation
- Consider the legal and other requirements, significant environmental aspects, technological options, financial, operational and business requirements and views of interested parties
- Assure consistency with the environmental policy, including the commitment to prevent pollution

the release of VOCs to the air, which can contribute to air pollution. Properly controlling the process will minimize the release of these VOCs.

Changes, or potential changes, to the environment are considered environmental impacts. Think of the environmental aspect as the cause, and the resultant effect as the impact. It is important to note here that one aspect may have several impacts — some beneficial environmental impacts, as well as detrimental.

ISO 14001 requires that we focus on significant environmental aspects — those aspects that have, or could have, a significant impact on the environment. In short, you must focus on those products, services and activities that result in significant changes to the environment.

Remember, the identification and evaluation of aspects is an ongoing activity in your EMS. Your procedure must address any changes to your products or processes that might result in new environmental aspects or different impacts to the environment, to ensure these are kept up-to-date.

Clearly understanding Element 4.3.1 is one of the most important keys to discovering what ISO 14001 is all about and how an ISO 14001 EMS can result in improved environmental performance. When we look at how we can minimize our adverse environmental impacts, we normally focus on how we can modify the environmental aspect (the cause).

4.3.2 Legal and Other Requirements

This element states that you must identify legal and other requirements that apply to your organization and ensure you have access to these requirements. A process must exist for identifying legal and other requirements that apply to your environmental aspects. You must also have the ability to access these requirements when needed.

Some examples of national laws that apply in the United States and other countries include:

- US Environmental Protection Agency Clean Air Act (US EPA CAA).
- Canadian Environmental Protection Act (CEPA).
- Regulatory requirements at the national, regional or local level that may include air and wastewater discharge permitting, chemical use reporting and mandatory emissions reporting.

Examples of "other" requirements include any programs that you voluntarily abide by, such as the use of Energy Star™ compliant computer monitors that automatically power down when not in use (saving significant energy) or any environmentally-related customer requirement.

"Other" requirements might also include nonregulatory international, national, state, provincial and local industry programs or customer-supplier programs. Additional examples may include:

- Coalition for Environmentally Responsible Economies (CERES).
- Global Sullivan Principles of Corporate Responsibility.
- European Union's Eco-Management and Audit Scheme (EMAS) requirements.
- Global Reporting Initiative (GRI).

In the case of Ford suppliers, customer requirements include ISO 14001, materials of concern and recyclability.

This element makes you answer questions like: How do you know what requirements and laws apply to your business? Do you have access to these laws and requirements? Do you know what they require?

This element is also related to clause 4.2 Environmental Policy since your environmental policy must include commitments to environmental laws and regulations and to other requirements voluntarily adopted by your organization. In addition, it is related to Element 4.3.3 Objectives and Targets since legal and other requirements must be considered when setting your objectives. Finally, it is related to Element 4.5.1 Monitoring and Measurement (Regulatory Compliance Evaluation) since compliance with relevant environmental laws and regulations, as determined in 4.3.2, must be periodically evaluated.

4.3.3 Objectives and Targets

Here you are required to establish objectives and targets to improve your environmental performance throughout the organization. This is how you will drive continual improvement and where real business value can be derived from your EMS.

An environmental objective is defined as an overall environmental goal arising from the environmental policy that the organization sets, which must be quantified where practicable.

Examples of environmental objectives might include the elimination of PCB use by the end of 2001 or a 30 percent reduction in water use by December, 2002.

Environmental targets, on the other hand, are defined as detailed performance requirements quantified where practicable and applicable to the organization or parts thereof arising from environmental objectives and necessary to meet those objectives.

Examples of environmental targets based on our objectives as stated above might include the removal of all PCB-containing capacitors in a particular plant by the end of 2000 or the installation of a closed-loop water reuse system in an industrial washer by September, 2001.

ISO 14001 doesn't specify how many objectives and targets you should have or what they should be though they must be established at each relevant function and level within the organization and must be documented.

While allowing you a certain amount of discretion in developing your objectives and targets, ISO 14001 requires that you consider the following:

- Legal and regulatory requirements as determined in Element 4.3.2.
- Significant environmental aspects as determined in Element 4.3.1.
- The environmental policy as required by Element 4.2.
- The views of interested parties as determined in Element 4.4.3. Interested parties are defined as individuals or groups concerned with or affected by the environmental performance of your organization. They may include employees, the local community, regulators, shareholders, customers and anyone else who has a potential interest in your organization's environmental performance.
- Your technological options and business and financial requirements.

The intent of these considerations is to ensure alignment between your objectives, targets, significant aspects, environmental policy and the resources and requirements of your business.

This element is related to Element 4.2 Environmental Policy, which requires that the policy must provide a framework for setting objectives and targets; Element 4.4.6 Operational Control, which provides operations and activities associated with significant environmental aspects must be identified in line with your objectives and targets; and Element 4.5.1 Monitoring and Measurement, which requires the tracking of your conformance with objectives and targets.

In addition, this element also is related to Element 4.4.3 Communication and Element 4.4.2 Training, Awareness and Competence since environmental objectives and targets must be appropriately communicated by some means throughout the organization. This can involve a communications procedure or training or both.

Employees must be aware of their responsibilities and actions required to achieve the objectives and targets relevant to them.

4.3.4 Environmental Management Programs

EMPs must be established for the purpose of meeting objectives and targets as defined in Element 4.3.3.

This element requires that your EMPs address who is responsible for achieving each specific objective and target, when each will be achieved and what resources will be needed to support their achievement.

Once established, your EMPs must allow you to track progress with respect to meeting objectives and targets. Based on reviews of new projects and/or changing conditions, your EMPs may need modifications to ensure continued appropriateness.

4.4 Implementation and Operation

This element focuses on the core implementation elements of an ISO 14001 EMS. As previously stated, the seven elements under this element form the "Do" part in a "Plan-Do-Check-Act" cycle. They also represent opportunities to integrate your existing quality management system, if desired.

4.4.1 Structure and Responsibility

This element provides the organizational foundation of an effective EMS. It has three main requirements:

- Everyone involved in the development or maintenance of the EMS must fully understand their documented role, responsibility and authority.
- Management must provide the necessary resources to properly maintain the EMS.
- Management must appoint one or more management representatives.

Top management must appoint a specific management representative who will be in charge of the environmental system. The management representative is given overall responsibility to ensure that the EMS is properly implemented and maintained but this does not mean that the management representative is responsible for doing all of the work. He or she should be responsible for ensuring the work is done. The standard allows you to assign more than one management representative. Such an approach might be preferred in the case of a multisite implementation.

Ford & ISO 14001

In any case, the management representative:

- Reports to management on the performance of the EMS.
- Ensures that EMS requirements are established, implemented and maintained.

Roles and responsibilities can be defined in several documents, such as job descriptions, organization charts or documented procedures and instructions. The reason

---

ISO 14001 STANDARDS

5. ENVIRONMENTAL MANAGEMENT PROGRAMME

- Establish and maintain a programme for achieving objectives and targets
- Designate responsibility for achieving objectives and targets at each relevant function and organisational level
- Establish the means and time frame by which targets and objectives are to be achieved
- If a project relates to new developments and new or modified activities, products or services the Programme shall be amended where relevant to ensure that environmental management applies to such projects

6. STRUCTURE AND RESPONSIBILITY

- Define, document and communicate roles, responsibility and authorities to facilitate effective environmental management
- Provide resources essential to the implementation and control of the environmental management system, including human resources and specialized skills, technology and financial resources
- Ensure that the environmental management system requirements are established, implemented and maintained in accordance with this standard
- Report on the performance of the environmental management system to top management for review and as a basis for improvement of the environmental management system

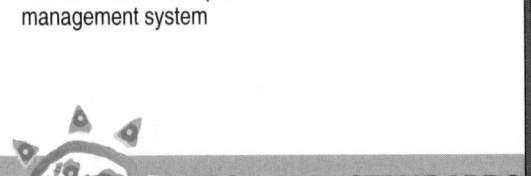

ISO 14001 STANDARDS

- Appoint specific management representatives who will have defined roles, responsibility and authority to ensure that environmental management system requirements are established, implemented and maintained in accordance with this standard. Representatives will report on the performance of the environmental management system to operating management for review and as a basis for improvement of the system

7. TRAINING, AWARENESS AND COMPETENCE

- Identify training needs and require all personnel whose work may create a significant impact on the environment to receive appropriate training
- Establish and maintain procedures to make employees at each relevant function and level aware of the importance of conformance with the environmental policy and procedures and with the requirements of the environmental management system
- Make employees aware of the significant environmental impacts, actual or potential, of their work activities and the environmental benefits of improved personal performance
- Ensure employees know their roles and responsibilities in achieving conformance with the environmental policy and with the requirements of the environmental management system including emergency preparedness and response requirements
- Make clear the potential consequences of departure from specified operating procedures

for defining them is to promote better understanding of everyone's responsibilities, and what authority each individual has relative to that responsibility.

Management demonstrates its commitment to the EMS largely, but not solely, through the provision of adequate resources. Essential resources include:

- Human resources and specialized skills
- Technology resources
- Financial resources

This element also relates to Element 4.3.4 Environmental Management Programs, which requires programs to include a designation of responsibility for achieving objectives and targets at each relevant organizational function and level; Element 4.4.6 Operational Control, which provides responsibilities and authorities can be documented in operational control procedures or specific work instructions; Element 4.5.2 Nonconformance, Corrective and Preventive Action, which requires you to establish and define the responsibility and authority for handling and investigating nonconformances; and Clause 4.6 Management Review, which states the management representative is specifically charged with reporting on the performance of the EMS to top management for the purposes of periodic management reviews.

4.4.2 Training, Awareness and Competence

This element requires that all personnel whose work could significantly impact the environment must receive appropriate training, and must be competent on the basis of their education, experience and/or training. All relevant personnel must have:

- The appropriate mix of education, training and/or experience in order to ensure competency.
- An awareness of the impact their work has or could have on the environment, including the consequences of not following the practices and procedures established under the EMS.

This means that all employees whose work could have a significant impact on the environment must receive some form of environmental awareness training. You must identify the necessary training to support the environmental policy, objectives, EMPs and EMS. Training must be provided to employees at each relevant level and function within the organization to include:

- An understanding of the importance of complying with policies, procedures and other requirements of the EMS.

- The significant environmental impacts that their work has, or could have on the environment.
- The environmental benefits of improved personal performance.

Awareness training must be conducted to instruct personnel with respect to how their actions or inactions might impact the environment or affect the organization's ability to achieve objectives and targets.

This element also relates to Element 4.5.3 Records, which requires environmental records, including those related to training, to be identified, maintained and disposed of according to procedures; Element 4.4.1 Structure and Responsibility, which provides for the communication of roles, responsibilities and authorities to occur through training activities; Element 4.4.6 Operational Control, which stipulates that personnel associated with operations and activities related to significant aspects may need training on related procedures; and Element 4.4.7 Emergency Preparedness and Response, which states that personnel associated with emergency preparedness and response procedures may require specialized training.

4.4.3 Communication

The purpose of this element is to ensure that your organization has working mechanisms to communicate information about your EMS.

Your procedures must address both internal communication (disseminating and receiving information within your organization) and external communication (receiving and responding to external requests for information about your EMS).

Management must decide if it will provide information about your significant environmental aspects to the general public, and that decision must be recorded. Internal communication systems can take many forms that are probably already well established within your organization including:

- Company communication vehicles such as newsletters, memos and bulletins can be effective tools for conveying information about your company's policies, objectives and values. They can also be used to raise environmental awareness among your employees.
- Meetings between senior management and employees can be an effective means of conveying the importance of your organization's EMPs and policies. In a similar fashion, periodic environmental awareness training can help communicate information about the organization's significant environmental aspects and potential impacts.
- Suggestion boxes are an easy and effective method to collect environmental improvement ideas.

- Gantt charts can communicate progress related to your environmental objectives and targets, as well as your EMPs for achieving them.

With respect to external communications, your procedure must address:

- How communications from interested parties are to be received, responded to and documented.
- Whether you will communicate information relating to your significant environmental aspects to external parties, defined as an individual or group concerned with or affected by the environmental performance of your organization. These may include employees, the local community, regulators, shareholders, customers and anyone else who has a potential interest in your organization's environmental performance. Your decision must be recorded.

Documented procedures may establish relationships, reporting responsibilities and communications needed to properly carry out tasks essential to the operation of the EMS.

This element also relates to Clause 4.2 Environmental Policy, which requires that the policy be communicated to employees and the public; Element 4.4.2 Training, Awareness and Competence, which provides for training using an internal communication procedure and Element 4.4.6 Operational Control, which requires relevant environmental requirements to be communicated to contractors and suppliers.

4.4.4 Environmental Management System Documentation

This element requires you to develop written information relative to your EMS. Typically, such information takes the form of an EMS manual and associated procedures. This information may be in paper or electronic format.

Documenting your environmental policies, practices and methods provides the following benefits:

- Promotes consistency in the way tasks are performed.
- Permits the clear identification of roles, responsibilities and authorities.
- Permits a high level of control during the performance of critical operations.
- Provides for the description of actions that may be necessary during nonroutine operations.

Ford & ISO 14001

At a minimum, your documentation must:

- Describe the core elements of the EMS and their interaction.
- Provide direction with respect to related documentation.

A common method of satisfying this requirement is through the development of an environmental manual, though one is not explicitly required. In fact, the standard does not specify any particular format for this information nor does it stipulate that

---

¥ Ensure personnel performing the tasks which can cause significant environmental impacts are competent on the basis of appropriate education, training and/or experience

¥ Facilitate access to legal and other requirements to which the organisation subscribes directly applicable to the environmental aspects of its activities, products or services

8. COMMUNICATION

¥ Establish and maintain procedures for internal communication between the various levels and functions of the organisation

¥ Receive, document and respond to relevant communication from external interested parties regarding environmental aspects and the environmental management system

¥ Consider processes for external communication on significant environmental aspects and record decision

9. ENVIRONMENTAL MANAGEMENT SYSTEM DOCUMENTATION

¥ Establish and maintain information, in paper or electronic form, to describe the core elements of the management system and their interaction

¥ Provide direction to related documentation

---

10. DOCUMENT CONTROL

¥ Establish and maintain procedures for controlling all documents required by this standard

¥ Ensure that documents can be located, periodically reviewed, revised as necessary and approved for adequacy by authorized personnel

¥ Make available current versions of relevant documents at all locations where operations essential to the effective functioning of the system are performed

¥ Promptly remove obsolete documents at all points of issue and points of use or otherwise assure against unintended use

¥ Identify any obsolete documents retained for legal and/or knowledge preservation purposes

¥ Assure documents are legible, dated (with dates of revision) and readily identifiable, maintained in an orderly manner, and retained for a specified period

¥ Establish and maintain procedures and responsibilities for the creation and modification of various types of documents

such information even be kept in a single binder. EMS documentation is referenced in several elements of the standard. At minimum, the requirements of this element apply to all parts of the standard in which the terms "documented procedure" and "documentation" are used.

In some places, "procedures," or systematic processes, are specified that may also be addressed in documented procedures. This is especially true of companies that already have an ISO 9000 or QS-9000 system since much of the existing documentation may be easily modified to address additional EMS requirements.

This element also relates to Element 4.3.1 Environmental Aspects, which requires a procedure(s) to identify and evaluate environmental aspects; Element 4.3.2 Legal and Other Requirements, which requires a procedure(s) to identify and provide access to legal and other requirements; Element 4.4.2 Training, Awareness and Competence, which requires a procedure(s) for employee "awareness" training; Element 4.4.3 Communication, which requires a procedure(s) for internal communication and a procedure(s) for receiving, documenting and responding to relevant communication from external interested parties; Element 4.4.5 Document Control, which requires a procedure(s) for controlling all documents required by the ISO 14001 standard; Element 4.4.6 Operational Control, which requires a procedure(s) to control and maintain operations and activities to ensure adherence to the environmental policy and objectives and targets and a procedure(s) related to the identifiable significant aspects of goods and services used, including suppliers and contractors; Element 4.4.7 Emergency Preparedness and Response, which requires a procedure(s) to identify the potential for and response to accidents and emergencies; Element 4.5.1 Monitoring and Measurment, which requires a procedure(s) to monitor and measure key characteristics of operations and activities that have a significant environmental impact and which requires a procedure(s) to perform periodic environmental compliance assessments; Element 4.5.2 Nonconformance, Corrective and Preventive Action, which requires a procedure(s) for defining responsibility and authority for addressing nonconformance and corrective/preventive action; Element 4.5.3 Records, which requires a documented procedure(s) for identifying, maintaining and disposing of environmental records; Element 4.5.4 Environmental Management System Audit, which requires a documented procedure(s) for EMS Audits.

4.4.5 Document Control

This is a requirement to control documentation used to describe and operate your EMS. The intent here is to ensure that everyone is "on the same page" regarding standard operating procedures or work practices, etc. In essence, documents must be reviewed and approved by the right people before they are issued, and must be available to those who need them and removed when they become obsolete. These requirements apply to all documents relating to your ISO 14001 EMS. At a minimum, this control must provide for:

- Location of your documentation. Since documents must be updated and removed as necessary, you must know where your documents are located.
- Creation and modification of documentation, including responsibilities for review and approval of documents. Specifying who must be involved in the review and approval of documents increases the likelihood that documentation will be accurate and complete.
- Assurance that current versions of documents are available at all locations where needed. If documents are maintained electronically, personnel must have access to computer terminals and know how to find all necessary documents.
- Removal of obsolete documents, except where other means are provided, to assure unintentional usage.
- Suitable identification of obsolete documents retained for legal or other purposes.

All documentation must be:

- Legible.
- Dated by revision.
- Readily identifiable.
- Maintained in an orderly fashion. This might involve adequately marked filing cabinets and document containers, indexing and/or some other consistent filing and/or archival system.
- Retrievable.
- Retained for a specified period. Many organizations retain documents for specified periods of time as a historical reference or for legal purposes. Retention times must be specified.

Document control relates to every element of ISO 14001 that generates written procedures and instructions including those that specify a requirement for documented procedures:

- Element 4.4.6 Operational Control
- Element 4.5.1 Monitoring and Measurement (two specific requirements for documented procedures)

As mentioned earlier, many of the remaining elements require "procedures" or systematic processes. These can all be described by documented procedures, which would then be subject to document control.

4.4.6 Operational Control

Operational control refers to the manner in which a facility controls its operations to ensure that the environmental policy, objectives and targets are consistently met. Operational control focuses on the activities and operations associated with your significant environmental aspects.

Operations and activities that are related to your significant environmental aspects and policies, or which could affect your ability to achieve your environmental objectives and targets, must be identified, planned and controlled.

How you control your operations and activities strongly influences your environmental performance. Those operations and activities associated with your significant environmental aspects should have already been identified as part of your initial environmental planning under Clause 4.3. Here you will establish how you will control those operations and activities.

This element establishes minimum considerations for such operations and activities which require the following:

- Suitable maintenance. Improperly maintained pollution control or production equipment may not effectively control your operation's environmental impacts. For example, equipment that's not properly maintained may produce excessive waste material or scrap, or use too much energy. Plans for maintaining the equipment associated with your significant aspects must be developed and implemented.
- Documented procedures where needed.
- Definition and documentation of operating criteria in documented procedures.

Operating criteria may take the form of set points, operating limits or an operating range for a particular process. It may represent operating guidance to achieve your environmental objectives and targets (e.g., print on both sides of the paper to minimize paper usage and waste).

This requirement allows you some flexibility in determining where you need documented procedures and instructions. Whether a documented procedure is needed depends on several factors, including the:

- Complexity of the work.
- Potential consequences of incorrectly performed work.
- Skills and training of personnel conducting the operations.

Complex, high-risk operations are typically documented, even when relying on highly trained and/or experienced personnel. Similarly, activities performed infrequently or by personnel with limited training and/or experience must be documented if they could result in a significant environmental impact. Documented procedures also provide a baseline for process improvements. You must also identify environmental aspects related to purchased goods and services and establish procedures to cover relevant requirements that must be communicated to suppliers and contractors.

Objectives and targets and/or operational controls can be established from those aspects determined to be significant. Examples include:

- Establishing minimum percentages for the use of recycled content in purchased materials.
- Identifying hazardous or material that is to be avoided in purchased products.
- Specifying the use of returnable dunnage and/or minimizing the amount of disposable packaging material.
- Specifying necessary training, proper disposal and handling techniques, for contractors working on-site or representing your company in the field.

This element is also related to Element 4.3.4 Environmental Management Programs, which allows for the documentation of means and time to achieve objectives and targets in operational control procedures; Element 4.4.3 Communication, which describes the communication of requirements to contractors and suppliers; and Element 4.4.2 Training, Awareness and Competence, which specifies that employees be trained in specific operational controls.

4.4.7 Emergency Preparedness and Response

This requirement is to develop procedures relative to accidents and emergencies. Examples include:

- Spills of hazardous chemicals or solvents.
- Explosions, fires or flooding, especially in areas where hazardous materials are present.
- Unanticipated loss of electrical power to pollution control equipment, monitoring equipment or other devices needed to ensure operation of your processes.

You must identify potential accident and emergency situations and develop appropriate procedures to prevent and/or mitigate any adverse environmental impacts that may result.

Consider abnormal operating conditions, such as process startup or shutdown. Some or all of this analysis may already have been performed during the identification of environmental aspects.

Emergency preparedness and response procedures must be periodically reviewed and revised where necessary, and particularly following accidents or emergencies. These procedures must also be tested periodically where practicable to do so.

At minimum, this element requires you to periodically review your emergency preparedness and response procedures. Revisions or process improvements must be made where appropriate.

Many organizations already have some type of essential emergency planning and response procedures. Examples include a prevention and response procedure for spills of oil or hazardous waste and an emergency action plan, which may be required by regulation. These procedures must be reviewed, updated and tested as part of your EMS activities where practicable.

This element is also related to Element 4.3.1 Environmental Aspects. Potential environmental impacts related to emergency situations may be identified during the identification of environmental aspects; Element 4.4.2 Training, Awareness and Competence, which requires employees to be trained in emergency response procedures. Some emergency response training may also be required by environmental regulation as identified in Element 4.3.2 Legal and Other Requirements.

4.5 Checking and Corrective Action

The intent of this clause is to find out if your EMS is producing the intended results.

This clause focuses on monitoring the effectiveness of your EMS and taking action to address weaknesses or opportunities for improvement where appropriate. The requirements form the "Check" and part of the "Act" links in the "Plan-Do-Check-Act" cycle.

4.5.1 Monitoring and Measurement

This element requires you to monitor the key characteristics of your operation that could have a significant impact on the environment. You must also record data and information to track operational performance as it relates to your significant environmental objectives and targets and calibrate and properly maintain your environmental monitoring equipment.

Ford & ISO 14001

In addition, this element requires you to periodically evaluate compliance with applicable environmental regulations. Although the focus of ISO 14001 is on your EMS, and not environmental compliance, the standard requires you to make a commitment to complying with all legislation and regulations pertinent to your operations and to periodically monitor your performance in that regard. You must monitor and measure the key characteristics of any operations and/or activities that could have a significant impact on the environment This must be described in your documented procedures.

11. Operational Control

- Identify operations and activities that are associated with the identified significant environmental aspects in line with the Company's policy, objectives and targets
- Plan these activities, including maintenance, in order to ensure that they are carried out under specified conditions by establishing and maintaining documented procedures to cover situations where their absence could lead to deviations from the environmental policy and the objectives and targets
- Establish and maintain procedures related to the identifiable significant environmental aspects of goods and services used by the organisation and communicating relevant procedures and requirements to suppliers and contractors

12. Emergency Preparedness and Response

- Establish and maintain procedures to identify potential for and respond to environmental accidents and emergency situations, and for preventing and mitigating the environmental aspects that may be associated with them
- Review and revise, where necessary, emergency preparedness and response procedures, in particular, after the occurrence of environmental accidents or emergency situations
- Periodically test such procedures, where practicable

13. Monitoring and Measurement

- Establish and maintain documented procedures to monitor and measure on a regular basis the key characteristics of operations and activities that can have a significant impact on the environment
- Record information to track performance, relevant operational controls and conformance with objectives and targets
- Calibrate and maintain monitoring equipment and retain records according to established procedures
- Establish and maintain documented procedures for periodically evaluating compliance with relevant environmental legislation and regulations
- Identify and have access to legal and other requirements directly applicable to the environmental aspects of activities, products or services

14. Non-Conformance and Corrective and Preventive Action

- Establish and maintain procedures for defining responsibility and authority for handling and investigating non-conformance, taking action to mitigate any impacts and causes, and initiating and completing corrective and preventive action
- Assure corrective or preventive action to eliminate the causes of actual or potential non-conformances appropriate to the magnitude of problems and commensurate with the environmental impact encountered
- Implement and record any changes in the documented procedures resulting from corrective and preventive action

This requirement relates to the need to establish operating criteria for operations and activities that could have a significant environmental impact as defined in Element 4.4.6 Operational Control. The method and frequency of monitoring key characteristics and/or operating criteria must be established in written procedures or instructions.

An example of a key characteristic that might require measurement to prevent an adverse environmental impact would be the concentration of a chemical in discharged wastewater; the analysis of the discharged wastewater is the measuring tool of this key characteristic.

Your procedures must include requirements to record information relative to your environmental performance, including information on relevant operational controls and how well you are doing in achieving and/or complying with your environmental objectives and targets.

As noted above, monitoring and measuring the key characteristics of important operations and activities will help you achieve your environmental objectives and targets. To ensure this, the standard requires that you record relative information and review it to establish environmental performance.

Examples include the monitoring of energy usage (e.g., kwh) and/or volume of solid waste generated (e.g., pounds/month, kilograms/year). Note that monitoring may involve reviewing nonnumeric data, such as tank inspections, facility walk-throughs as well as visual observations of air or wastewater discharges.

Monitoring equipment must be calibrated and properly maintained. Calibration and maintenance records must be retained in accordance with procedures.

The environmental performance data you obtain may likely be used to make critical decisions relating to your EMS and/or your operations and processes. It is important that this information be accurate. Properly maintaining your equipment and keeping it calibrated helps to ensure the accuracy and validity of data used to establish environmental performance.

You can easily fold your environmental monitoring equipment into your existing calibration and maintenance program if your organization already complies with ISO 9000 or QS-9000 quality requirements.

This element also requires that environmental compliance reviews be conducted periodically to evaluate compliance to relevant environmental legislation and regulations. These reviews must be described in a documented procedure to ensure that you have a systematic and consistent process for performing reviews.

4.5.2 Nonconformance, Corrective and Preventive Action

This element requires you to establish procedures for investigating and dealing with any nonconformities associated with your EMS. This includes taking corrective action to eliminate the cause and mitigate the impact of problems as well as taking preventive action to avoid potential problems and/or prevent recurrence of related problems.

You must have a structured method to deal with nonconformances, noncompliances and other problems with respect to your EMS. That's the corrective action. The method you develop to head off problems before they happen is the preventive action.

Procedures must be established to provide for the proper handling and investigation of instances of nonconformance and to allow for appropriate action to mitigate any adverse environmental impacts that result. The procedures must define responsibilities and authorities for action and must also provide for the initiation of appropriate corrective and preventive action.

Occasional problems with your EMS and your operations and/or activities will arise. As this occurs, you must minimize any adverse environmental impact and put in place controls to prevent a recurrence as needed. Possible steps include:

- Documenting the problem.
- Taking immediate action to contain the problem or mitigate its impact.
- Investigating the problem and identifying its root cause.
- Taking appropriate corrective action to restore the system and eliminate the root cause.
- Investigating the need for and take preventive action to ensure this or similar problems do not occur elsewhere.

Any corrective and preventive measures must be appropriate to the magnitude of the problem presented by associated environmental impacts. The level of effort taken to address the problem must be appropriate to the nature of the problem and the potential environmental risk involved. A high level of attention must be given to problems that could result in significant impact to the environment.

Any change to your documented procedures resulting from the corrective and/or preventive action must be recorded.

Revisions to documented procedures must follow your document control procedures as specified in Element 4.4.5 Document Control.

This element is also related to Element 4.5.4 Environmental Management System Audit, which specifies that nonconformances found during internal audits may be corrected using the nonconformance, checking and corrective action processes.

Noncompliance with environmental regulations found during the periodic compliance evaluation can also be corrected using the nonconformance, checking and corrective action process as specified in Element 4.5.1 Monitoring and Measurement.

4.5.3 Records

Records provide you with the ability to monitor your performance and to prove that you are "walking the talk." They also provide information for you to track whether you are improving. The ISO 14001 standard requires that you maintain records to demonstrate that you are conforming to your EMS requirements.

Environmental records must be legible and traceable to the activity that generated the record. They must also be appropriately stored and maintained and protected against damage, deterioration or loss. Finally, records must have a retention period specified.

Procedures to identify, maintain and dispose of your environmental records must be established.

Records provide evidence that you are following your EMS. They also provide information needed to evaluate your environmental performance and identify areas for potential improvement. Records allow you to make decisions based on fact, not our sometimes-faulty memories.

Your environmental records must include, but are not limited to, training records, audit results and reviews. Other records that are needed to demonstrate conformance to the requirements of ISO 14001 must also be maintained.

At a minimum, records must be maintained everywhere the ISO 14001 standard says you must keep records. Beyond these requirements, records must be kept to show that you are maintaining your system.

Environmental records must be:

- Legible.
- Identifiable and traceable to the originating activity.
- Retained in accordance with documented retention periods.

Records must also be stored and maintained so that they will be:

- Readily retrievable.
- Protected against damage, deterioration or loss.

What constitutes "readily retrievable" depends on how the record may potentially be used. For example, training records needed daily for job assignments must be quickly retrievable, while records retained under certain regulatory requirements may not require quick access and could be archived off-site.

EMS records may be related to every element of the ISO 14001 standard.

Specifically, Element 4.3.3 which requires the documentation of objectives and targets; Element 4.4.2 Training, Awareness and Competence, which requires training records to be kept; Element 4.4.3 Communication, which requires the decision on communicating significant aspects to be recorded; Element 4.5.1 Monitoring and Measurement, which requires that performance information be tracked; Element 4.5.4 Environmental Management System Audit, which requires EMS audit records to be kept; and Clause 4.6 Management Review, which requires management reviews to be documented.

4.5.4 Environmental Management System Audit

EMS audits must be conducted periodically to identify if what you say you are doing is actually happening. Objectively collected evidence generated through audits can shed light on any gaps or weaknesses in your system or show opportunities for improvement. Audits generally examine:

- Conformance to ISO 14001.
- Conformance to EMS policies and procedures.
- Effective implementation of your EMS as measured by the intended results.

During an internal audit, you may identify activities or documentation not conforming to your EMS requirements and/or parts of the EMS that are working very well. Any nonconformances noted can be processed through your established corrective action process under Element 4.5.2 Nonconformance, Corrective and Preventive Action. At minimum, periodic EMS audits must be conducted to determine:

- Whether the EMS conforms to the ISO 14001 standard and any other planned arrangements.
- Whether the EMS has been properly implemented and maintained.

Internal audits are a vital component of your EMS. The term "planned arrangements" includes anything that you say you will conform with — your policies, procedures and work instructions.

Audits also look for proper implementation. The system is implemented properly when everyone is conforming to the system and the EMS is getting the expected results. The environmental audit program, including scheduling, must be based on the environmental importance of the areas and/or activities concerned and past audit findings.

Areas with a higher potential degree of environmental risk (e.g., certain manufacturing areas where hazardous substances are present, bulk unloading operations, etc.) should be considered for more frequent reviews than areas of lower risk.

Likewise, areas or activities with a history of compliance may not need to be audited as frequently as those areas that have been a source of nonconformities.

Audit procedures must include the scope, frequency, methodology and responsibilities for conducting audits and reporting results. Audit results must be reported to management.

This element also relates to Element 4.5.3 Records, which requires that EMS audit records be kept and Element 4.5.2 Nonconformance, Preventive and Corrective Action, which permits nonconformances identified by internal auditing activities to be corrected using the nonconformance, checking and corrective action processes. Results of audits must also be reviewed during management review as required by Clause 4.6 Management Review.

4.6 Management Review

The last element requires you to conduct periodic management reviews. The management review process is critical to continual improvement of your EMS.

Management review is the process whereby top management reviews the EMS to determine its effectiveness and to identify any changes needed to respond to changing circumstances or for system improvement.

Your environmental policy, objectives and/or targets may require revision as new opportunities or concerns arise within the organization. The management review provides a systematic method to identify the need for such changes and to develop appropriate responses.

Information normally considered during the management review includes, but is not limited to:

- EMS audit results.
- Summary of operational performance trends.
- Results of any compliance audits.
- Status of achieving stated environmental objectives and targets.
- Concerns and comments of external parties (e.g., the community, regulators, shareholders, etc.).

The review itself must seek to answer three questions with respect to your EMS:

- Is it suitable? Suitability looks at whether the system, as designed, meets the requirements of ISO 14001 and your environmental policy.
- Is it adequate? Adequacy looks at whether the system, as implemented, is capable of meeting these requirements.
- Is it effective? Effectiveness evaluates whether the system is getting the intended results. An effective system is likely to produce measurable improvements in environmental performance, achieve environmental objectives and targets and meet business goals.

Top management must perform periodic management reviews of the EMS to ensure the system's continuing suitability, adequacy and effectiveness. If the system is not getting results, as indicated by declining environmental performance or failure to meet objectives and targets, then the review must look for reasons why the system is not getting the expected results and what actions should be taken. Note that this review must be performed by top management. It cannot be delegated down to the lower levels of the organization. In addition, the review must be documented.

The management review must consider the need for changes to policies, objectives and other elements of the EMS, taking into account the results of EMS audits, changing circumstances and the organization's commitment to continual improvement.

Note that this review will often identify the need to modify procedures and policies. This reinforces the notion that your EMS is not a static collection of procedures and documentation, but rather a dynamic system that is constantly reshaping itself to suit the needs of the organization and the changing external environment in which the organization operates.

The management review should be a primary monitoring point for assessing your status in achieving environmental objectives and targets. New objectives and targets may be established as old ones are achieved. Actions can be assigned to get programs back on track when reviews indicate that progress is lacking.

This element is related to Clause 4.2 Environmental Policy, which requires that the policy must be considered during management review; Clause 5.4 Environmental Management System Audit, which requires that audit records be reviewed in management review; Element 4.4.1 Structure and Responsibility, which requires that management provide resources to meet the objectives and targets established under Element 4.3.3 Objectives and Targets; Element 4.3.4 Environmental Management

---

15. RECORDS

- Establish and maintain documented procedures for the identification, maintenance and disposition of environmental records
- Include training records and the results of audits and reviews
- Ensure environmental records are legible, identifiable and traceable to the activity, product or service involved
- Store and maintain environmental records in such a way that they are readily retrievable and protected against damage, deterioration or loss. Establish and record retention times
- Maintain records, as appropriate, to demonstrate conformance to the requirements of this standard

16. ENVIRONMENTAL MANAGEMENT SYSTEM AUDIT

- Establish and maintain programmes and procedures for periodic environmental management system audits
- Determine whether or not the environmental management system conforms to planned arrangements for environmental management including the requirements of this standard
- Determine if the system has been properly implemented and maintained

ISO 14001 STANDARDS

ISO 14001 STANDARDS

- Provide information on the results to management
- Base audit programme and schedule on the environmental importance of the activity concerned and the results of previous audits
- Cover the audit scope, frequency and methodologies as well as the responsibilities and requirements for conducting audits and reporting results

17. MANAGEMENT REVIEW

- At intervals it determines, top management reviews the environmental management system to ensure its continuing suitability, adequacy and effectiveness
- Ensure necessary information is collected to allow management to carry out this evaluation. This review shall be documented
- Address the possible need for changes to policy, objectives and other elements of the environmental management system in light of the audit results, changing circumstances and the commitment to continual improvement

Programs further requires that EMPs be amended as relevant new developments warrant, such as those identified during management review.

Once you have designed your EMS, you can use the following checklist to make sure that all of the requirements have been covered.

ISO 14001 SYSTEM CHECKLIST

1. Environmental Policy

Define your environmental policy and ensure that it:

- Is appropriate to the nature, scale and environmental impacts of your activities, products or services.
- Includes a commitment to continual improvement and the prevention of pollution.
- Includes a commitment to comply with relevant environmental legislation and regulations and with other requirements to which the supplier subscribes.
- Provides the framework for setting and reviewing environmental objectives and targets.
- Is documented, implemented, maintained and communicated to all employees.
- Is made available to the public.

2. Environmental Aspects

Establish and maintain procedures to identify the environmental aspects of your activities, products or services that you can control, and which you can be expected to influence, in order to determine those that have, or can have, significant impacts on the environment. Ensure that the aspects related to these significant impacts are considered in setting your environmental objectives. Keep this information up to date.

3. Legal and Other Requirements

Establish and maintain a procedure to identify and have access to legal and other requirements to which you subscribe that are directly applicable to the environmental aspects of your activities, products or services.

4. Objectives and Targets

Establish and maintain documented environmental objectives and targets at each relevant function and level within your organization. Establish and review your objectives taking into consideration legal, financial, operational and business requirements, without losing sight of significant environmental aspects, technological options and the views of interested parties.

The objectives and targets must be consistent with your environmental policy, including the commitment to prevention of pollution.

5. Environmental Management Programs

Establish and maintain programs for achieving your objectives and targets. They should include:

- Designation of responsibility for achieving objectives and targets at each relevant function and level of the organization.
- Means and time by which they are to be achieved.
- Amending programs where new developments and/or modified activities, products or services relate to a project to ensure that environmental management is applied.

6. Structure and Responsibility

Define, document and communicate roles, responsibilities and authorities in order to facilitate effective environmental management.

Provide resources essential to the implementation and control of the EMS. Resources include human resources and specialized skills, technology and financial resources.

Appoint specific management representatives who, irrespective of their other responsibilities, shall have defined roles, responsibilities and authority for:

- Ensuring that EMS requirements are established, implemented and maintained in accordance with ISO 14001.
- Reporting on the performance of the EMS to top management for review, and as a basis for improvement, of the EMS.

7. Training, Awareness and Competence

Identify training needs. Require that all personnel whose work may create a significant impact on the environment have received appropriate training.

Establish and maintain procedures to make your employees at each relevant function and level aware of:

- The importance of conformance with environmental policy and procedures and with the requirements of the EMS.
- The significant environmental impacts, actual or potential, of their work activities and the environmental benefits of improved personal performance.
- Their roles and responsibilities in achieving conformance with the environmental policy and procedures and the EMS including emergency preparedness and response requirements.
- The potential consequences of departure from specified operating procedures.

Personnel performing tasks that can cause significant environmental impacts should be competent on the basis of appropriate education, training and/or experience.

8. Communication

Establish and maintain procedures for:

- Internal communication between the various levels and functions of the organization.
- Receiving, documenting and responding to relevant communication from external interested parties.

Consider processes for external communication on your significant environmental aspects and record your decision.

9. EMS Documentation

Establish and maintain information, in paper or electronic form, to:

- Describe the core elements of your management system and their interaction.
- Provide direction to related documentation.

10. Document Control

Establish and maintain procedures for controlling all documents required by ISO 14001 to ensure that:

- They can be located.
- They are periodically reviewed, revised as necessary and approved for adequacy by authorized personnel.

- Current versions of relevant documents are available at all locations where essential operations of the system are performed.
- All obsolete documents are promptly removed from all points of issue and otherwise assured against unintended use.
- All obsolete documents retained for legal and/or knowledge preservation purposes are suitably identified.

Documentation shall be legible, dated (with revision dates), readily identifiable and maintained in an orderly manner for a specified period.

Establish and maintain procedures and responsibilities concerning the creation and modification of the various types of documents.

11. Operational Control

Identify those operations and activities that are associated with the identified significant environmental aspects, in line with your policy, objectives and targets.

Plan these activities, including maintenance, to ensure that they are carried out under specified conditions by:

- Establishing and maintaining documented procedures to cover situations where their absence could lead to deviations from your environmental policy and objectives and targets.
- Stipulating operating criteria in the procedures.
- Establishing and maintaining procedures related to the identifiable, significant environmental aspects of goods and services the organization uses.
- Communicating relevant procedures and requirements to your suppliers and contractors.

12. Emergency Preparedness and Response

Establish and maintain procedures to identify the potential for and response to accidents and emergency situations. This is important for preventing and mitigating the environmental impacts that may be associated with emergency situations and accidents.

Review and revise, where necessary, your emergency preparedness and response procedures particularly after the occurrence of accidents or emergency situations. Where practicable, occasionally test such procedures.

13. Monitoring and Measurement

Establish and maintain documented procedures to monitor and measure on a regular basis key characteristics of your operations and activities which can have a significant impact on the environment.

This shall include the recording of information to track performance, relevant operational controls and conformance with your environmental objectives and targets.

Calibrate and maintain monitoring equipment and retain records of this process according to your procedures.

Establish and maintain a documented procedure for periodically evaluating compliance with relevant environmental legislation and regulations.

14. Nonconformance and Corrective and Preventive Action

Establish and maintain procedures for defining responsibility and authority for handling and investigating nonconformances, mitigating any impacts caused, initiating and completing corrective and preventive action.

Any corrective or preventive action taken to eliminate the causes of actual and potential nonconformances should be appropriate to the magnitude of the problem and commensurate with the environmental impact encountered. Implement and record any changes in your documented procedures resulting from corrective and preventive action.

15. Records

Establish and maintain procedures for the identification, maintenance and disposition of environmental records, including training records and the results of audits and reviews.

Environmental records shall be legible, identifiable and traceable to the activity, product or service involved.

Store these records and maintain them in such a way that they are readily retrievable and protected against damage, deterioration or loss. Establish and record their retention times. Maintain records, as appropriate to your system and organization, to demonstrate conformance to the requirements of ISO 14001.

16. Environmental Management System Audit

Establish and maintain programs and procedures for periodic EMS audits to be carried out in order to:

- Determine whether or not the EMS conforms to planned arrangements for environmental management (including the requirements of ISO 14001) and has been properly implemented and maintained.
- Provide information on the results of the audits to management.

Base your audit program, including any schedule, on the environmental importance of the activity concerned and the results of previous audits.

Cover the audit scope to be comprehensive. Frequency and methodologies, as well as the responsibilities and requirements for conducting audits and reporting results should be covered in the audit procedures.

17. Management Review

Top management shall, at self-determined intervals, review the EMS to ensure its continuing suitability, adequacy and effectiveness.

All necessary information should be collected to allow management to carry out the management review evaluation. The review should also be documented.

The management review should address the possible need for changes to policy, objectives and other elements of the EMS in light of environmental management audit results, changing circumstances and the commitment to continual improvement.

THE REGISTRATION PROCESS

1. Filing an Application

Start the process of registering your company or facility's EMS by filing an application with the registrar or certifying body. The application solicits basic information about your company or facility such as its size, the scope of its operations (in the United States, this is defined by Standard Industrial Classification [SIC] codes) and the desired time frame for achieving registration. Once the application is filed (Step 1), the registrar will either conduct a pre-assessment (Step 2) or begin the documentation process (Step 3).

2. Documentation Review

Submit a controlled copy of your company or facility's environmental manual or key EMS procedures four to six weeks before the scheduled registration assessment. Although the ISO 14001 standard does not require creation of an environmental manual, many registrars do. *Check with your registrar.*

Registrars often require an environmental manual because it aids the audit team in making preparations for the actual on-site registration assessment by:

- Providing general information about the company or facility.
- Presenting the company's or facility's environmental policy.
- Outlining the company's or facility's significant environmental aspects and associated objectives and targets.
- Describing the structure of the company or facility, including responsibilities, authorities and their interrelationships.
- Describing all applicable EMS elements.

During this "desk-top audit" the registrar's audit team will examine your environmental manual or EMS procedures to determine if the system conforms to requirements — ISO 14001, legal, regulatory, company, policies, etc. The registration process cannot proceed until the registrar has confirmed that the company or facility's EMS documentation accurately reflects the requirements of ISO 14001.

If the documentation review process points to some potential nonconformances, the registrar will describe the nature of the failures in a report.

For every nonconformance, proof must be provided to the registrar demonstrating that corrective action was implemented. When the registrar is satisfied that all corrective actions were effective, the registration assessment can proceed.

3. Pre-Assessment (Optional)

Before initiating the actual registration assessment, your company or facility can opt to have a pre-assessment, sometimes also referred to as a gap analysis, baseline or benchmark audit.

A pre-assessment can be a full or partial evaluation of your EMS to determine your company or facility's state of readiness for registration.

The only difference between a pre-assessment and a gap analysis, baseline or benchmark audit is timing. The pre-assessment is held just before the registration assessment, while the gap analysis, baseline or benchmark audit is conducted earlier in the process, usually during the developmental or implementational phases of the EMS.

Though labeled with different titles, the underlying goal of each assessment is the same: to identify areas where improvements are needed to bring the EMS into a state of full conformance.

Pre-assessments can be conducted by registrars or independent consulting firms. Each has its own advantages.

By having the registrar's audit team conduct the pre-assessment, your company or facility can be assured that direct feedback is coming from the same group of people who, presumably, will conduct the actual registration assessment of your EMS.

As long as your company or facility addresses any identified nonconformities with a satisfactory plan of corrective/preventive action, the registrar will close out those deficiencies. More than likely the registrar will not revisit them at the time of the registration assessment.

If your company or facility is looking for direct, hands-on guidance, you may want to seek the services of a competent consultant because third-party auditors are not permitted to advise or provide consultation as part of an assessment.

In the long run, a pre-assessment of your EMS can save your company or facility time and money, and increase your chances of securing registration on your first attempt.

4. Registration Assessment

This is the culmination of all registration activities. The registrar's audit team, at this stage, will visit your company or facility to take a concentrated look at the day-to-day operations of your EMS.

The number of days required to complete the registration assessment depends on the size and complexity of your company or facility's operations.

Registration assessment begins with a formal meeting with members of your company or facility's management team. During this meeting, members of the audit team are introduced, the scope and objectives of the registration assessment are reviewed, the assessment process is explained and questions are answered.

At the conclusion of this opening meeting, the actual assessment begins. The audit team will collect objective audit evidence — through interviews, examination of documents, and observations of activities and conditions — to determine whether the environmental management activities of your company or facility comply with planned arrangements, including ISO 14001 requirements, and whether these arrangements are effective and suitable for achieving your stated environmental objectives.

When the audit team has completed its assessment, a closing meeting is held to reveal the audit team's findings, including the identification of any nonconformances, and its recommendation for registration.

The audit team's recommendation may include one of three possible outcomes: approval, conditional approval or disapproval. Conditional approval requires a company or facility to take corrective action against any nonconformances within a certain time frame as determined by the registrar. Registration cannot be granted until all nonconformances have been "closed out" by the registrar.

5. Nonconformances

A nonconformance is the nonfulfillment of a specified requirement. Nonconformances are generally classifed by two categories: major and minor.

A major nonconformance is something that can jeopardize the performance of the EMS, resulting in the nonfulfillment of environmental objectives. It may be the absence of a required procedure or the total breakdown of a procedure.

A minor nonconformance is a single, observed lapse of a procedure. Minor nonconformances are usually easy to correct and do not pose a serious threat to the performance of the EMS — unless a number of minor nonconformities are uncovered against the same requirement, which can represent a total breakdown of the system, constituting an upgrade to a major nonconformance classification.

The auditor may cite an observation in addition to nonconformances. This is a concern raised by the auditor against an existing condition that, in the auditor's judgment, warrants clarification or further investigation. Observations may lead to eventual nonconformances and should be addressed by the company or facility. However, a formal response usually is not required by the registrar.

When a nonconformance or observation is made, the details surrounding the area of concern are described in a written report, usually one page per nonconformance. It is then up to the company or facility to take the appropriate corrective/preventive action.

6. Corrective Action

Before a certificate of registration can be awarded to a company or facility, all non-conformances — major and minor — must be closed out by the registrar, via subsequent on-site surveillance visit or acceptance of the corrective action in writing.

Corrective action is considered to be effective when the nonconforming situation is eliminated altogether or, at best, recurrence is minimized.

Corrective action is the responsibility of the company or facility being audited, not the registrar. It involves the assignment of responsibility, an investigation to find the root cause(s) of the nonconformance, analysis of the problem, a plan of action to eliminate the cause and avoid recurrence and a timetable to implement the corrective action.

When the registrar has verified the effectiveness of all corrective actions and can close out all nonconformities, a recommendation for registration approval can be delivered.

7. Achieving Registration

To protect the objectivity of the certification process, the decision to extend or withhold registration is determined by registrar personnel independent of the assessment process itself.

Some registrars form a separate and impartial authoritative body, known as the Executive Committee or Advisory Board, to make registration decisions. When an audit team has completed its registration assessment of a company or facility it forwards its recommendation and a full report of the assessment results to the decision-making authority.

Upon reviewing the company or facility's application and the audit report, and considering the audit team's recommendation, this impartial body ultimately determines whether all requirements for ISO 14001 registration have been met.

If the decision-making body determines that a company or facility's EMS is functioning satisfactorily, a certificate of registration is issued.

The certificate is good for three years and serves as written proof that a company or facility's EMS conforms to specified requirements for environmental management recognized on an international basis.

The certificate displays the registration marks (logos) of the registrar and its own accreditation agencies, and can be used in advertising, promotional literature and stationary.

8. Surveillance

Once your company or facility has attained registration status, your relationship with the registrar has not ended. You must continually work to improve and maintain the EMS.

The registrar typically conducts a surveillance visit to verify that your EMS is still in conformance to stated requirements and that it is achieving a satisfactory environmental performance level every six months to one year.

The surveillance does not represent a full reassessment of your EMS; it is more a sampling on parts of the system. Over three years, all elements of the EMS must have been reviewed.

Your company or facility's registration certificate will never expire so long as you can demonstrate continued conformance during these surveillance visits.

9. Special Assessments

In addition to conducting periodic surveillance visits, the registrar has the right to schedule special assessments. These evaluations usually are conducted if significant changes have occurred at your company or facility which, in the registrar's judgment, could impact the EMS.

Special assessments also can be scheduled if situations arise (e.g., customer complaints, regulatory violations, etc.) that indicate that your EMS is not conforming to specified requirements.

10. Re-certification Assessment

A company or facility must normally undergo a complete reassessment every three years when its certificate of registration expires.

Conclusion

Obtaining registration is not an easy task. It requires a lot of time and commitment. The road to registration can be shortened as long as your company or facility believes in the philosophy behind the FES and the ISO 14001 standard and pays close attention to the requirements.

Chapter 9

Achieving ISO 14001 registration will earn your company or facility worthwhile recognition and a solid competitive edge in the international marketplace.

10 Sample Documentation

EMSs are only as good as their supporting documentation. From the identification of environmental aspects and potential impacts to establishing specific objectives and targets to be addressed through EMPs, good documentation allows you to assess whether your system is functioning as intended. It summarizes legal and other environmental requirements that affect your site and provides a history of system nonconformances and how each is addressed. It provides a history of problem avoidance and establishes who in your organization is responsible for carrying out specific duties related to the EMS. Finally, it gives management specific performance data to assess which environmental programs and practices are providing the greatest returns on investment and arms management with the facts to identify opportunities for improvement.

If your company has an existing ISO 9000 or QS-9000 system you may consider modifying some of your existing documentation to address the additional EMS requirements. Refer to Chapter 9: Ford's Approach to Implementation for greater detail on specific ISO 14001 requirements.

To support our worldwide implementation of ISO 14001, Ford developed a number of sample EMS documents for training purposes, including an environmental policy, EMS manual and various checklists and forms.

Our manufacturing facilities found these documents to be useful starting points for implementation. Specific documentation will vary according to the nature of the organization, its product, service mix and the complexity of the EMS.

We have selected a range of sample EMS documents for inclusion in this section with the understanding that they are provided only as a training resource.
We begin with a sample EMS manual. Nowhere in the standard is one explicitly

required nor does the standard specify any particular format for this information, but it's been helpful in keeping us on the same page. It should be noted that the sample documents presented in this section reflect Ford's interpretation of the standard. Registrars or auditors may disagree with some content. Consult your own expert in adapting these documents to your business or organizational needs.

TABLE OF CONTENTS

1.0   Purpose
2.0   Scope
3.0   Issue and Update
4.0   Environmental Policy
5.0   Environmental Aspects
6.0   Legal and Other Requirements
7.0   Environmental Objectives and Targets
8.0   Environmental Management Programs
9.0   Organizational Structure and Responsibility
10.0 Training, Awareness and Competence
11.0 Communication
12.0 Environmental Management System Documentation
13.0 Document Control
14.0 Operational Control
15.0 Emergency Preparedness and Response
16.0 Monitoring and Measurement
17.0 Nonconformance and Corrective and Preventive Action
18.0 Records
19.0 Environmental Management System Audit
20.0 Management Review
21.0 Record of Revisions

SUPPLEMENTS

Supplement A   Environmental Policy
Supplement B   Aspects, Objectives and Targets
Supplement C   Legal and Other Requirements
Supplement D   Environmental Management Programs
Supplement E   Structure and Responsibilities
Supplement F   Training Matrix
Supplement G   Master Document List
Supplement H   Master Records List
Supplement I   Procedures
Supplement J   Work Practices

Ford & ISO 14001

1.0 Purpose

This manual defines the scope of the *Facility/Plant*'s Environmental Management System (EMS) and provides a linkage of system documents to the elements of the ISO 14001:1996 standard.

The principal elements of the system described in this manual are:

- Environmental Policy
- Environmental Aspects
- Legal and Other Requirements
- Environmental Objectives and Targets
- Environmental Management Programs (EMPs)
- Organizational Structure and Responsibility
- Training, Awareness and Competence
- Communication
- EMS Documentation
- Document Control
- Operational Control
- Emergency Preparedness and Response
- Monitoring and Measurement
- Nonconformance, Corrective and Preventive Action
- Records
- EMS Audit
- Management Review

2.0 Scope

The *Facility/Plant* EMS provides a mechanism for environmental management throughout all areas and departments. The EMS is designed to cover environmental aspects that a facility can control and directly manage, and those it does not control or directly manage but can be expected to influence.

3.0 Issue and Update

The control of this manual is in accordance with the *Facility/Plant* environmental procedure EP-016 Environmental Document Control. All copies of this manual not marked "Controlled Document" are uncontrolled and should be used for reference purposes only. Amendments to this manual will be issued by the Environmental Management Representative (EMR) or designee following approval by the *Facility/Plant* Manager.

4.0 Environmental Policy

The *Facility/Plant* Environmental Policy (Policy) is endorsed by the *Facility/Plant* Manager. The Policy covers all activities at the facility. The Policy includes a commitment to continual improvement and prevention of pollution, as well as a commitment to meet or exceed relevant environmental legislation, regulations and other requirements. The Policy will be reviewed annually by top management, communicated to all employees and made available to the public in accordance with the Environmental Communication procedure. (See Supplement A: Policy for a copy of the *Facility/Plant* Environmental Policy.)

Reference Material: ISO 14001 Standard (4.2)

Applicable Procedures: EP-010 Environmental Communication

5.0 Environmental Aspects

The *Facility/Plant* Cross-Functional Team (CFT) identifies the environmental aspects which the facility controls and over which it may be expected to have an influence and determines which of those aspects are considered significant. Discussions regarding significance are recorded in CFT meeting minutes. These aspects are reviewed semi-annually by the CFT or when there is a new or changed process or activity at the facility. The EMR maintains CFT minutes and other records. (See Supplement B - Aspects, Objectives and Targets for a list of all aspects by area and department.)

Reference Material: ISO 14001 Standard (4.3.1)

Applicable Procedures: EP-002 Environmental Aspects, Objectives and Targets, and Management Programs; EP-008 Environmental Review of Projects

6.0 Legal and Other Requirements

The *Facility/Plant* has established an environmental procedure for the purpose of identifying, accessing and communicating legal and other requirements that are applicable to the facility. Additional information is also available through legal publications. Local regulations are identified, accessed and communicated by the Environmental Coordinator.

The Environmental Coordinator will review the most current national, regional, provincial, state and local legal and other requirements applicable to the *Facility/Plant*, at least annually. (See Supplement C: Legal and Other Requirements for a complete list.)

Reference Materials: Legal and Other Requirements; ISO 14001 Standard (4.3.2)

Applicable Procedures: EP-007 Environmental Regulations and Other Requirements

7.0   Environmental Objectives and Targets

The CFT has developed objectives and targets for each significant environmental aspect. These objectives and targets define:

1. Performance objectives (Investigate/Study, Control/Maintain or Improve) for each significant environmental aspect.
2. Specific, quantified targets which define those performance objectives.
3. Planned deadlines for the achievement of those targets.

Objectives and targets are developed considering significant environmental aspects, technological options and financial, operational and business plans and the views of interested parties. (See Supplement B: Aspects, Objectives and Targets for the facility's objectives and targets.)

Reference Material: ISO 14001 Standard (4.3.3)

Applicable Procedures: EP-002 Environmental Aspects; Objectives and Targets; Management Programs; EP-008 Environmental Review of Projects

8.0   Environmental Management Programs

The CFT establishes EMPs as a means for achieving objectives and targets. These programs define the principal actions to be taken, those responsible for undertaking those actions and scheduled times for their implementation. The EMPs are developed by the CFT and approved by the *Facility/Plant* Management Team (refer to Section 5.0 Environmental Aspects). (See Supplement D: Management Programs for the EMP.)

Reference Material: ISO 14001 Standard (4.3.4)

Applicable Procedures: EP-002 Environmental Aspects, Objectives and Targets; Management Programs; EP-008 Environmental Review of Projects

9.0   Organizational Structure and Responsibility

EMS roles, responsibilities and authorities are defined at relevant functions and levels within the organization. The *Facility/Plant* Management Team jointly provides the resources essential to the implementation and control of the EMS including: training, human resources, specialty services, financial resources, technical and informational services. The EMR has primary responsibility for establishing, operating and maintaining the EMS. A CFT provides routine EMS support and reports directly to the EMR. (See Supplement E: Structure and Responsibilities for documentation describing the various positions.)

Reference Material: ISO 14001 Standard (4.4.1)

10.0 Training, Awareness and Competence

The *Facility/Plant* identifies, plans, monitors and records training needs for personnel whose work may create a significant impact upon the environment. The *Facility/Plant* has an environmental procedure to train employees at each relevant function and level so that they are aware of the environmental policy, significant environmental aspects, their roles and responsibilities in achieving conformance with the policy, procedures and the requirements of the EMS. The training coordinator is responsible for maintaining employee training records. Appropriate records are monitored and reviewed on a scheduled basis. Competency is determined by the employee's supervisor as specified in EP-021. (See Supplement F: Training Matrix for an environmental training plan.)

Reference Material: ISO 14001 Standard (4.4.2)

Applicable Procedures: EP-014 Environmental Training and Awareness

11.0 Communication

The *Facility/Plant* has established and will maintain a procedure for internal and external communications regarding environmental aspects and the EMS.

Reference Material: ISO 14001 Standard (4.4.3)

Applicable Procedures: EP-010 Environmental Communication

12.0 Environmental Management System Documentation

This manual identifies all documents relevant to the EMS. A copy of EMS documents, other than visual aids and records, can be obtained from the EMR or designee. (See Supplements I: Procedures and J: Work Practices.)

Reference Material: ISO 14001 Standard (4.4.4)

13.0 Document Control

The *Facility/Plant* has established an environmental procedure for controlling all documents related to the environmental system. This procedure describes where documents can be located and how and when they are reviewed. The procedure ensures that current versions are available and that obsolete documents are promptly removed from use or are suitably identified. Controlled documents are obtainable from the EMR or designee. A list of controlled documents is provided in Supplement G: Master Document List.

Reference Material: ISO 14001 Standard (4.4.5)

Applicable Procedures: EP-001 Formatting Environmental Procedures; Work Practices & Forms; EP-012 Environmental Document Control

14.0 Operational Control

The CFT is responsible for identifying operations and activities associated with significant environmental aspects that require operational controls in procedures, work practices or EMPs.

These documents define the mechanisms for the establishment, implementation and maintenance of the EMS and ensure that the system is maintained in accordance with the environmental policy and objectives and targets and is communicated to suppliers and contractors.

- System Procedures (See Supplement I: Procedures): Cover the management and control of both the EMS and the principal environmental aspects which the system manages. These procedures are *Facility/Plant*-wide in application.

- Work Practices (See Supplement J: Work Practices): Cover the environmental control of specific operational activities and are usually activity specific in their application.

Reference Material: ISO 14001 Standard (4.4.6)

15.0 Emergency Preparedness and Response

The *Facility/Plant* has an environmental procedure to identify potential for and response to accidents and emergency situations, and for preventing and mitigating the environmental impacts that may be associated with them. Emergency methods are reviewed by the CFT on an annual basis and after the occurrence of accidents or emergency situations.

Reference Material: ISO 14001 Standard (4.4.7)

Applicable Procedures: EP-006 Emergency Preparedness and Response

16.0 Monitoring and Measurement

The *Facility/Plant* has established an environmental procedure to monitor and measure the key characteristics of its operations and activities that can have a significant impact on the environment. This procedure includes calibration and maintenance requirements and ensures that records will be retained.

The *Facility/Plant* has established an Environmental Regulatory Compliance Program. Procedure EP-003 outlines the requirements of the program and submits a periodic review on regulatory compliance to management on a yearly basis.

Reference Material: ISO 14001 Standard (4.5.1)

Applicable Procedures: EP-003 Environmental Management System and Regulatory Compliance Audits; EP-015 Monitoring and Measurement

17.0 Nonconformance and Corrective and Preventive Action

The *Facility/Plant* has an environmental procedure for defining responsibility and authority for handling and investigating nonconformances, for taking action to mitigate impacts and for initiating and completing corrective and preventive action. Any changes in procedures resulting from corrective and preventive actions are implemented and recorded. The Audit Program Leader maintains these records.

Reference Material: ISO 14001 Standard (4.5.2)

Applicable Procedures: EP-004 Nonconformance and Corrective and Preventive Action

18.0 Records

The *Facility/Plant* has an environmental procedure for the identification, maintenance and disposal of environmental records. These records include training records and the results of audits and reviews. They are readily retrievable and protected against damage, deterioration and loss. The areas and departments maintain their own environmental records. Record and document retention is also specified in the procedure. (See Supplement H: Master Records List for a list of relevant records.)

Reference Material: ISO 14001 Standard (4.5.3)

Applicable Procedures: EP-013 Environmental Records

19.0 Environmental Management System Audit

Periodic system audits are conducted to ensure that the EMS has been properly implemented and maintained. The results of these audits are provided to management. Audits are performed according to a schedule, which is based on the environmental importance of an activity, the results of previous audits and the audit schedule. All auditors are trained and audit records are kept with the Audit Program Leader.

Reference Material: ISO 14001 Standard (4.5.4)

Applicable Procedures: EP-003 Environmental Management System and Regulatory Compliance Audits

20.0 Management Review

The *Facility/Plant* Management Team reviews all elements of the EMS annually to ensure its continuing suitability, adequacy and effectiveness. Meeting minutes record these reviews and are kept by the EMR or designee.

Reference Material: ISO 14001 Standard (4.6)

Applicable Procedures: EP-005 Environmental Management System Management Review

21.0 Record of Revisions

Revision Date, Description, Sections Affected

Supplement A: ENVIRONMENTAL POLICY

The following policy is only an example. It must be modified to address facility-specific conditions and requirements.

The following are tips on structuring the Environmental Policy:

- Include a title, such as "(*Facility/Plant*) Environmental Policy."

- Include an opening paragraph that briefly describes the activities, products and/or services of the facility.

- Include a statement that communicates the facility's commitment to complying with acceptable environmental practices, including the commitment to meet or exceed legal, regulatory and other requirements, to strive for continual improvements and to minimize the creation of waste and pollution.

- Include a list, in general terms, of objectives or programs relevant to significant environmental aspects, thus making the policy "facility specific."

- The policy should be signed by the *Facility/Plant* Manager.

- The policy should be made available to the public by:
    —Posting it at the facility entrance.
    —Providing copies to the public upon request.

FACILITY/PLANT NAME

ENVIRONMENTAL POLICY

The *Facility/Plant* (provide an opening paragraph that briefly describes the activities, products and/or services at the facility).

Our Environmental Policy is to be a responsible corporate citizen in protecting the environment. We are committed to complying with accepted environmental practices, including the commitment to meet or exceed applicable legal and other requirements, to strive for continual improvement in our EMS and to minimize the creation of wastes and pollution. We will, therefore, manage our processes, our materials and our people in order to reduce the environmental impacts associated with our work.

The *Facility/Plant* pledges to implement and operate the ISO 14001 EMS to further enhance environmental performance. Our main objectives are to:

- Investigate the reduction of hazardous and toxic chemicals.
- Reduce, reuse and recycle waste and packaging.
- Improve the efficiency of energy usage.

This policy will be communicated to all parties interested in the performance of our EMS.

Signed:_____   Date:_____
Facility/Plant Manager

Supplement B: ASPECTS, OBJECTIVES AND TARGETS

The following information on aspects, objectives and targets are only examples. The correct identification of aspects and determination of significance can only be made after proper consideration of national, regional and local conditions and requirements.

The documents provided in the supplement include a description of controlled and influenced environmental aspects and an example of environmental aspects for any engine assembly department.

ENVIRONMENTAL ASPECTS

1. The *Facility/Plant*'s environmental aspects are determined, and their significance evaluated, through implementation of EP-002: Environmental Aspects, Objectives and Targets and Management Programs.

2. The environmental aspects for the *Facility/Plant* EMS are recorded in the Environmental Aspects list maintained in this section of the EMS manual.

    Environmental aspects include:

    a) Controlled Environmental Aspects

    Controlled environmental aspects are aspects that the *Facility/Plant* can directly manage through its organizational structure and responsibilities. These aspects are controlled through the EMS consistent with the Environmental Policy.

    b) Influenced Environmental Aspects

    Influenced Environmental Aspects are aspects generated on-site that the *Facility/Plant* does not directly control, but over which the *Facility/Plant* has some authority (i.e., through contractual obligations) or persuasion.

Supplement B: Environmental Aspects, Objectives and Targets Determination

Form Completed by: Jane Doe
Department/Area: Engine Assembly
Date Completed: Sept. 24, 1999
Process/Activity: All

Aspect Identification			Significance		Objectives & Targets	
Category*/Aspect	Quantity/Volume	Rationale for Significance/ Nonsignificance**	S/NS ***	Objective	Target
AIR EMISSIONS					
Maintenance Paint Booth Exhaust		R	S	Maintain compliance to regulations; upgrade maint. paint booth exhaust system.	Ongoing 6/98
Air Discharge from Air Scrubber at Waste Treatment		NS	NS		
WASTEWATER DISCHARGE					
Sanitary Sewage Discharge to City		R	S	Maintain compliance to permits for life of permits. Investigate low flow shower heads.	Ongoing 1/99
LIQUID & SOLID WASTES					
Waste Gasoline Gen. by Hot Test, DYNO, IND. Garage and Tank Farms		R	S	Maintain compliance to hazardous waste regulations	Ongoing
Cartridge Filters		NS	NS		
MATERIAL USE					
Hydraulic, Lube Oil Usage		NS	NS		

*Aspect Categories: Air Emissions, Wastewater Discharges, Liquid and Solid Wastes, Energy Use, Stormwater Discharges, Water Use, Storage Tanks, Material Usage, Noise, Odor, Natural Environment, Land Condition
**Rationale for Significance/NonSignificance: R = Regulated/Other Req., A = Accidental Release, E = Energy, L = Environmental Load, NS = Does not meet significance criteria
***Abbreviations: S = Significant & NS = Not Significant

Supplement C: LEGAL AND OTHER REQUIREMENTS

ASPECT	REQUIREMENT	CITATION/ SOURCE
Material Usage	**General Environmental Requirements**	
	Hazardous Substances and Reportable Quantities (CERLA)	40 CFR Part 302
	Hazardous Chemical Reporting: Community Right to Know (SARA Title III)	40 CFR Part 370
	Toxic Chemical Release Reporting: Community Right to Know (SARA Title III)	40 CFR Part 372
Air Emissions	**Air Quality Requirements**	
	Air Quality (CAA)	40 CFR Parts 50-61
	CFC Containing Equipment	40 CFR Part 82
	State Air Permit #8580	State Act 336 Part 2
Stormwater Discharges	**Water Quality Requirements**	
	Discharge of Oil	40 CFR Part 110
	Spill, Pollution Control Countermeasures (CWA)	40 CFR Part 112
	Water Discharge Permits	40 CFR Part 122
	Test Procedures for Analysis of Pollutants	40 CFR Part 136
	Spillage of Oil and Polluting Material	State Act 245 Part 5
	State Stormwater Permit #8585	State Act 246 Part 2
	City Water & Sewerage Permit #123	City Ordinance 65
Wastewater Discharges	**Wastewater Requirements**	
	State NPDES Wastewater Permit #8587	State Act 255 Part 6

ASPECT	REQUIREMENT	CITATION/ SOURCE
Solid & Liquid Waste	**Waste Requirements**	
	Hazardous Waste RCRA	40 CFR Part 264-265
	Land Disposal Restrictions	40 CFR Part 268
	Used Oil Management Standards	40 CFR Part 279
	Hazardous Substances and Reportable Quantities	40 CFR Parts 302
	Toxic Substance Control Act	40 CFR Part 700
	PCB Waste Management	40 CFT Part 761
	Asbestos Management	40 CFT Part 763
	Hazardous Waste Management	State Act 299
	Solid Waste Management Act	State Act 451 Part 115
	Liquid Industrial Waste	State Act 451 Part 121
	Medical Waste Management	State Act 368 Part 138
	Universal Waste	State Act 451 Part 225
Material Usage, Solid & Liquid Waste and Storage Tanks	**Emergency Response Requirements**	
	Emergency Planning and Notifications	40 CFR Part 355
	Underground Storage Tank Management	State Act 505 Part 120

Supplement C: LEGAL AND OTHER REQUIREMENTS (continued)

REQUIREMENT	CITATION/ SOURCE
Other Requirements	
EMSs	ISO 14001:1996
Ford Global Terms and Conditions	Implementation and maintenance of ISO 14001 EMS. One facility certified by 12/31/01. All supplier manufacturing sites certified by 7/1/03.
Ford Restricted Substance Management Standard WSS-M99P9999-A1	Addresses chemicals and material involved in products or services delivered to Ford and indentifies those considered either restricted or prohibited.
Ford Worldwide Design Standard 00.00D28 Complete Vehicle Recycling	Outlines the requirements for developing and implementing recycling strategies and technologies.
Ford Engineering Standard E4	Outlines the requirements for properly marking plastic, polymeric and recycled content parts
Ford Packaging Guideline	Guideline addresses packaging solution to minimize the environmental impact for delivered products and services.
Production, Non-Production and Post Production Material Procedure, Ford Automotive Procedure 02-132	Outlines the material approval process prior to bringing materials into Ford facilities.

Supplement D: ENVIRONMENTAL MANAGEMENT PROGRAMS

Significant Aspect: All aspects determined significant based on legal requirements
Department/Area(s): All applicable
Objective: Maintain regulatory compliance
Program Plan: Regulatory Compliance Program
Champion: EMR
Process/Activity: All applicable
Target: Ongoing
Date: September 21, 1999

Task	Responsible Party	Schedule	Performance Monitoring	Key Characteristics/ Operational Controls/Comments
Identify applicable legal & other requirements	Env. Coordinator	Oct. 99 & annually thereafter	List of legal & other requirements	Prepare list as specified in EP-007
Communicate legal & other requirement changes to applicable area or department managers	Env. Coordinator	Ongoing	Communication record	Prepare memoranda or e-mail summarizing changes and provide to area or department managers per EP-007 & EP-010
Communicate legal & other requirement changes to applicable staff	Affected area or dept. managers	Ongoing	Communication record or meeting minutes	Report changes as specified in EP-010
Conduct internal compliance audits	EMR & Compliance audit team	As specified in audit schedule	Audit schedule, checklists, CARs & audit summary report	EMR reports noncompliance to management team
Prepare and maintain lists of monitoring and reporting requirements & schedules. Conduct monitoring and submit required reports as specified by legal & other requirements	Env. Coordinator	Ongoing	List of requirements & schedules, reports	List of monitoring and reporting requirements & schedules revised as needed. Reports to agencies reviewed & approved by EMR prior to submittal

Calibrate and maintain monitoring equipment as specified by legal & other requirements, and by manufacturer's instructions	Affected area or dept. manager	Ongoing	Calibration & maintenance schedules and records	Affected areas & depts. maintain list of monitoring equipment and calibration & maintenance schedules. Corresponding records maintained by area or dept.
Prepare permit applications and revise permits as necessary	Env. Coordinator	Ongoing	Applications & permit conditions	Permit applications prepared per applicable legal & other requirements. Permit conditions monitored per list of monitoring and reporting requirements & schedules
Respond to agency inquiries	Env. Coordinator	Ongoing	Communication records	Communications conducted per EP-010
Use project method statements to assess impact of new installations or equipment on compliance	EMR	Ongoing after Oct. 99	Project method statements & evaluation report	Method statements generated per EP-011. EMR prepares evaluation report and submits to Project Manager. Project must be modified if compliance not maintained.
Ensure CFC/HCFC and PCB containing equipment are serviced and maintained according to applicable requirements	Affected area or dept. managers	Ongoing	Maintenance schedules & records	Affected areas or depts. maintain maintenance records
Review wastestreams to ensure that waste materials are properly classified	Env. Coordinator	Per monitoring schedules	List of wastestreams	This review must be completed at least every 6 months prior to aspect identification
Ensure hazardous waste accumulation areas are maintained per applicable requirements	Affected area or dept. managers	Per monitoring schedules	Inspection log	Completed inspection logs submitted to Env. Coordinator for review
Ensure proper handling and disposal of wastes	Env. Coordinator	Per monitoring schedules	Waste manifests, inspection logs	Records maintained by Env. Coordinator

Supplement D: ENVIRONMENTAL MANAGEMENT PROGRAMS (continued)

Significant Aspect: Materials identified as significant
Department/Area(s): All applicable
Objective: Maintain regulatory compliance
Program Plan: Manage significant materials
Champion: EMR
Process/Activity: All applicable
Target: Ongoing
Date: September 21, 1999

Task	Responsible Party	Schedule	Performance Monitoring	Key Characteristics/ Operational Controls/Comments
Indentify materials used by facility and determine significance	CFT	Oct. 99 & every 6 months	Data recorded on EF-002.01	Type and annual quantity of materials recorded per EP-002. Materials determined significant are "managed materials."
Track managed material usage by area/department	CFT	Monthly, beginning Nov. 99	Monthly usage record	Type and monthly quantity of managed materials by area department. Results reported to EMR.
Investigate feasibility of reducing managed material usage	CFT	Nov. 99 & every 6 months	Report of investigation	Report results of investigation, with recommendations to EMR.
As appropriate, develop plan for reducing the use of selected managed materials per EMR direction	CFT	Dec. 99 & every 6 months	Reduction plan	Reduction plan submitted to EMR for approval.
Implement managed material usage reductions, as applicable	Affected area or dept. manager	Jan. 00 & upon issuance of new plan	Monthly usage record	Type and monthly quantity of managed materials by area department. Results reported to EMR.

Task	Responsible Party	Schedule	Performance Monitoring	Key Characteristics/ Operational Controls/Comments
Evaluate materials before they are used on-site	CFT & affected area or dept. manager	Ongoing	Evaluation record	Personnel who purchase materials for on-site use will establish a system approved by the CFT for evaluation and approval of materials before they are brought on-site. The established system will use EP-002 for the evaluation. Results of reviews are to be reported to EMR. Materials deemed too hazardous may be banned.

Supplement D: ENVIRONMENTAL MANAGEMENT PROGRAMS (continued)

Significant Aspect: Energy usage identified as significant
Department/Area(s): All applicable
Objective: Reduce energy
Program Plan: Energy Reduction Program
Champion: EMR
Process/Activity: All applicable
Target: 5% (rate basis & production normalized) from 1998 levels by Jan., 2002
Date: Sept. 21, 1999

Task	Responsible Party	Schedule	Performance Monitoring	Key Characteristics/ Operational Controls/Comment
Monitor energy usage	Controller	October through December, 1999	Utility bills	Rate of usage reported monthly to energy team
Identify high potential energy users and energy type. Prioritize areas for energy savings principally based on feasibility of energy reduction potential	CFT	January, 2000-February, 2000 and update semi-annually	Data recorded on EF-002.01	Type and rates of utility usage recorded per EP-002
Develop utility reduction plan to achieve energy usage objective & targets	CFT	March, 2000	Reduction plan	Plan submitted to management team by the EMR for approval
For energy process identified in utility plan and established baseline and performance metrics to track	Controller	April, 2000, track monthly	Monthly utility bills	Rate of usage and actual vs. baseline reported monthly to Utility Team
Implement reduction initiatives as specified in the plan	Affected area or dept. manager	As specified in reduction plan	Progress reports	CFT to monitor implementation progress and report findings each month to EMR

Task	Responsible Party	Schedule	Performance Monitoring	Key Characteristics/ Operational Controls/Comment
Use project method statements to assess impact of new installations or equipment on reduction initiatives	EMR	Ongoing after October, 1999	Project method statements & evaluation report	Method statements generated per EP-011. EMR prepares evaluation report and submits to project manager. Objective & target may be modified if project utilization rates adversely affect reduction initiatives and project utilization cannot be changed

Supplement D: ENVIRONMENTAL MANAGEMENT PROGRAMS (continued)

Significant Aspect: Solid and liquid identified as significant
Department/Area(s): All applicable
Objective: Reduce solid and liquid
Program Plan: Waste Minimization Program
Champion: EMR
Process/Activity: All applicable
Target: 5% (volume basis & production normalized) from 1998 levels by Dec. 2000
Date: Sept. 21, 1999

Task	Responsible Party	Schedule	Performance Monitoring	Key Characteristics/ Operational Controls/Comments
Identify solid & liquid wastes generated by facility and determine significance.	CFT	Oct. 99 & update every six months	Data recorded on EF-002.01	Types and annual quantities of wastes & emissions recorded per EP-002.
Evaluate current and potential waste minimization practices for significant solid & liquid wastes and air emissions (e.g., recycle, reuse, or changing process or practice to minimize, eliminate or substitute).	CFT	Nov. 99 & update every six months	Report of evaluation	Report results of evaluation with recommendations to EMR. Include a discussion of current wate and air emission minimization practices.
Select target waste streams and develop action plan to achieve 2000 target.	CFT	Dec. 99 & every six months	Minimization plan	Minimization plan submitted to Management Team by EMR for approval.
Establish traceable performance metrics for chosen waste streams.	Affected area or dept. manager	Monthly	Monthly record	Types and monthly quantities of wastes and emissions recorded by area or department. Results reported to EMR.
Implement minimization initiatives specified in the plan.	Affected area or dept. manager	As specified in minimization plan	Progress reports	CFT to monitor implementation progress and report findings each month to EMR.

Task	Responsible Party	Schedule	Performance Monitoring	Key Characteristics/ Operational Controls/Comments
Evaluate program effectiveness and need for program adjustments to meet target.	Waste Coordinator, CFT	Quarterly	CFT minutes	Comparison between actual and baseline is monitored and effectiveness of program evaluated.
Develop annual report for management review to include summary and status of action plans.	EMR, CFT	Aug. 00 and Aug. 01	Report	EMR to present the report to Management Team to assess progress of action plans and need for adjustments.
Use project method statements to assess impact of new installations or equipment on reduction initiatives.	EMR	Ongoing after Oct. 99	Project method statements & evaluation report	Method statements generated per EP-011. EMR prepares evaluation report and submits to Project Manager. Objective & targets may be modified if project utilization rates adversely affect reduction initiatives and project utilization cannot be changed.

Supplement E: STRUCTURE AND RESPONSIBILITIES

The following table and organization chart are only examples. They must be modified to properly address local conditions.

Structure and Responsibilities

Facility/Plant Manager
a) Has overall responsibility for the development and implementation of the EMS.
b) Allocates EMS resources.
c) Participates in the management review of the EMS for suitability, adequacy and effectiveness.
d) Sets the focus of environmental policy, objectives and targets for the facilities/stores.

Department/Area Managers
a) Participate on the Management Team in reviewing the plant's EMS.
b) Support the EMR in providing resources adequate to achieve environmental objectives and targets and proper implementation and maintenance of the EMS.

Controller
a) Manages the accounting and financial operations of the plant including the funding for projects and expenses to maintain compliance with regulations and adherence to company environmental policy.
b) Participates on the Management Team in reviewing the plant's EMS.

Human Resources Manager
a) Is responsible for providing industrial and public relations services for the plant.
b) Is responsible for external environmental communications with interested parties and the media.
c) Oversees the plant's training programs including environmental training.
d) Participates on the Management Team in reviewing the plant's EMS.

Material Handling Manager
a) Is responsible for the storage of production and nonproduction materials.
b) Ensures that delivery, transportation, handling and storage of all materials are properly managed.
c) Manages shipping of waste materials.
d) Maintains information on usages, storage and inventory of all production materials.
e) Manages warehouse layout optimization, facilitating material and waste flow.

f) Participates on the Management Team in reviewing the plant's EMS.

Structure and Responsibilities

Quality Manager
a) Manages the quality management system for the plant.
b) Manages and controls quality documents.
c) Coordinates the Records Retention system for the plant.
d) Participates on the Management Team in reviewing the plant's EMS.

Plant Safety Manager
a) Manages plant safety activities including coordination of Emergency Response Plan when appropriate.
b) Participates on the Management Team in reviewing the plant's EMS.

Information Systems Manager
a) Manages *Facility/Plant* computer systems including systems for the EMS.

Environmental Management Representative
a) Participates as a member of the Management Team.
b) Directs the CFT in the development, implementation and maintenance of the EMS.
c) Reports to the Management Team on the status of the EMS, including: environmental compliance, system audits and corrective action plans.

Environmental Coordinator
a) Monitors and interprets environmental legal requirements applicable to the *Facility/Plant*.
b) Monitors and interprets other requirements to which the *Facility/Plant* subscribes.
c) Supports the EMS by:
   —generating and submitting reports required by the government.
   —maintaining summary data and information on liquid and solid wastes, air emissions, and other key environmental performance measurables.
   —determining the appropriate disposal methods for all wastes at the *Facility/Plant*.
   —maintaining environmental records as required.
d) Maintains the EMS Manual.
e) Manages applicable permit applications.
f) Acts on behalf of the *Facility/Plant*, when assigned and as required, as the official representative with regulatory and local authorities.

Structure and Responsibilities

Cross-Functional Team
a) Periodically identifies aspects, determining significance, establishing environmental objectives and targets and creating EMS.
b) Maintains system procedures, including those for emergency response.
c) Develops, implements and maintains the EMS under the direction of the EMR.
d) Acts as the pollution prevention, waste minimization and energy team, where applicable.

Emergency Response/Safety Committee
a) Manages safety and security activities including coordination of the Emergency Response Plan.

Audit Program Leader
a) Schedules and coordinates internal environmental system audit program. Reports audit results to the EMR.
b) Monitors closures of nonconformances.

Internal System Audit Team
a) Audits environmental system elements as directed by the Environmental Audit Program Leader.
b) Reports system nonconformances and verifies corrective and preventive actions are implemented.

Project Managers
a) Reviews and characterizes environmental aspects of a project through the use of project environmental checklists.
b) Receives and reviews environmental method statements from contractors.
c) Forwards method statements and checklists to EMR.
d) Works with EMR to resolve environmental issues with contractors.

Supplement F: TRAINING MATRIX

The following training matrix tables are only examples. They must be modified to properly address national, regional or local conditions and requirements.

TRAINING NEEDS MATRIX
ENVIRONMENTAL COURSES

Course	Employees Requiring Training	Source of Training	Duration (hrs)	Frequency
A/C Refrigeration Servicing (Stationary)	A/C Maintenance			Once, each new maintenance staff
HAZWOPER: First Responder	Security			Annual
Environmental Awareness	(Bulk Materials, HAZWOPER 1st Responder Awareness, Integrated Emergency Response and Spill Contingency Plan, Prevention Plan, Waste Management, Energy Management, Asbestos Management)			Every other year
Incident Command Training	Security and Supervisors			Annual
Fire Brigade Training	Emergency Response Team			For all new team members
RCRA Awareness Training	Waste Management Coordinator			Annual
EMS Lead Auditor Training	Environmental Coordinator, Lead Internal Auditor			Initially
EMS Awareness Training	All employees & full-time on-site contractors			Initially, new hires and as necessary
EMS Document Training (see also "Applicable Procedures by Department")	Employees and full time on-site contractors whose work requires knowledge of the document			Initially, new hires and when document changes occur

Course	Employees Requiring Training	Source of Training	Duration (hrs)	Frequency
EMS Implementation Training	CFT & EMR			Initially
EMS Internal Auditor Training	EMS Internal Auditors			Initially & new auditors

TRAINING NEEDS MATRIX
PROCEDURES AND WORK INSTRUCTIONS BY AREA/DEPT.

Procedure/ Work Practice No.	Title	Tool & Die	Truck Shop	Paint Shop	Safety	Powerhouse Engineer	Maint./Facility Engineering	Production	Shipping
EV-01	CSP Asbestos Management				X				
EV-02	PCB Management					X	X		
EV-03	Bulk Material Management					X			X
EV-04	Outside Equipment Storage Management	X					X		
EV-05	Material Usage/ Tox # Assignment	X		X	X	X	X		
WI02-01	PCB-Containing Transformer Instructions						X		
WI03-01	Bulk Chemical Truck Deliveries					X	X		
WI03-02	Bulk Truck Deliveries of Petroleum Products						X		
WI03-04	Bulk Propane Delivery and Storage						X		
WI04-01	Scrap Metal	X					X		
WP03-05	Machining Coolants	X	X				X		
WP03-06	Road Salt						X		
WP03-07	Power House/ Cooling Tower Chemical Usage					X			
WP05-01	Review/Approve "Special" Biocide Additions to CSP Coolant Systems				X	X	X		
WP06-01	KECKES Boilers					X	X		

Chapter 10

Supplement G: MASTER DOCUMENT LIST

The following master document list is only an example. It must be modified to properly address national, regional or local conditions and requirements.

ID	Title	Issue Date	Location	Authorized By
Policy				
	Environmental Policy			
Manuals & Plans				
	EMS Manual			
	Integrated Spill Plan			
Procedures				
EP-001	Formatting Environmental Procedures and Work Practices			
EP-002	Environmental Aspects, Objectives and Targets, and Management Programs			
EP-003	EMS and Regulatory Compliance Audits			
EP-004	Nonconformance and Corrective and Preventive Action			
EP-005	EMS Management Review			
EP-006	Emergency Preparedness and Response			
EP-007	Environmental Regulations and Other Requirements			
EP-008	Environmental Review of Projects			
EP-009	Agency Approvals			
EP-010	Environmental Communication			
EP-011	Contractor Control			
EP-012	Environmental Document Control			
EP-013	Environmental Records			
EP-014	Environmental Training and Awareness			
EP-015	Monitoring and Measurement			

ID	Title	Issue Date	Location	Authorized By
Work Practices				
EWP-020.01	Servicing of Stationary Refrigeration Equipment			
EWP-023.01	Waste Drum Shipments			
EWP-024.01	Bulk Material Loading and Unloading			
Forms				
EF-002.01	Environmental Aspects			
EF-003.01	Audit Checklist			
EF-003.02	Corrective and Preventative Action Request (CAR)			
EF-003.03	Internal Environmental Audit Summary Report			
EF-003.04	Audit Schedule			
EF-005.01	Attendee Sheet			
EF-008.01	Project Environmental Checklist			
EF-010.01	External Communications Log			
EF-011.01	Environmental Briefing Packet and Contractor Method Statement Template			
EF-012.01	Master Document List			
EF-013.01	Index of Environmental Records			
EF-014.01	Training Matrix			
EF-999.01	Management Review Meeting			
	Service Order			
	Evacuation Label			
	Appliance Input			
	Refrigerant Cylinder Input			
	Refrigerant Transfer			

ID	Title	Issue Date	Location	Authorized by
	Bulk Material Inspection Log			
Audit Checklists				
ACEP-002	Audit Questions for Procedure EP-002			
ACEP-003	Audit Questions for Procedure EP-003			
ACEP-004	Audit Questions for Procedure EP-004			
ACEP-005	Audit Questions for Procedure EP-005			
Records	(see Supplement H - Master Records List)			
References				
ISO 14001:1996	EMSs - Specification with Guidance for Use			

Supplement H: MASTER RECORDS LIST

The following master records list is only an example. It must be modified to properly address national, regional or local conditions and requirements.

Document	Record	Retention (yrs)	Controlled By	Location
EP-002	Environmental aspects			
	CFT meeting agenda, minutes and attendance sheets			
	EMPs, management review agenda, attendance sheets, meeting minutes and assignments			
EP-003	Audit checklists			
	Corrective & preventative action requests			
	Audit schedule			
	Original copies of internal environmental audit records			
	Internal environmental audit summary report			
EP-004	Corrective & preventative action requests			
	Action plans, where used			
EP-005	Management review agenda, attendance sheets, meeting minutes and assignments			
EP-006	Incident reports			
	Records of emergency response tests and drills			
	Training records			
EP-007	List of relevant environmental legal & other requirements			
EP-008	Project appropriation requests			
	Project environmental checklist			
EP-009	Environmental permits & applications			
	Regulatory communications			
EP-010	Records of internal communications			
	Records of external communications			
	Log of external communications			
EP-011	Contractor method statements			
	Contractor records pertaining to environmental training, etc.			
EP-012	Master document list			
EP-013	Index of environmental records			
EP-014	Training matrix			
	Training schedule			
EP-015	Key characteristics and environmental performance of significant aspects			
	Compliance audit documents			

Document	Record	Retention (yrs)	Controlled By	Location
EWP-020.01	Calibration & maintenance records			
	Refrigeration technician certification card			
	Weight logs			
	Appliance input			
	Refrigerant cylinder input			
	Refrigerant transfer			
EWP-023.01	Tank certifications			
EWP-024.01	Waste manifests			
	Shipping manifests			
	Waste manifests			
	Weekly inspection logs			

Supplement I: PROCEDURES

FORMATTING ENVIRONMENTAL PROCEDURES, WORK PRACTICES AND FORMS, EP-001

1.0   Purpose/Scope

This procedure defines the format to be used in creating *Facility/Plant* environmental procedures (EPs), environmental work practices (EWPs) and forms (EFs).

The control of these documents is addressed in environmental procedure EP-016: Environmental Document Control.

2.0   Activities Affected: All

3.0   Forms Used: None

4.0   References: ISO 14001:1996, Element 4.4.5

5.0   Definitions: None

6.0   Exclusions: None

7.0   Procedure

    7.1   Environmental Procedures shall:

        a) Have a unique reference number in the bottom corner of the page in the format "EP-###" where:
            EP = *Facility/Plant* Environmental Procedure identifier
            EP-### = Environmental Procedure Number and each # is a digit.
        b) Be paginated in the format "Page # of #" in the bottom center of the page.
        c) Be dated as per date of issue/revision in the bottom corner of the page.
        d) Have a title at the top of the page.
        e) Have the following sections:

            1.0   Purpose/Scope
            2.0   Activities Affected
            3.0   Forms Used

4.0 References
5.0 Definitions
6.0 Exclusions
7.0 Procedure
8.0 General Rules
9.0 Records
Record of Revisions

7.2 Environmental Work Practices shall:

a) Have a unique reference number in the bottom corner of the page in the format "EWP-###" where:
   EWP = *Facility/Plant* Environmental Work Practice identifier.
   EWP-### = Environmental Work Practice Number, each # is a digit.
b) Have a title at the top of the page.
c) Be paginated in the format "Page # of #" in the bottom center of the page.
d) Be dated as per date of issue/revision in the bottom corner of the page.
e) Be written in whatever form is considered to be appropriate to the operational circumstances.

7.3 Environmental Forms shall:

a) Have a unique reference number in the bottom corner of the page in the format "EF-###.##" where:
   EF = *Facility/Plant* Environmental Form identifier.
   EF-###.## = Environmental Form Number, each # is a digit.
b) Have a title at the top of the page.
c) Be paginated in the format "Page # of #" in the bottom center of the page.
d) Be dated as per date of issue/revision in the bottom corner of the page.
e) Be written in whatever form is considered to be appropriate to the operational circumstances.

8.0 General Rules: None

9.0 Records: None

Record of Revisions: Revision Date, Description, Sections Affected

Supplement I: ENVIRONMENTAL ASPECTS, OBJECTIVES AND TARGETS, AND MANAGEMENT PROGRAMS, EP-002

1.0   Purpose/Scope

This procedure defines the mechanism for the identification and significance evaluation of the environmental aspects of the *Facility/Plant* operations, in order to determine those aspects which have actual or potential significant impacts upon the environment.

It also defines the framework within which the *Facility/Plant* shall establish and maintain environmental objectives and targets and EMPs.

2.0   Activities Affected: All Areas and Departments

3.0   Forms Used

    3.1   Environmental Aspects, Objectives and Targets Determination

    3.2   Environmental Management Programs

4.0   References

    4.1   EP-005   Environmental Management System Management Review

    4.2   EP-006   Emergency Preparedness and Response

    4.3   EP-007   Environmental Regulations and Other Requirements

    4.4   EP-008   Environmental Review of Projects

    4.5   EP-010   Environmental Communication

    4.6   EP-014   Environmental Training and Awareness

    4.7   EP-015   Monitoring and Measurement

    4.8   ISO 14001:1996, Elements 4.3.1, 4.3.3 and 4.3.4

5.0   Definitions

    5.1   Environmental Aspect: element of an organization's activities, products or services that can interact with the environment.

5.2 Environmental Objective: overall environmental goal, arising from the environmental policy, that an organization sets itself to achieve and which is quantified where practicable.

5.3 Environmental Target: detailed performance requirement, quantified where practicable, applicable to the organization or parts thereof, that arises from the environmental objectives and that needs to be set and met in order to achieve those objectives.

5.4 EMP: the means, time frames and personnel responsible for achieving an objective and target.

6.0 Exclusions: None

7.0 Procedure

    7.1 Identification of Environmental Aspects

        7.1.1 A CFT championed by the EMR shall identify environmental aspects of operations that can be controlled or influenced. This information will be documented on the Environmental Aspects form.

        7.1.2 Using pertinent plant information (e.g., process flow diagrams, plant layout maps, etc.) the facility/plant CFT will document all relevant activities, processes and services in which to identify aspects.

        7.1.3 The CFT will identify the specific environmental aspects using General Aspect Categories. General Aspect Categories shall include, but not necessarily be limited to, the following:

- Air Emissions
- Liquid & Solid Wastes
- Stormwater Discharges
- Storage Tanks
- Noise
- Natural Environment
- Wastewater Discharges
- Energy Usage
- Water Usage
- Material Usage
- Odor
- Land Condition

        7.1.4 Lists of the aspects identified shall be maintained and shall be reviewed by the CFT at least every six months to identify any new aspects that should be added and any old aspects that should be deleted. Aspects identified through implementation of EP-008 shall be incorporated into the lists of aspects.

7.2 Determination of Significant Aspects

7.2.1 The CFT shall review and evaluate the aspects identified and shall determine their significance using the criteria in 7.2.2 below. Where a new aspect is incorporated into the lists of aspects (see 7.1.4 above) it shall be reviewed and evaluated by the CFT to determine significance.

7.2.2 The environmental aspects of the facility/plant may be considered by the CFT to be "significant" where the aspect:

7.2.2.1 Is subject to relevant legislation, regulation, permit requirements, and/or other requirements. This will likely include aspects associated with processes and activities if: (1) environmental regulations or other requirements specify controls and conditions, (2) information must be provided to outside authorities, and/or, (3) there are or may be periodic inspections or enforcements by these authorities. This will also include aspects that are addressed in the facility business plan or other applicable documents.

7.2.2.2 Is subject to a potential accidental release (liquid or gas only) that is regulated or that could be of sufficient quantity to cause environmental concern. These aspects shall be managed and controlled through implementation of environmental procedure EP-006: Emergency Preparedness and Response.

7.2.2.3 Pertains to energy usage.

7.2.2.4 Is subject to high environmental loading due to one or more of the following criteria:

- Toxicity (compositional characterization of materials and wastes)
- Ford Engineering Specification WSS-M99P9999-A1 (Restricted Substance Management Standard)
- Amounts (volumes and masses of releases)
- Amounts (consumption of renewable and non-renewable resources)

- Frequencies of episodes
- Severity of actual or potential impacts

7.2.3 The rationale for significance and insignificance will be documented on the Environmental Aspects, Objectives and Targets Determination form.

7.3 Establishing and Maintaining Objectives and Targets

7.3.1 The CFT shall establish and maintain environmental objectives and targets for all significant aspects. Objectives and targets shall be consistent with the *Facility/Plant* environmental policy and shall be one of three types: control, improve or investigate.

7.3.2 In establishing objectives and targets consideration shall be given to:

- Environmental legal and other requirements
- Technological options
- Financial, operational and business requirements
- Views of interested parties

7.3.3 Performance against objectives and targets shall be reviewed at least every six months by the CFT and reported at the management review meeting. (See EP-005: Environmental Management System Management Review). The management review shall endorse the facility environmental objectives and targets.

7.4 Establishing and Maintaining EMPs

7.4.1 The CFT shall establish and maintain EMPs for achieving the objectives and targets developed for the significant environmental aspects identified and updated every six months.

7.4.2 EMPs shall identify the means, time frames and those responsible for achieving associated objectives and targets. Responsibility will be identified at each relevant function and level of the organization.

8.0 General Rules

    8.1 The CFT shall include representation from all appropriate functional areas and departments.

    8.2 The environmental aspects and significant aspects associated with the operations of semipermanent on-site contractors are covered by this procedure.

    8.3 Interested parties include employees and the community. Their input is obtained through the implementation of EP-010.

    8.4 All records pertaining to the development and determination of aspects, significant aspects, objectives and targets, and EMPs will be marked "Environmental Audit Report: Privileged Document" (US only).

    8.5 The EMPs that address the following areas should be created if applicable objectives and targets are developed:

        8.5.1 Compliance Assurance

        8.5.2 Pollution Prevention/Waste Minimization

        8.5.3 Energy Management

        8.5.4 Materials Management

9.0 Records: Records shall be retained consistent with EP-013.

Record of Revisions: Revision Date, Description, Sections Affected

Facility/Plant Name
Environmental Aspects, Objectives and Targets Determination

Form Completed by: *Date Completed:*
Department/Area: *Process/Activity:*

Aspect Identification		Significance		Objectives & Targets	
Category*/Aspect	Quantity/ Volume	Rationale for Significance/ Nonsignific- ance**	S/NS ***	Objective	Target

*Aspect Categories:
**Rationale for Significance/Non-Significance: R = Regulated/Other Req., A = Accidental Release, E = Energy, L = Environmental Load, NS = Does not meet significance criteria
***Abbreviations: S = Significant & NS = Not Significant

Ford & ISO 14001

Facility/Plant Name
Environmental Management Program

Significant Aspect: 　　　　　　　　Champion:
Department/Area: 　　　　　　　　　Process/Activity:
Objective: 　　　　　　　　　　　　 Target:
Date:
Program Plan:

Task	Responsible Party	Schedule	Performance Monitoring	Key Characteristics/ Operational Controls/ Comments

Supplement I: ENVIRONMENTAL MANAGEMENT SYSTEM AND REGULATORY COMPLIANCE AUDITS, EP-003

1.0   Purpose/Scope

This procedure defines the mechanism for the planning and implementation of internal EMS and regulatory compliance audits at the *Facility/Plant*.

2.0   Activities Affected: All Areas and Departments

3.0   Forms Used

    3.1   Audit Checklist

    3.2   Corrective and Preventive Action Request (CAR)

    3.3   Internal Environmental Audit Summary Report

    3.4   Audit Schedule

4.0   References

    4.1   EP-004: Nonconformance and Corrective and Preventive Action

    4.2   EP-005: Environmental Management System Management Review

    4.3   ISO 14001:1996, Elements 4.5.1 and 4.5.4

    4.4   Compliance Assurance Program Guideline

5.0   Definitions

    5.1   Auditee: individual audited.

    5.2   Auditor: audit team member performing the audit.

    5.3   Audit Criteria: policies, practices, procedures or other requirements against which the auditor compares objective evidence about the subject matter.

    5.4   Audit Program Leader: individual responsible for maintaining the Environmental Audit Program.

5.5 CAR: corrective and preventive action request that identifies observed nonconformances.

5.6 Finding: an existing condition supported by objective evidence.

5.7 Nonconformance: the nonfulfillment of specified system requirements.

5.8 Objective Evidence: qualitative or quantitative information records, or statements of fact pertaining to the existence and implementation of an EMS element which is based on measurement or test and which can be verified.

6.0 Exclusions: None

7.0 Procedure

7.1 Conducting the Internal EMS Audit

7.1.1 The Quality Manager or designee shall plan, schedule and implement internal EMS audits. The audit schedule will be used to identify the frequency and location of internal EMS audits and will be revised as necessary. Revisions to the audit schedule may be based on the results of prior audits.

7.1.2 Audit frequency will be established on a priority basis, taking into account previous audit results and the relative importance of the area or department, and will not be less than once per year for each location. Each area or department will be audited at least once every three years on all system elements.

7.1.3 For each area or department within the facility, an audit team will be formed whose membership has no responsibility within the area or department to be audited. This independence will be documented by indicating on the audit report or other audit record the organization to which the auditors belong.

7.1.4 Competent audit teams shall perform internal environmental audits.

7.1.4.1 At least one member of the team shall be competent in the environmental auditing process through either training and/or experience.

7.1.4.2 All members of the audit team shall have an awareness and understanding of the *Facility/Plant*'s EMS by virtue of formal and informal training.

7.1.5 Audit scope and criteria will be established for each area or department prior to each audit. Audit criteria may be documented by the audit team in an Audit Checklist and the checklist used during the audits.

7.1.6 During the audit, the audit team will record audit information, such as: items checked, individuals interviewed, any concerns identified and any corrective or preventive actions completed during the audit. The audit team shall promptly notify the EMR or designee of any possible regulatory noncompliance. Upon verification of noncompliance, the EMR shall notify facility management.

7.1.7 Upon completion of the internal audit, the audit team will review their findings with the auditee and responsible and accountable area or department representative. The team will then initiate a CAR for each finding of nonconformance (Note: a noncompliance is a nonconformance) using the CAR form.

7.1.8 The Quality Manager or designee will track the status of all outstanding CARs using the Internal Environmental Audit Summary Report form (see also EP-004: Nonconformance, Corrective and Preventive Action).

7.1.9 The responsible and accountable area or department representative is to identify the route cause of the nonconformance (where applicable), corrective and preventive actions to be undertaken and the dates by which these actions will be completed. This information will be documented on the original CAR and the CAR sent to the applicable area or department manager. A copy of the CAR will also be provided to the Quality Manager or designee within the time frame established during the audit review meeting.

7.1.10 Upon completion of the corrective and preventive actions, the area or department manager will acknowledge completion of these actions by signing the orignal CAR and returning it to the Quality Manager or designee.

7.1.11 Corrective and preventive actions will be verified during the next internal audit or the area or department manager may contact the Quality Manager to schedule verification of actions prior to the next audit.

7.1.12 When full conformance is determined or corrective and preventative actions accepted, the audit team leader will sign the original CAR and return it to the Quality Manager or designee for closure and filing.

7.1.13 At least annually, the EMR or designee will summarize system audit results with facility management as specified in EP-005: Environmental Management System Review.

7.2 Conducting the Compliance Assessment Audit

7.2.1 The EMR or designee is responsible for planning, scheduling and implementing internal environmental regulatory compliance assessment audits, including the identification of required resources.

7.2.2 The EMR or designee develops and maintains the environmental compliance assurance program and issues program support documents, based on company environmental compliance assurance guidelines, where available.

7.2.3 During a compliance assessment audit, assessment team members will record information, such as: items checked, individuals interviewed, any possible regulatory noncompliance issues. The assessment team shall promptly notify the EMR or designee of any possible regulatory noncompliance. Upon verification of noncompliance, the EMR shall notify facility management.

7.2.4 The assessment team reviews possible regulatory noncompliance issues with the responsible and accountable area or department representative. The team also prepares a CAR identifying the issues, corrective and preventive actions required, and the individuals responsible for completing the actions. The EMR or designee and area or department manager will concur with the CAR before its issuance.

7.2.5 Upon completion of the corrective and preventive actions, the area or department manager will acknowledge completion of these actions by signing the original CAR and returning it to the EMR or designee.

    7.2.6 Corrective and preventive actions will be verified in a timely manner by a member of the assessment team. When full compliance is determined or corrective and preventive actions accepted, the assessment team member will sign the original CAR and return it to the EMR or designee for closure and filing.

    7.2.7 Each calendar quarter, the EMR or designee will present a summary of open CARs that are based on regulatory noncompliance to facility management for review.

8.0   General Rules

    8.1 Records, including CARs, relating to potential or actual noncompliance issues will be treated as confidential and will be kept separate from those relating to internal EMS audits.

    8.2 Potential nonconformance issues (Note: a noncompliance is a nonconformance) must receive prompt attention and timely corrective and preventive action.

    8.3 All audit records shall be marked "Environmental Audit Report: Privileged Document" (US only) and distributed to individuals with a need to know their contents in order to assess, respond to or remedy a potential or actual nonconformance.

9.0   Records: Records shall be retained consistent with EP-013: Environmental Records.

Record of Revisions: Revision Date, Description, Sections Affected

Ford & ISO 14001

Facility/Plant Name
Internal Audit Checklist

Date: Area/Department:

Auditee:	Audit Date:	Audit Criteria:
Requirements	Questions	Findings/Observations

Audit Team Leader Signature: _____ Date: _____

Facility/Plant Name
Corrective and Preventive Action Request (CAR)

A. Audited Area/Department:	
Audit Date: *Auditee(s):*	*Auditor(s):* *Date:*
B. Description of Nonconformance: Audit Criteria: Applicable ISO 14001 Element:	**C. Root Cause Analysis:**
D. Corrective Action: Date of Implementation:	
E. Preventive Action: Date of Implementation:	
F. Verification: Date of Verification:	
Auditor (signed):	*Date:*

Facility/Plant Name
Internal Environmental Audit Summary Report

CAR #	Issue Date	Area/ Department	Problem Description	Corrective Action Completion Date	Preventive Action Completion Date	Closure Date

Facility/Plant Name
Audit Schedule

X = System Audit
Y = Compliance Audit to be Conducted

Department	AUDIT FREQUENCY												
	JAN	FEB	MAR	APRIL	MAY	JUNE	JULY	AUG	SEPT	OCT	NOV	DEC

Supplement I: NONCONFORMANCE AND CORRECTIVE AND PREVENTIVE ACTION, EP-004

1.0   Purpose/Scope

This procedure defines the responsibilities and process for identifying and investigating nonconformances with the *Facility/Plant* EMS, for taking action to mitigate any negative impacts caused and for applying corrective and preventive actions.

2.0   Activities Affected: All Areas and Departments

3.0   Forms Used: Corrective and Preventive Action Request (CAR)

4.0   References

    4.1   EP-003 Environmental Management System and Regulatory Compliance Audits

    4.2   EP-006 Emergency Preparedness and Response

    4.3   EP-010 Environmental Communication

    4.4   EP-012 Environmental Document Control

    4.5   EP-015 Monitoring and Measurement

    4.6   ISO 14001:1996, Element 4.5.2

5.0   Definitions: None

6.0   Exclusions: None

7.0   Procedure

    7.1   Where nonconformances or noncompliances are identified through the environmental audit process, the responsible and accountable area or department representative, affected area or department manager, audit team member or EMR, as specified in EP-003, is responsible for:

        a) Identifying the root cause(s) of nonconformances or noncompliances.
        b) Identifying appropriate corrective and preventive actions

(including modifying or creating environmental procedures and work practices).
c) Planning and implementing corrective and preventive actions.
d) Verifying the close-out and effectiveness of corrective and preventive actions.

7.2 Where nonconformances are identified outside the environmental audit process, the Quality Manager or designee will generate a CAR, as appropriate, in accordance with EP-003: Environmental Management System and Regulatory Compliance Audits. The affected area or department manager or designee is responsible for:

a) Identifying the root cause(s) of these nonconformances
b) Identifying appropriate corrective and preventive actions (including modifying or creating environmental procedures and work practices)
c) Planning and implementing corrective and preventive actions
d) Verifying the close-out and effectiveness of corrective and preventive actions. The Quality Manager or designee will verify proper implementation of corrective and preventive actions.

7.3 Where noncompliances are identified outside the environmental audit process, the EMR or designee will generate a CAR, as appropriate. The CAR will then be addressed as specified in EP-003.

8.0 General Rules

8.1 All incidents, accidents, spills, releases and emergencies shall be dealt with through environmental procedure EP-006: Emergency Preparedness and Response.

8.2 A CAR shall be used for recording nonconformances (Note: a noncompliance is a nonconformance) and corrective and preventive actions as indicated in EP-003 or in step 7.2 of this procedure.

8.3 Action Plans may be used where appropriate for planning, scheduling and managing corrective and preventive actions.

8.4 Environmental procedures, environmental work practices and/or training programs shall be modified and/or created where necessary to establish adequate controls for avoiding repetition of nonconformances and noncompliances.

9.0   Records: Records shall be retained consistent with EP-013: Environmental Records.

Record of Revisions: Revision Date, Description, Sections Affected

Supplement I: ENVIRONMENTAL MANAGEMENT SYSTEM MANAGEMENT REVIEW, EP-005

1.0   Purpose/Scope

This procedure defines the process for the periodic review and evaluation of the *Facility/Plant* EMS by the *Facility/Plant* Management Team, to ensure its continuing suitability, adequacy and effectiveness.

2.0   Activities Affected: All Areas and Departments

3.0   Forms Used: Attendee Sheet

4.0   References

   4.1   EP-002 Environmental Aspects, Objectives and Targets, and Management Programs

   4.2   EP-003 Environmental Management System and Regulatory Compliance Audits

   4.3   EP-004 Nonconformance and Corrective and Preventive Action

   4.4   EP-007 Environmental Regulations and Other Requirements

   4.5   EP-015 Monitoring and Measurement

   4.6   ISO 14001:1996, Element 4.6

5.0   Definitions: None

6.0   Exclusions: None

7.0   Procedure

   7.1   The *Facility/Plant* Manager and *Facility/Plant* Management Team shall conduct a review of the EMS at least once each year.

   7.2   Management review meetings shall be scheduled in advance by the EMR and an agenda issued to ensure appropriate preparation and attendance.

7.3 The meeting shall review all applicable components of the *Facility/Plant* EMS. The EMR shall present information for review and concurrence, which may include but not be limited to:

    a) Environmental Policy
    b) Environmental Aspects
    c) Objectives and Targets and Programs
    d) Legal and Other Requirements
    e) Training, Awareness and Competence
    f) Operational Control
    g) Emergency Preparedness and Response
    h) Monitoring and Measurement
    i) Nonconformance and Corrective and Preventive Action
    j) Environmental System and Regulatory Compliance Audits

7.4 The *Facility/Plant* Manager and *Facility/Plant* Management Team shall review and confirm their approval and the continual suitability, adequacy and effectiveness of the environmental policy, environmental objectives and targets, EMPs and other elements of the system as well as regulatory compliance requirements are met.

7.5 The EMR or designee will publish and maintain meeting minutes identifying issues discussed and corrective and preventive actions to be taken. Required actions will be assigned to the responsibility of process, area and functional management.

7.6 Timely decisions will be made.

8.0 General Rules: None

9.0 Records: Records shall be retained consistent with EP-013: Environmental Records.

Record of Revisions: Revision Date, Description, Sections Affected

Facility/Plant Name
EMS Management Review Sign-In Sheet

Name (please print)	Area/Department	Title/Function

Supplement I: EMERGENCY PREPAREDNESS AND RESPONSE, EP-006

1.0 Purpose/Scope

This procedure defines the framework for preparing for and responding to emergencies involving potential environmental incidents at the *Facility/Plant*.

2.0 Activities Affected: All Areas and Departments

3.0 Forms Used: None

4.0 References

   4.1 EP-002 Environmental Aspects, Objectives and Targets, and Management Programs

   4.2 EP-004 Nonconformance and Corrective and Preventive Action

   4.3 EP-010 Environmental Communication

   4.4 ISO 14001:1996, Element 4.4.7

5.0 Definitions

   5.1 Environmental Incident or Emergency Situation: environmental releases that require an emergency response

   5.2 Emergency Response: actions taken by personnel outside of the immediate work area to address an environmental incident.

6.0 Exclusions: None

7.0 Procedure

   7.1 Potential environmental incidents and emergencies likely to occur at the facility shall be identified semiannually by the CFT and documented according to EP-002 and Emergency Response and Planning requirements.

   7.2 Methods to respond to, mitigate and prevent environmental emergencies shall be established and maintained at the facility in the Security Office by the Emergency Response Coordinator.

7.3 Roles and responsibilities for communications within the facility and for obtaining outside support services shall be established and maintained at the facility via the emergency plans.

7.4 Environmental emergency methods and communications will be tested at least annually. The Security Office shall maintain records of these tests. Methods to respond to, mitigate and prevent environmental emergencies shall be amended as required based on the results of these tests.

7.5 Following an environmental emergency, the cause of the emergency and corresponding emergency methods shall be reviewed. Corrective/preventive actions will be identified and undertaken by implementing EP-004. Methods to respond to, mitigate and prevent releases that arise as a consequence of an environmental emergency shall be amended as required and the EMR or Environmental Coordinator notified.

7.6 Where applicable, regulatory agencies shall be notified by the Environmental Coordinator of environmental incidents consistent with EP-010.

8.0 General Rules

8.1 All emergency response activities are to be conducted within boundaries of training levels, appropriate procedures, and governmental regulations.

8.2 The facility manager shall designate an emergency response coordinator.

9.0 Records: Records shall be retained consistent with EP-013: Environmental Records.

Record of Revisions: Revision Date, Description, Sections Affected

Supplement I: ENVIRONMENTAL REGULATIONS AND OTHER REQUIREMENTS, EP-007

1.0 Purpose/Scope

This procedure defines the mechanism for identifying and maintaining current legal and other requirements and regulations applicable to the *Facility/Plant*, and for maintaining access to up-to-date editions of those requirements.

2.0 Activities Affected: Environmental Coordinator

3.0 Forms Used: None

4.0 References

    4.1 EP-010 Environmental Communication

    4.2 Governmental/commercially available publications

    4.3 Other requirements to which *Facility/Plant* subscribes (e.g., Ford requirements)

    4.4 ISO 14001:1996, Element 4.3.2.

5.0 Definitions: None

6.0 Exclusions: None

7.0 Procedure

    7.1 The Environmental Coordinator shall maintain up-to-date listings of applicable environmental legal and other requirements through the maintenance, access and review of the relevant references listed in Section 4.0 above at least annually.

    7.2 The Environmental Coordinator may undertake additional activities as appropriate to ensure that all applicable legal and other requirements are available.

    7.3 Access to, or copies of, all applicable legal and other requirements shall be readily available.

    7.4 The Environmental Coordinator shall communicate legal and other requirements to all applicable areas and departments consistent with EP-010.

8.0   General Rules: None

9.0   Records: Records shall be retained consistent with EP-013: Environmental Records.

Record of Revisions: Revision Date, Description, Sections Affected

Supplement I: ENVIRONMENTAL REVIEW OF PROJECTS, EP-008

1.0 Purpose/Scope

This procedure defines the method for identifying and evaluating the environmental issues of new projects at the *Facility/Plant* to:

a) Ensure that appropriate consideration is given to environmental issues prior to project approval and funding.
b) Ensure that new environmental aspects generated by projects are identified and their significance evaluated.
c) Provide a mechanism for the amendment of EMS elements and programs, where relevant, to ensure that the EMS applies to such projects.

2.0 Activities Affected: All Areas and Departments

3.0 Forms Used: Project Environmental Checklist

4.0 References: EP-002 Environmental Aspects, Objectives and Targets, and Management Programs

5.0 Definitions: None

6.0 Exclusions: None

7.0 Procedure

    7.1 Areas/departments initiate Project Appropriation Requests when the need for project funding becomes apparent.

    7.2 The initiating activity or designee shall identify and evaluate environmental issues associated with the project. A summary of this evaluation shall be documented on a project environmental checklist form and the form added to the appropriation request. This process may be undertaken in liaison with the Environmental Coordinator (or other competent individual) at the discretion of the initiating activity, and shall include an identification of environmental aspects and requirements for obtaining approvals from environmental regulatory agencies.

    7.3 The initiating activity shall submit the appropriation request and completed Project Environmental Checklist for review to the EMR.

7.4 The EMR, or designee, shall review the proposed project to ensure that all relevant environmental issues have been identified, and if incomplete, shall return the Appropriation Request and Project Environmental Checklist to the initiating activity for alteration.

7.5 The EMR, or designee, shall review the environmental aspects of the project, considering their significance in line with EP-002.

7.6 Following appropriate review, the EMR or designee may approve the project by returning the Appropriation Request to the initiating activity for further processing. If a project is not acceptable, the initiating activity will coordinate any necessary actions to satisfy concerns identified. The initiating activity in conjunction with the EMR or designee will coordinate any necessary prevention, mitigation or control activities associated with the project.

8.0 General Rules

8.1 Environmental aspects associated with projects shall be evaluated for significance by the CFT per EP-002.

8.2 Changes to the EMS resulting from an environmental review of a project will be approved by the *Facility/Plant* Management Team.

9.0 Records: Records shall be retained consistent with EP-013: Environmental Records.

Record of Revisions: Revision Date, Description, Sections Affected

Ford & ISO 14001

Facility/Plant Name
Review of Projects

Project Description:

Project Number:

AIR EMISSIONS

Yes	No

Will this project/process change produce air emissions?
Will this project/process change require an air permit or permit modification?
Does the change require air pollution controls?
Does the project/process change require the use or purchase of ozone depleting substances?

WATER DISCHARGES

Yes	No

Does the project/process change result in wastewater, sanitary or stormwater discharges?
Will the project/process change result in changes to water discharge flow rates?
Will the discharge require a permit modification?
Will new or additional pretreatment be required?
Are facility discharges to a common sewer altered?

STORAGE TANKS

Yes	No

Will underground storage tanks be installed?
Will tanks be installed to store hazardous waste or materials, petroleum products or propane?

WASTE GENERATION

Yes	No

Will the project/process change produce waste or recyclable materials?
Will the waste be classified as special or hazardous?
Will off-site disposal be required?
Are special handling, abatement or disposal measures required?

ENERGY USAGE

Yes	No

Will the project/process change affect facility energy usage?

OTHER CONSIDERATIONS

Yes	No

Do recycling options and costs need to be considered?
Does the project/process change require use of toxic, hazardous or carcinogenic materials?
Do project/process materials require special handling or storage?
Does the project cause land disturbances?
Do pollution prevention issues need to be addressed?
Does the project/process change impact the surrounding community (e.g., odor, noise etc.)?
Are there any wildlife or land use issues?
Does the project/process change alter or add to current facility aspects?
Does the project/process change require a change to Emergency Response methods?

_____   _____
Initiating Activity Manager   Date

_____   _____
Environmental Management Representative   Date

Supplement I: AGENCY APPROVALS, EP-009

1.0   Purpose/Scope

This procedure describes the method to be implemented to secure approval from regulatory agencies for processes and activities at the *Facility/Plant* affecting air emissions, waste management or water discharges, as well as the method for other environmental approvals.

2.0   Activities Affected: All Areas and Departments

3.0   Forms Used: None

4.0   References

   4.1   EP-002 Environmental Aspects, Objectives and Targets and Programs

   4.2   EP-007 Environmental Regulations and Other Requirements

   4.3   EP-008 Environmental Review of Projects

   4.4   EP-010 Environmental Communication

   4.5   ISO 14001:1996, Elements 4.3.4, 4.4.6, 4.5.1

5.0   Definitions

   5.1   Regulatory Agency: governmental unit delegated authority for implementing regulations related to ambient air quality, waste management and/or water discharge quality.

   5.2   Process: materials, activities, equipment associated with operations.

   5.3   Permit: permit, licenses, certifications or other authorizations issued by a governmental regulatory body.

6.0   Exclusions: None

7.0   Procedure

   7.1   Where operations are identified as potentially requiring environmental permits the Environmental Coordinator shall coordinate the investigation and permitting process through the use of an informal "permit team" comprising of at least the Environmental Coordinator and as appropriate, a representative from the *Facility/Plant* function responsible for the operation concerned.

7.2   All communications in connection with permits, and specifically those with the relevant regulatory agencies shall be undertaken in conformance with EP-010.

7.3   The "permit team" shall develop a strategy to secure permits in concurrence with existing operational timing plans. The EMR is responsible for timely communicating issues to the *Facility/Plant* Management Team.

7.4   The Environmental Coordinator shall coordinate the preparation, submission and negotiation of permit applications, operating through the "permit team." Permits obtained shall be reviewed to ensure that they adequately cover the operation(s) concerned.

7.5   The "permit team" will review the terms and conditions in new permits and modify or establish operational controls necessary to ensure compliance with the permit.

8.0   General Rules: None

9.0   Records: Records shall be retained consistent with EP-013: Environmental Records.

Record of Revisions: Revision Date, Description, Sections Affected

Supplement I: ENVIRONMENTAL COMMUNICATION, EP-010

1.0 Purpose/Scope

This procedure defines the process for:

a) Internal environmental communication/awareness within the *Facility/Plant*.
b) External environmental communication between the *Facility/Plant* Name and external interested parties, such as regulatory authorities and the public/local community groups.

2.0 Activities Affected: All Areas and Departments

3.0 Forms Used: External Communication Log

4.0 References

    4.1 Environmental Policy

    4.2 EP-002 Environmental Aspects, Objectives and Targets and Programs

    4.3 EP-005 Environmental Management System Management Review

    4.4 EP-006 Emergency Preparedness and Response

    4.5 EP-007 Environmental Regulations and Other Requirements

    4.6 EP-008 Environmental Review of Projects

    4.7 EP-009 Agency Approvals

    4.8 EP-011 Contractor Control

    4.9 EP-012 Environmental Document Control

    4.10 EP-014 Environmental Training and Awareness

    4.11 ISO 14001:1996, Element 4.4.3

5.0 Definitions: External Communications: written or electronic correspondence, telephone conversations and oral discussions or meetings with anyone external to the company.

6.0   Exclusions: None

7.0   Procedure

   7.1   Internal Communications/Awareness

      7.1.1   Internal environmental communications shall be implemented to ensure those personnel at each relevant level and function are aware of the following:

      7.1.1.1 The EMS.

      7.1.1.2 The importance of conformance with the environmental policy, procedures and system.

      7.1.1.3 The potential consequences of system nonconformances.

      7.1.1.4 Individual roles and responsibilities in achieving conformance with procedures, including emergency preparedness and response.

      7.1.1.5 Significant environmental aspects associated with work activities and the environmental benefits of improved personal performance.

      7.1.2   Internal environmental communications may be accomplished by the use of:

      7.1.2.1 Notice boards.

      7.1.2.2 Awareness training of facility personnel, as appropriate in line with job function.

      7.1.2.3 Environmental training of relevant job functions, as appropriate. (See environmental procedure EP-014: Environmental Training and Awareness.)

      7.1.2.4 Newsletters.

7.1.2.5 Electronic notes.

7.1.2.6 Team meetings and meeting minutes.

7.1.2.7 Management reviews and meeting minutes.

7.1.2.8 Corrective Action Requests.

7.1.3 Communication of environmental issues from employees to the *Facility/Plant* Management Team shall be handled by the CFT member representing the affected area, in coordination with the EMR. These communications shall be documented.

7.1.4 Communication of changes to legal and other requirements to employees shall be handled by the area or department manager or designee. These communications shall be documented.

7.2 External Communications

7.2.1 External communications concerning the environmental aspects of the facility should be directed to the Security Manager, Human Resources Manager or the EMR.

7.2.2 The EMR or Environmental Coordinator is responsible for responding to inquiries from interested parties and regulatory agencies.

7.2.3 The human resources manager or designee is responsible for sending current copies of the environmental policy to interested parties. These requests will be documented on the external communications log.

7.2.4 The human resources manager, in consultation with the EMR, is responsible for responding to media communications.

7.2.5 Where community concerns relate to an environmental emergency, EP-004 shall be implemented.

7.2.6 The EMR or designee is responsible for determining the need for and preparation of any notification to regulatory agencies on an as needed basis.

8.0   General Rules

    8.1   CFT members and area or department managers shall maintain their own internal communication records.

    8.2   The EMR shall maintain records of external environmental communication with interested parties and the media.

    8.3   The Environmental Coordinator shall maintain records of external environmental communications with regulatory agencies.

9.0   Records: Records shall be retained consistent with EP-013: Environmental Records.

Record of Revisions: Revision Date, Description, Sections Affected

Facility/Plant Name
External Communications Log

Date: _____ Time: _____
Type of Contact: _____
Meeting: _____ E-mail: _____
Tel: _____
Other (describe): _____

Contact Name(s): _____

Person Completing Form: _____

Environmental Issue/Concern:

Actions to be Taken:

Type of Follow-up Required:

Supplement I: CONTRACTOR CONTROL, EP-011

1.0   Purpose/Scope

This procedure defines the process for controlling the environmental aspects of on-site contractors and their subcontractors at the *Facility/Plant*.

2.0   Activities Affected: All areas and departments authorizing contractors to work on-site.

3.0   Forms Used: Environmental Briefing Packet and Contractor Method Statement template

4.0   References: ISO 14001:1996, Element 4.4.6

5.0   Definitions
        Method Statement: a written statement prepared by a contractor which outlines the work to be undertaken and the method(s) for minimizing and managing environmental impacts. The method statement includes an assessment of the environmental issues associated with specified work activities and measures necessary to minimize environmental impacts.

6.0   Exclusions

    6.1   Contractor activities and services that are not performed at the *Facility/Plant*.

    6.2   Contractors performing emergency services.

    6.3   Contractors providing clerical, accounting or similar administrative services.

7.0   Procedure

    7.1   A CFT led by the EMR or designee develops a process to obtain and review contractor method statements.

    7.2   The need for contractor services is identified and a request for a Method Statement is prepared by the initiating activity.

    7.3   Information related to contractor on-site activities shall be documented by the contractor using a Contractor Method Statement.

7.4 Completed contractor method statement forms will be submitted to the initiating activity. The EMR or designee will evaluate method statements to identify potential environmental issues and concerns.

7.5 Prior to on-site work contractors shall:

7.5.1 Be provided with information and documents to ensure their awareness of the *Facility/Plant* EMS and their conformance to it.

7.5.2 Submit a completed Contractor Method Statement to the initiating activity.

7.6 While on-site, contractors shall conform to the *Facility/Plant* EMS and to all applicable legal and other requirements.

7.7 Contractors shall maintain records as specified by the EMS and by contract requirements.

8.0 General Rules: Contractors shall ensure their on-site staff is aware of EMS requirements.

9.0 Records: Records shall be retained consistent with EP-013: Environmental Record.

Record of Revisions: Revision Date, Description, Sections Affected

Supplement I: ENVIRONMENTAL DOCUMENT CONTROL, EP-012

1.0   Purpose/Scope

This procedure defines the mechanism for controlling EMS documents. The purpose of this procedure is to ensure that those personnel requiring access to EMS documents have the most up-to-date issues and are aware of the document control process.

2.0   Activities Affected: All Areas and Departments

3.0   Forms Used: Master Document List

4.0   References

    4.1   EP-001 Formatting Environmental Procedures, Work Practices and Forms

    4.2   ISO 14001:1996, Element 4.4.5

5.0   Definitions: None

6.0   Exclusions: None

7.0   Procedure

    7.1   The EMR or designee shall be responsible for coordinating, developing, issuing and controlling EMS documents.

    7.2   Procedures shall be in the format specified by environmental procedure EP-001.

    7.3   The EMR or designee shall maintain a master set of EMS documents.

    7.4   Each area or department manager or designee should maintain a list of, or have access to, all EMS documents relevant to their area or department, as applicable.

    7.5   Relevant documents are available at the locations where they are needed.

7.6   Personnel ensure current versions are available and used.

7.7   The CFT shall review and approve changes to EMS documents.

7.8   All controlled documents shall be marked with the words "Controlled Document."

7.9   Controlled versions of system documents may be placed on the computer system for access by area or department personnel.

7.10 All controlled documents issued by the EMR or designee shall be recorded on a Master Document List.

7.11 The EMR or designee shall:

   7.11.1 Provide notice to affected personnel to ensure they are aware of the new or revised document.

   7.11.2 Issue controlled copies of those documents to appropriate personnel.

8.0   General Rules: All documents not marked with the words "Controlled Document" shall be considered uncontrolled.

9.0   Records: Records shall be retained consistent with EP-013: Environmental Records.

Record of Revisions: Revision Date, Description, Sections Affected

Ford & ISO 14001

Facility/Plant Name
Master Documents List

ID	Title	Issue Date	Location	Authorized By
Policy				
Manuals & Plans				
Procedures				
Work Practices				
Forms				
Audit Checklist				
Records (See Master Records List)				
References				

Supplement I: ENVIRONMENTAL RECORDS, EP-013

1.0 Purpose/Scope

This procedure identifies the management of environmental records at the *Facility/Plant*.

2.0 Activities Affected: All Areas and Departments

3.0 Forms Used: Index of Environmental Records

4.0 References: ISO 14001:1996, Element 5.5.3

5.0 Definitions

> Records: documented information that:
> (a) is evidence of an environmental activity or event that has been or is being performed.
> (b) is required to be retained for future reference. It is information on environmental performance.

6.0 Exclusions: None

7.0 Procedure

   7.1 Records shall be maintained and retained as specified in the Index of Environmental Records.

   7.2 Record retention will be consistent with applicable legal and other requirements.

   7.3 Each area or department manager or designee shall have access to a master list of all EMS records relevant to their area or department, as applicable.

   7.4 Each activity responsible for maintaining a record has the responsibility for establishing the method for filing and indexing records to ensure accessibility.

8.0 General Rules: Records shall be legible, readily retrievable and stored and maintained so as to prevent damage, deterioration or loss as appropriate to the importance of the record.

9.0   Records: Records shall be retained as specified in this procedure.

Record of Revisions: Revision Date, Description, Sections Affected

Facility/Plant Name
Index of Environmental Records

Document	Record	Retention (yrs)	Controlled By	Location

Supplement I: ENVIRONMENTAL TRAINING AND AWARENESS, EP-014

1.0   Purpose/Scope

This procedure defines the process for identifying and planning environmental training and awareness at the *Facility/Plant*.

2.0   Activities Affected: All Areas and Departments

3.0   Forms Used

    3.1   Training Needs Matrix — Environmental Courses

    3.2   Training Needs Matrix — Procedures and Work Practices by Area/Department

4.0   References

    4.1   EP-002   Environmental Aspects, Objectives and Targets and Programs

    4.2   EP-007   Environmental Regulations and Other Requirements

    4.3   EP-008   Environmental Review of Projects

    4.4   EP-010   Environmental Communication

    4.5   ISO 14001:1996, Element 4.4.2

5.0   Definitions: None

6.0   Exclusions: None

7.0   Procedure

    7.1   Training

        7.1.1   A training needs analysis (TNA) and training schedule shall be completed and maintained by the Training Department to identify the level of instruction needed by personnel whose jobs may create a significant impact on the environment.

7.1.2 The TNA and training schedule shall be reviewed and updated where necessary at least annually, and when requested by the EMR or designee, in consultation with the Training Department to ensure its continuing adequacy.

7.1.3 The TNA shall be developed by knowledgeable individuals with appropriate expertise and experience in: operational environmental management; relevant environmental legal requirements for environmental training; and training provision at the *Facility/Plant*.

7.1.4 New, part-time and transferred employees, as well as permanent on-site contractors, shall be included in the environmental training program.

7.1.5 The Training Department shall maintain records of each individual's environmental training.

7.2 Awareness: Environmental awareness shall be implemented as specified in EP-010.

7.3 Competence: Employee competence relevant to the EMS is determined through applicable training and through observation of performance by the employee's supervisor.

8.0 General Rules

8.1 The Training Department shall maintain the current copy of the TNA and training schedule.

8.2 The Training Department shall maintain records of the environmental training which individuals have received.

8.3 The EMR and Training Department shall maintain data/record elements that together comprise an environmental training program.

8.4 The Training Department will maintain curriculum and class objectives for all training courses.

9.0 Records: Records shall be retained consistent with EP-013: Environmental Records.

Record of Revisions: Revision Date, Description, Sections Affected

Ford & ISO 14001

Facility/Plant Name
Training Needs Matrix
Environmental Courses

Course	Employees Requiring Training	Source of Training	Duration (hrs)	Frequency

Facility/Plant Name
Training Need Matrix
Procedures and Work Instructions by Area/Dept.

Procedure/ Work Practice No.	Title	Area/Department

Supplement I: MONITORING AND MEASUREMENT, EP-015

1.0 Purpose/Scope

This procedure defines the mechanism for the monitoring and measurement of significant environmental aspects associated with the *Facility/Plant* operations and activities; the calibration and maintenance of monitoring equipment; and the evaluation of compliance with relevant environmental legal and policy requirements.

2.0 Activities Affected: All Areas and Departments

3.0 Forms Used: None

4.0 References

    4.1 EP-002 Environmental Aspects, Objectives and Targets and Management Programs

    4.2 EP-003 Environmental Management System and Regulatory Compliance Audits

    4.3 EP-004 Nonconformance and Corrective and Preventive Action

    4.4 EP-005 Environmental Management System Management Review

    4.5 EP-006 Emergency Preparedness and Response

    4.6 EP-007 Environmental Regulations and Other Requirements

    4.7 EP-008 Environmental Review of Projects

    4.8 EP-010 Environmental Communication

    4.9 EP-011 Contractor Control

    4.10 EP-014 Environmental Training and Awareness

    4.11 ISO 14001:1996, Element 4.5.1

5.0 Definitions: None

6.0 Exclusions: None

7.0　Procedure

　　7.1　Monitoring and Measurement of Significant Aspects, Objectives and Targets and Operational Controls

　　　　7.1.1　The monitoring and measurement of key characteristics and environmental performance associated with significant aspects will be specified in EMPs.

　　　　7.1.2　The monitoring and measurement of conformance to specified environmental objectives and targets will be accomplished through the internal system audit process, as specified in EP-003 and through the creation of CARs, as specified in EP-004.

　　　　7.1.3　Operational controls will be monitored and measured as indicated in applicable EMPs, procedures, work practices or visual aids. The methods, frequencies and responsible parties for completing the monitoring and measuring activities will be specified in these documents.

　　7.2　Calibration and Maintenance of Environmental Monitoring Equipment

　　　　7.2.1　Relevant areas and departments shall ensure that environmental monitoring equipment is calibrated and maintained at a frequency consistent with manufacturers' recommendations, or at least every 12 months if those recommendations are unknown. Relevant areas and departments shall maintain calibration and maintenance records as necessary to prove conformance with this procedure.

　　　　7.2.2　Calibration and maintenance of environmental monitoring equipment shall be addressed in area and department preventive maintenance programs, where applicable, or in local work practices, if desired.

　　　　7.2.3　Each applicable area and department will maintain a list of EMS equipment requiring calibration and the corresponding calibration frequency.

7.3 Evaluation of Compliance

    7.3.1 The evaluation of compliance with relevant environmental legal requirements shall be accomplished through the implementation of EP-003.

8.0   General Rules: None

9.0   Records: Records shall be retained consistent with EP-013: Environmental Records.

Record of Revisions: Revision Date, Description, Sections Affected

Supplement J: WORK PRACTICES

The following work practices are only examples. Actual work practices to be developed by the *Facility/Plant* will depend on the particular significant aspects established, the types of operational controls and monitoring required, and legal and other requirements applicable.

Environmental Work Practice Index

Work Practice No.	Work Practice Title	ISO 14001 Element
EWP-020.01	Servicing of Stationary Refrigeration Equipment	4.4.6
EWP-023.01	Waste Drum Shipments	4.4.6
EWP-024.01	Bulk Material Loading and Unloading	4.4.6

Supplement J: *Facility/Plant* ENVIRONMENTAL WORK PRACTICE, EWP-020.01

Operation: Servicing of Stationary Refrigeration Equipment

1.0 Only trained and certified refrigeration technicians (CRT) may service refrigeration systems.

2.0 CRTs are responsible for ensuring that their tools are in good working condition. They must check that:

2.1 All hoses and gauges are free of damage or possible leaks.

2.2 Recovery cylinders are in good condition, of the proper type, and the retest date has not expired.

2.3 Recovery equipment is approved, certified, properly oiled and filters are in good condition.

3.0 When a CRT is adding or removing refrigerant from a refrigeration system or cylinder, methods prescribed by legal requirements and best engineering practice shall be followed.

4.0 CRTs shall use appropriate scales and measuring devices to determine the amounts of refrigerant transferred during servicing. The amount of refrigerant use shall be recorded.

5.0 Appliance Servicing:

5.1 When adding or removing refrigerant from an appliance, the CRT shall complete all required information on the service order form.

5.2 If equipment is to be scrapped or shipped off-site, the CRT shall evacuate the refrigerant and affix a signed and dated evacuation label to the equipment. Scrapped equipment shall have their refrigeration lines cut after refrigerant is removed.

5.3 All required information on the appliance input form shall be completed by the CFT for new refrigeration equipment.

5.4 CRTs will immediately notify area or department managers of any significant appliance leaks or unintentional venting of refrigerant.

6.0 Cylinder Management:

6.1 All required information on a refrigerant cylinder input form must be completed by a CRT when new refrigerant cylinders are received.

6.2 If a cylinder is not clearly marked with the type of refrigerant it contains, a CRT shall properly label or tag the cylinder to identify refrigerant type.

6.3 All required information on a refrigerant transfer form will be completed when refrigerant is transferred from one cylinder to another.

6.4 Shipment of refrigerants off-site for recycling or disposal must be coordinated with designated waste handlers.

7.0 Contractor Control:

7.1 A copy of the contractor's CRT card is required to be on file with the area or department prior to any work being performed.

7.2 The contractor is responsible for performing work in compliance with all legal and other requirements.

7.3 A *Facility/Plant* CRT shall observe the work performed by the Contractor and shall complete a contractor input form.

7.4 All refrigerant reclaiming shall be accomplished using certified tanks.

7.5 All required information on a service order shall be completed or supplied by the contractor.

8.0 Unless otherwise specified in this procedure, CRTs shall maintain refrigeration records.

Supplement J: *Facility/Plant* ENVIRONMENTAL WORK PRACTICE, EWP-023.01

Operation: Waste Drum Shipments

1.0   The designated waste handler contacts the proper disposal facility and transporter to schedule the waste drum shipments.

2.0   The designated waste handler will direct the transporter to the pickup location.

3.0   The transporter will verify proper labeling and cleanliness of drums before they are loaded and prepare the proper waste manifests.

4.0   The designated waste handler or designee stages and loads the drums onto the transportation vehicle.

5.0   In the event of a nonincidental spill, the emergency response coordinator will be notified.

6.0   After the transportation vehicle has been loaded, the transporter will provide the completed waste manifests to the waste handler.

7.0   If required, the driver will placard the transportation vehicle. The waste handler will determine when and what placarding is required.

8.0   The EMR or designee shall review the waste manifests and sign them when appropriate.

The EMR shall retain copies of the waste manifests.

Supplement J: *Facility/Plant* ENVIRONMENTAL WORK PRACTICE, EWP- 024.01

Operation: Bulk Material Loading and Unloading

1.0 When the Bulk Material Transporter arrives at the facility, an area or department representative will direct the transporter to the appropriate tank.

2.0 The transporter and area or department representative will follow this transfer procedure:

    2.1 The transporter is responsible for ensuring that the truck has appropriate Department of Transportation (DOT) placarding prior to entering the facility.

    2.2 The transporter is instructed by the area or department representative regarding the facility's bulk material transfer protocol.

    2.3 The area or department representative indicates proper tanker spotting.

    2.4 The area or department representative verifies that the volume available in the bulk storage tank is greater than the volume of product to be transferred from the delivery tank. The transporter is responsible for ensuring the capacity of the tank truck is not exceeded.

    2.5 The area or department representative will remove pipeline caps and assure connection to the correct delivery transfer lines.

    2.6 The area or department representative inspects facility transfer connections for damage or material leaks.

    2.7 The transporter will make all connections necessary for material transfer.

    2.8 The area or department representative will stay alert and have a clear unobstructed view of the operation at all times during the transfer.

    2.9 The area or department representative will verify the transporter is in attendance monitoring the transfer operations.

    2.10 The area or department representative is authorized to order the transporter to terminate the transfer and have the driver move the tanker during an emergency.

    2.11   The transporter will remove transfer lines such that excess material will flow back toward the receiving tank or catchment basin.

    2.12   The area or department representative will monitor the termination process.

3.0   Copies of shipping manifests are retained by the appropriate area or department. Waste manifests are retained by the EMR or designee.

4.0   The bulk material storage area is inspected weekly by the appropriate area or department and an inspection log is completed.

Ford's Registered Sites

Editor's note: The following may include single or multiple facilities under a single certificate.

Australia

Broadmeadows Assembly
Certificate Number: 402578
Date Issued: 12/14/97
Accreditation: Joint Accreditation System of Australia and New Zealand
Scope: Site activities associated with the assembly, subassembly and painting of passenger and light commercial vehicles including the management of the office activities at the head office, Research Centre and Customer Service Division, in accordance with the publicly available environmental policy
Registrar: Lloyd's Register Quality Assurance

Broadmeadows and Geelong Product Development
Certificate Number: 402581
Date Issued: 12/14/97
Accreditation: Joint Accreditation System of Australia and New Zealand
Scope: Services and facilities in support of the development and testing of automotive vehicles, subsystems, parts and accessories for general passenger and light commercial use, including office activities of the Design Department, in accordance with the publicly available environmental policy
Registrar: Lloyd's Register Quality Assurance

Geelong Powertrains Operations
Certificate Number: 402580
Date Issued: 12/14/97
Accreditation: Joint Accreditation System of Australia and New Zealand
Scope: Stamping, machining, tooling, aluminum casting, assembly operations and supporting services in accordance with the publicly available environmental policy
Registrar: Lloyd's Register Quality Assurance

Geelong Stamping
Certificate Number: 402580
Date Issued: 12/14/97
Accreditation: Joint Accreditation System of Australia and New Zealand
Scope: Stamping, machining, tooling, aluminum casting, assembly operations and supporting services in accordance with the publicly available environmental policy
Registrar: Lloyd's Register Quality Assurance

Belgium

Genk Body and Assembly
Certificate Number: 51305
Date Issued: 10/22/98
Accreditation: Dutch Council for Accreditation
Scope: The manufacture of passenger and estate motorcars and light and medium commercial vehicles including body and wheel pressings, body and wheel fabrications, plastic mouldings, paint and assembly
Registrar: Bureau Veritas Quality International

Canada

Casting Process Development Centre
Certificate Number: E54
Date Issued: 04/12/00
Accreditation: United Kingdom Accreditation Service
Scope: The development, design and launch of manufacturing processes to support new and existing programs for powertrain components
Registrar: Vehicle Certification Agency

Essex Aluminum Plant
Certificate Number: E50
Date Issued: 01/08/99
Accreditation: United Kingdom Accreditation Service
Scope: The manufacturing of automotive aluminum castings including heat treatment
Registrar: Vehicle Certification Agency

Essex Engine Plant
Certificate Number: E12
Date Issued: 06/23/98
Accreditation: United Kingdom Accreditation Service
Scope: The manufacture of automotive engines including machining, assembly and testing
Registrar: Vehicle Certification Agency

Oakville Assembly
Certificate Number: 110404
Date Issued: 12/20/96
Accreditation: US National Accreditation Program
Scope: The assembly of automobiles
Registrar: Lloyd's Register Quality Assurance

Ontario Truck
Certificate Number: 111074
Date Issued: 08/07/98
Accreditation: US National Accreditation Program
Scope: Manufacture of trucks, including

body construction, paint and assembly
Registrar: Lloyd's Register Quality Assurance

Windsor Aluminum Plant
Certificate Number: E43
Date Issued: 12/21/98
Accreditation: United Kingdom Accreditation Service
Scope: The manufacture of automotive aluminum castings
Registrar: Vehicle Certification Agency

Windsor Casting Plant
Certificate Number: E11
Date Issued: 04/15/98
Accreditation: United Kingdom Accreditation Service
Scope: The manufacture of iron casting, including crank shafts and engine blocks. Also including wastewater treatment plant and powerhouse operations
Registrar: Vehicle Certification Agency

Windsor Engine Plant
Certificate Number: E19
Date Issued: 08/07/98
Accreditation: United Kingdom Accreditation Service
Scope: Component machining, assembly and testing of passenger vehicle engines
Registrar: Vehicle Certification Agency

France

Bordeaux Plant
Certificate Number: E37
Date Issued: 12/15/98
Accreditation: United Kingdom Accreditation Service
Scope: The manufacture of transmissions
Accreditation: United Kingdom Accreditation Service
Registrar: Vehicle Certification Agency

Ford France Automobiles S.A.S
Certificate Number: E13
Date Issued: 06/18/98
Accreditation: United Kingdom Accreditation Service
Scope: The supply and distribution of parts and accessories to the network of Ford dealers in France and the French overseas territories
Registrar: Vehicle Certification Agency

Germany

Cologne Tool & Die
Certificate Number: 260301
Date Issued: 10/12/98
Accreditation: Deutscher AkkreditierungsRat
Scope: Tool and die operation Cologne-Niehl, manufacturer for stamping dies, jigs, checking fixtures, aluminum die-cast tools, models and special tools for body/assembly plants and powertrain operations and corresponding services
Registrar: Lloyd's Register Quality Assurance

Cologne Engine Plant
Certificate Number: 260352
Date Issued: 09/23/98
Accreditation: Deutscher AkkreditierungsRat
Scope: Manufacturing of V6 and in-line engines
Registrar: Lloyd's Register Quality Assurance

Cologne Transmission Plant
Certificate Number: 260259
Date Issued: 09/23/98
Accreditation: Deutscher AkkreditierungsRat
Scope: The transmission and chassis plant with all its manufacturing areas including the corresponding services
Registrar: Lloyd's Register Quality Assurance

Cologne Pilot Plant
Certificate Number: 260264
Date Issued: 10/27/98
Accreditation: Deutscher AkkreditierungsRat
Scope: Pilot plant with its core business "body in white manufacturing" and related supporting activities garage shop and "vehicle recycling"
Registrar: Lloyd's Register Quality Assurance

Cologne Product Development
Certificate Number: 260261
Date Issued: 11/02/98
Accreditation: Deutscher AkkreditierungsRat
Scope: Development and production of vehicles and components including all supporting activities
Registrar: Lloyd's Register Quality Assurance

Cologne Body and Assembly
Certificate Number: 260257
Date Issued: 07/06/98
Accreditation: Deutscher AkkreditierungsRat
Scope: Body and assembly plant niehl with press shop, body shop, plastic-parts, paint shop, trim and final-assembly, logistic and corresponding services excluding central work-shop
Registrar: Lloyd's Register Quality Assurance

Cologne Central Workshop
Certificate Number: 260300
Date Issued: 10/27/98
Accreditation: Deutscher AkkreditierungsRat
Scope: Central maintenance for vehicle operations and powertrain operations; utility supply; wastewater treatment and waste services; building maintenance and estate maintenance; office services; construction services; car-conditioning center
Registrar: Lloyd's Register Quality Assurance

Saarlouis Body & Assembly
Certificate Number: 09 104 6002
Date Issued: 08/30/96
Accreditation: Deutscher AkkreditierungsRat
Scope: Vehicle operation
Registrar: TUV Rheinland

India

Ford India Limited
Certificate Number: I-60343
Date Issued: 6/8/00
Accreditation: United Kingdom Accreditation Scheme
Scope: Manufacture of motorcars and associated site activities
Registrar: Lloyd's Register Quality Assurance

Mexico

Chihuahua Engine Plant
Certificate Number: E29
Date Issued: 10/30/98
Accreditation: United Kingdom Accreditation Service
Scope: The manufacture of automotive engines
Registrar: Vehicle Certification Agency

Cuautitlan Assembly
Certificate Number: 111066
Date Issued: 10/01/98
Accreditation: US National Accreditation Program
Scope: Assembly of automobiles and trucks and manufacture of assembly tooling
Registrar: Lloyd's Register Quality Assurance

Hermosillo Assembly & Stamping
Certificate Number: 111068
Date Issued: 07/07/98
Accreditation: US National Accreditation Program
Scope: Stamping and assembly of automobiles in accordance with the publicly available environmental policy
Registrar: Lloyd's Register Quality Assurance

New Zealand

Manukau Alloy Wheel
Certificate Number: 52126
Date Issued: 11/18/98
Accreditation: Joing Accrediation System of Austrailia and New Zealand
Scope: The design and manufacture of alloy wheels and cast aluminum components for the automotive industry
Registrar: Bureau Veritas Quality International

Philippines

Ford Motor Co. Philippines, Inc.
Certificate Number: 09 104 9344
Date Issued: 09/07/99
Accreditation: Deutscher Akkreditierungs Rat
Scope: Vehicle assembly and parts plant and associated facilities
Registrar: TUV Rheinland

South America

Ford Brasil Ipiranga
Certificate Number: 701103
Date Issued: 11/27/98
Accreditation: US National Accreditation Program
Scope: Manufacture of commercial vehicles
Registrar: Lloyd's Register Quality Assurance

Ford Brasil LTDA
Certificate Number: 701104
Date Issued: 12/03/98
Accreditation: US National Accreditation Program
Scope: Stamping and body and assembly of vehicles and pick-ups
Registrar: Lloyd's Register Quality Assurance

Metcon Foundry
Certificate Number: 702039
Date Issued: 12/11/98
Accreditation: US National Accreditation Program
Scope: Manufacture of casting parts for automotors
Registrar: Lloyd's Register Quality Assurance

Pacheo
Certificate Number: 702040
Date Issued: 12/04/98
Accreditation: US National Accreditation Program
Scope: Stamping, painting and assembly of automobiles and trucks, and distribution of service parts to dealers
Registrar: Lloyd's Register Quality Assurance

Taubaté
Certificate Number: 701105
Date Issued: 12/18/98
Accreditation: US National Accreditation Program
Scope: Manufacturing of engines, transmissions and mechanical components for car and truck applications
Registrar: Lloyd's Register Quality Assurance

Ford Motor de Venezuela
Certificate Number: 701381
Date Issued: 11/13/98
Accreditation: US National Accreditation Program
Scope: Assembly of automotive vehicles and distribution of automotive parts and accessories
Registrar: Lloyd's Register Quality Assurance

Spain

Valencia
Certificate Number: 260236
Date Issued: 07/20/98
Scope: Manufacturing of vehicles and engines; parts distribution
Registrar: Lloyd's Register Quality Assurance

Taiwan

Lio Ho Engine
Certificate Number: 72025
Date Issued: 6/25/97
Accreditation: Swiss Certification Accreditation
Scope: The significant activities at the following sites of operation — 705 Chung-hwa Road Section 1, Chung-li, Taiwan, ROC. (H/O, assembly, body, paint, engine, FCSD, administration)
Registrar: SGS International Certification Services

Turkey

Ford-Otosan
Certificate Number: 53116
Date Issued: 12/22/98
Accreditation: United Kingdom Accreditation Service
Scope: The design, manufacture and assembly of passenger cars, minibuses and commercial vehicles, including pressings, paint, tool, die and trim manufacture. The design, manufacture and assembly of engines, transmissions, chassis frames and axles for motor vehicles and engines for motor vehicles and marine applications
Registrar: Bureau Veritas Quality International

United Kingdom

Aston Martin Lagonda
Certificate Number: 772332
Date Issued: 12/02/99
Accreditation: United Kingdom Accreditation Service
Scope: Development, manufacture, assembly and servicing of vehicles at the Newport, Pagnell and Bloxham sites
Registrar: Lloyd's Register Quality Assurance

Aveley
Certificate Number: 772409
Date Issued: 05/06/99
Accreditation: United Kingdom Accreditation Service
Scope: Automotive manufacture at Aveley plant
Registrar: Lloyd's Register Quality Assurance

Bridgend
Certificate Number: 772242
Date Issued: 10/23/98
Accreditation: United Kingdom Accreditation Service
Scope: The manufacture of engines for passenger and estate motor cars, light and medium commercial vehicles and industrial applications in accordance with the publicly available environmental policy
Registrar: Lloyd's Register Quality Assurance

Dagenham Estate & Croydon Plant
Certificate Number: E34
Date Issued: 11/25/98
Accreditation: United Kingdom Accreditation Service
Scope: The manufacture of motor

vehicles and the manufacture of engines and associated components
Accreditation: United Kingdom Accreditation Service
Registrar: Vehicle Certification Agency

Jaguar Cars Limited
(Including sites at: Castle Bromwich; Engineering Centre, Whitley; warranty operations facility at Baginton, Coventry; workshop facilities at MIRA, Nuneaton)
Certificate Number: E25
Date Issued: 09/25/98
Accreditation: United Kingdom Accreditation Service
Scope: The design, development, manufacture and marketing of Jaguar vehicles and parts
Registrar: Vehicle Certification Agency

Halewood
Certificate Number: 770276
Date Issued: 02/15/96
Accreditation: United Kingdom Accreditation Service
Scope: Manufacture and assembly of Escort saloon cars and vans, together with transmission systems and associated components for use elsewhere within the organization in accordance with the publicly available environmental policy
Registrar: Lloyd's Register Quality Assurance

Leamington Plant
Certificate Number: E20
Date Issued: 11/10/98
Accreditation: United Kingdom Accreditation Service
Scope: The manufacture of grey and S.G. iron castings
Registrar: Vehicle Certification Agency

Southampton Assembly Plant
Certificate Number: E17
Date Issued: 07/27/98
Accreditation: United Kingdom Accreditation Service
Scope: The manufacture of passenger and light and medium commercial vehicles, including body fabrications, paint and assembly
Registrar: Vehicle Certification Agency

United States

Atlanta Assembly
Certificate Number: 111063
Date Issued: 06/25/98
Accreditation: US National Accreditation Program
Scope: Manufacture of passenger vehicles in accordance with the publicly available environmental policy
Registrar: Lloyd's Register Quality Assurance

Automatic Transmission New Product Center
Certificate Number: E52
Date Issued: 03/31/99
Accreditation: United Kingdom Accreditation Service
Scope: Activities associated with building, assembly and testing of prototype automatic transmissions
Registrar: Vehicle Certification Agency

Brownstown Parts Redistribution Center (PRC)
Certificate Number: E63
Date Issued: 07/13/00
Accreditation: United Kingdom Accreditation Service
Scope: The receiving, storing, sheet metal primer coating, packaging and shipping of service parts and accessories
Registrar: Vehicle Certification Agency

Buffalo Stamping
Certificate Number: 111064
Date Issued: 04/23/98
Accreditation: US National Accreditation Program
Scope: The production of sheet metal stampings and subassembly of automotive and light truck components in accordance with the publicly available environmental policy
Registrar: Lloyd's Register Quality Assurance

Chicago Assembly Plant
Certificate Number: E22
Date Issued: 09/10/98
Accreditation: United Kingdom Accreditation Service
Scope: The manufacture of passenger vehicles including body construction, paint and assembly
Registrar: Vehicle Certification Agency

Chicago Stamping
Certificate Number: 111065
Date Issued: 08/06/98
Accreditation: US National Accreditation Program
Scope: The production of sheet metal stamping and subassembly of automobile and truck components
Registrar: Lloyd's Register Quality Assurance

Cleveland Casting Plant
Certificate Number: E9
Date Issued: 04/15/98
Accreditation: United Kingdom Accreditation Service
Scope: The manufacture of automotive engine castings
Registrar: Vehicle Certification Agency

Cleveland Engine Plant 2
Certificate Number: E16
Date Issued: 07/15/98
Accreditation: United Kingdom Accreditation Service
Scope: The machining of engine components and final assembly of internal combustion engines
Registrar: Vehicle Certification Agency

Dearborn Assembly Plant
Certificate Number: E44
Date Issued: 12/21/98
Accreditation: United Kingdom Accreditation Service
Scope: The assembly of motor vehicles
Registrar: Vehicle Certification Agency

Dearborn Engine Plant
Certificate Number: E49
Date Issued: 12/21/98
Accreditation: United Kingdom Accreditation Service
Scope: The manufacture of engines and steel fuel tanks for automobiles and trucks
Registrar: Vehicle Certification Agency

Dearborn Frame Plant
Certificate Number: E32

Date Issued: 12/02/98
Accreditation: United Kingdom Accreditation Service
Scope: The manufacture and fabrication of chassis frames, their components and hinges
Registrar: Vehicle Certification Agency

Dearborn Stamping Plant
Certificate Number: E31
Date Issued: 12/08/98
Accreditation: United Kingdom Accreditation Service
Scope: The manufacture of automotive stamping and subassemblies including North Yard Baling Operation
Registrar: Vehicle Certification Agency

Dearborn Technical & Transportation Services
Certificate Number: E33
Date Issued: 12/02/98
Accreditation: United Kingdom Accreditation Service
Scope: The transportation, construction, environmental services, industrial services and power and utility operations at the River Rouge Complex
Registrar: Vehicle Certification Agency

Dearborn Tool & Die Plant
Certificate Number: E27
Date Issued: 10/09/98
Accreditation: United Kingdom Accreditation Service
Scope: The manufacture of stamping dies including machining, tooling and assembly
Registrar: Vehicle Certification Agency

Edison Assembly
Certificate Number: 111067
Date Issued: 09/04/98
Accreditation: US National Accreditation Program
Scope: Manufacture of trucks, including body construction, paint, and assembly
Registrar: Lloyd's Register Quality Assurance

Engine Manufacturing Development Operations Plant
Certificate Number: E10
Date Issued: 04/15/98
Accreditation: United Kingdom Accreditation Service
Scope: Engine prototype design and testing including machining, plastic molding, engine assembly and off-site toolroom
Registrar: Vehicle Certification Agency

Kansas City Assembly
Certificate Number: 111069
Date Issued: 06/18/98
Accreditation: US National Accreditation Program
Scope: Manufacture of passenger and commercial automobiles, including body construction, paint, and assembly in accordance with the publicly available environmental policy
Registrar: Lloyd's Register Quality Assurance

Kentucky Truck
Certificate Number: 111070
Date Issued: 07/30/98
Accreditation: US National Accreditation Program
Scope: Manufacture of trucks, including production of sheet metal stamping, body construction, paint and asssembly
Registrar: Lloyd's Register Quality Assurance

Lima Engine Plant
Certificate Number: E4
Date Issued: 12/20/96
Accreditation: United Kingdom Accreditation Service
Scope: Vehicle engine manufacture
Registrar: Vehicle Certification Agency

Livonia Transmission Plant
Certificate Number: E42
Date Issued: 01/08/99
Accreditation: United Kingdom Accreditation Service
Scope: The manufacture of automatic transmissions, including machining, heat treatment and assembly
Registrar: Vehicle Certification Agency

Lorain Assembly Plant
Certificate Number: E51
Date Issued: 01/08/99
Accreditation: United Kingdom Accreditation Service
Scope: The assembly of light commercial vehicles
Registrar: Vehicle Certification Agency

Louisville Assembly Plant
Certificate Number: E14
Date Issued: 07/15/98
Accreditation: United Kingdom Accreditation Service
Scope: The manufacturing of automotive vehicles
Registrar: Vehicle Certification Agency

Michigan Truck Assembly Plant
Certificate Number: E21
Date Issued: 09/17/98
Accreditation: United Kingdom Accreditation Service
Scope: The manufacturer of trucks including body construction, painting and assembly
Registrar: Vehicle Certification Agency

Norfolk Assembly
Certificate Number: 111072
Date Issued: 07/23/98
Accreditation: US National Accreditation Program
Scope: Manufacture of trucks, including body construction, paint and assembly
Registrar: Lloyd's Register Quality Assurance

Ohio Assembly Plant
Certificate Number: E45
Date Issued: 12/21/98
Accreditation: United Kingdom Accreditation Service
Scope: The assembly of motor vehicles
Registrar: Vehicle Certification Agency

Romeo Engine Plant
Certificate Number: 110671
Date Issued: 06/20/97
Accreditation: US National Accreditation Program
Scope: The manufacture of automotive engines
Registrar: Lloyd's Register Quality Assurance

St. Louis Assembly Plant
Certificate Number: E18
Date Issued: 07/15/98
Accreditation: United Kingdom Accreditation Service
Scope: The manufacture of commercial vehicles and trucks, including body construction, paint and assembly
Registrar: Vehicle Certification Agency

St. Thomas Assembly
Certificate Number: 111075

Date Issued: 09/25/98
Accreditation: US National Accreditation Program
Scope: Manufacture of passenger vehicles, including body construction, paint and assembly
Registrar: Lloyd's Register Quality Assurance

Sharonville Transmission Plant
Certificate Number: E46
Date Issued: 12/21/98
Accreditation: United Kingdom Accreditation Service
Scope: The manufacture of automatic transmissions including machining, heat treatment and assembly
Registrar: Vehicle Certification Agency

Twin Cities Assembly Plant
Certificate Number: E8
Date Issued: 04/15/98
Accreditation: United Kingdom Accreditation Service
Scope: The manufacturer of vehicles including body construction, paint and assembly
Registrar: Vehicle Certification Agency

Van Dyke Plant
Certificate Number: E3
Date Issued: 12/20/96
Accreditation: United Kingdom Accreditation Service
Scope: The manufacture of automatic transaxles and suspension components for passenger cars
Registrar: Vehicle Certification Agency

Vulcan Forge Plant
Certificate Number: E48
Date Issued: 12/21/98
Accreditation: United Kingdom Accreditation Service
Scope: The manufacture of automotive engine connecting rods
Registrar: Vehicle Certification Agency

Walton Hills Stamping Plant
Certificate Number: E41
Date Issued: 12/21/98
Accreditation: United Kingdom Accreditation Service
Scope: The manufacture of automotive stampings and welded and clinched sub-assemblies
Registrar: Vehicle Certification Agency

Wayne Assembly & Stamping
Certificate Number: 111076
Date Issued: 05/07/98
Accreditation: US National Accreditation Program
Scope: Manufacture of passenger vehicles, including stamping, body construction, paint and assembly in accordance with the publicly available environmental policy
Registrar: Lloyd's Register Quality Assurance

Wixom Assembly Plant
Certificate Number: E26
Date Issued: 10/09/98
Accreditation: United Kingdom Accreditation Service
Scope: The manufacture of passenger vehicles, including body construction, paint and assembly
Registrar: Vehicle Certification Agency

Woodhaven Forging Plant
Certificate Number: E47
Date Issued: 12/21/98
Accreditation: United Kingdom Accreditation Service

Scope: The manufacture of automotive engine crankshafts
Registrar: Vehicle Certification Agency

Woodhaven Stamping
Certificate Number: 111077
Date Issued: 11/19/98
Accreditation: US National Accreditation Program
Scope: Sheet metal stamping and sub-assembly of automobile and light duty truck components
Registrar: Lloyd's Register Quality Assurance

Glossary

Awareness Training Training intended to communicate an understanding of ISO 14001 throughout the implementing organization.

BS 7750 Framework of an EMS developed by British Standards Institution; the forerunner to ISO 14001.

Compliance The act of meeting a specified requirement. In auditing, the term is used to indicate that a specific requirement or procedure has been met.

Conformance A positive condition where a product or process meets a specified requirement.

Continual Improvement The process by which the EMS is improved.

Contractor Management Corporate requirements for managing the environmental aspects of contractors and their subcontractors.

Corporate-Level Core Procedures Seventeen corporate-level EMS procedures of the Ford Motor Company intended to harmonize environmental management practices among all manufacturing facilities.

Corrective and Preventive Action	The process of investigating and dealing with any nonconformities associated with your EMS as well as the prevention of future nonconformities.
Cross-Functional Team (CFT)	A specially tasked team comprised of representatives of key functions at each Ford Motor Company site to assist the EMR with ISO 14001 implementation activities.
Document and Data Control	Responsibilities and actions that provide assurances that documents and data are controlled, including the need to make relevant documents available as needed.
Draft International Standard (DIS)	One of a series of designations given to draft ISO standards to indicate status in the consensus-building process.
Eco-Management and Audit Scheme (EMAS)	EU regulation establishing a voluntary environmental program to improve environmental performance through better management and public disclosure.
Emergency Preparedness and Response	The process of identifying potential accident and emergency situations and developing appropriate procedures to prevent and/or mitigate any adverse environmental impacts that may result.
EMS Documentation	Includes the corporate environmental policy, facility environmental policies, core environmental procedures, facility specific procedures and facility-specific work practices associated with the EMS.
EMS Implementation Plan	Strategic plan of action at each Ford Motor Company site to define how each implementation activity would be accomplished.

EMS Internal Audit	Internal evaluation system to ensure that the EMS is properly implemented and performing as intended.
EMS Manual	Written information relative to an EMS; typically includes associated procedures and may be in paper or electronic format.
Energy Management Efficiency	Corporate requirements for implementing an energy management efficiency program at a Ford Motor Company facility, including information and reporting requirements.
Environmental Aspect	An element of an organization's activities, products or services that can interact with the environment.
Environmental Impact	Any change to the environment, whether adverse or beneficial, wholly or partially resulting from an organization's activities, products or services.
Environmental Management Programs (EMP)	Programs intended to help achieve the environmental objectives and targets developed by the implementing organization.
Environmental Management Representative (EMR)	At least one person at each Ford Motor Company site responsible for overseeing and guiding all aspects of ISO 14001 implementation.
Environmental Management System (EMS)	The part of the overall management system that includes organizational structure, planning activities, responsibilities, practices, procedures, processes and resources for developing, implementing, achieving, reviewing and maintaining the environmental policy

Environmental Performance	Measurable results of the EMS, related to an organization's control of its environmental aspects, based on its environmental policy, objectives and targets.
Environmental Quality Office (EQO)	Corporate environmental staff of the Ford Motor Company offices in the United States, Europe, Canada, Mexico, Latin America and Asia Pacific.
Environmental Objective	Overall goal arising from the environmental policy, which is quantifiable where practicable.
Environmental Target	Detailed performance requirement, quantifiable where practicable, that needs to be set and met in order to achieve the stated objective.
Ford 2000	Ford Motor Company's strategic decision to globalize its business.
Ford Environmental System (FES)	Common global environmental management system of Ford Motor Company; implemented at all company manufacturing facilities by the end of 1998; includes the requirements of ISO 14001.
Global Core Team	Assisted in the implementation of ISO 14001 throughout Ford Motor Company sites; designed the FES.
GreenZone	Ford dealership in Europe believed to be the first purposely built "green" dealer facility that employs a combination of different environmental technologies, to demonstrate that energy requirements can be reduced by 60 to 70 percent.
Implementation Training	Training on the ISO 14000 standards, environmental management systems and implementation techniques.

International Organization for Standardization (ISO)	A worldwide federation of national standards bodies that develops and maintains international standards, including ISO 14001.
ISO 14000 Family of Standards	A series of standards published by the International Organization for Standardization dealing with environmental management systems. Documents address everything from environmental labeling to lifecycle assessment, environmental auditing and environmental performance evaluation.
ISO 14001 Supplier Requirement	All production and nonproduction suppliers with manufacturing facilities are required to certify a minimum of one manufacturing site to ISO 14001 by December 31, 2001. All supplier manufacturing sites are required to attain ISO 14001 certification by July 1, 2003.
ISO 14004	Provides guidance on the development and implementation of EMSs and principles, and their coordination with other management systems.
ISO 9000 Family of Standards	Series of standards first published by ISO in 1987 with respect to quality assurance and quality management.
Legal Requirements	Country, regional, federal, state, provincial and local environmental laws and regulations, operating permits, licenses, ordinances, authorizations, consent orders, insurance policies, contractual requirements, memorandums of agreement, etc.
Management Commitment	The process of obtaining senior management consensus to proceed to subscribe to the principles of the FES and ISO 14001.

Management Review	Periodic evaluation by the plant manager and each facility's operating committee to review all elements of the EMS, including the requirements of ISO 14001.
Mandatory Requirements	Identified in ISO 14001 by such words as "shall," "must" or "is required."
Materials Management	Corporate requirements for identifying and monitoring materials and chemical substances that may be of regulatory significance.
Monitoring and Measurement	The process of monitoring the key characteristics of your operations that could have a significant impact on the environment.
Nonconformity	Nonfulfillment of a specified requirement, generally classified as major or minor.
Objectives and Targets	Overall goals and detailed performance requirements established by the implementing organization to improve environmental performance.
Operational Control	The manner in which a facility controls its operations to ensure that the environmental policy, objectives and targets are consistently met.
Organizational Responsibilities	Roles, responsibilities and structure of the environmental management system.
Other Requirements	In the context of ISO 14001 environmental commitments made as a result of participation in industry associations, also public commitments, commitments as a result of company directives, policy requirements, etc.

Pilot Plants	Selected Ford Motor Company sites that participated in ISO 14001 implementation prior to worldwide implementation.
Plan-Do-Check-Act Cycle	Management cycle that serves as the foundational approach of ISO 14001; promotes continual improvement.
Planning	Identifying environmental aspects, legal and other requirements and establishing environmental objectives and targets.
Policy Letter No. 17	Issued August 28, 1996, to define Ford Motor Company policy with respect to protecting health and the environment.
Preventive Action	Action taken to mitigate a potential problem before it occurs.
Prevention of Pollution/ Waste Minimization	Worldwide, coordinated procedure of the Ford Motor Company for implementing and documenting a site-specific prevention of pollution and waste minimization program.
Procedures	Comprised of core environmental procedures and facility-specific procedures. Core environmental procedures serve as the basis for facility-specific procedures, satisfy requirements of ISO 14001 and ensure global consistency. Facility-specific procedures address the individual needs of plant-specific operations and activities.
Re-certification Assessment	Reassessment of an EMS by a third-party registrar when certificate of registration expires.
Recommended Requirements	Identified in ISO 14001 by such words as "should," "is suggested" or "it is recommended."

Records Maintenance	Responsibilities and actions for assuring that records are properly retained and accessible.
Registrars	Organizations that perform ISO 14001 audits (e.g., Lloyd's Register Quality Assurance). They may be accredited by one or more internationally recognized organizations.
Second-Party Review	Evaluation of conformance to ISO 14001 by Ford personnel prior to a formal registration audit.
Special Assessments	Evaluations conducted by third-party registrars, usually after significant changes which, in the registrar's judgment, could impact the EMS.
Surveillance	Periodic audit by third-party registrar to verify continued conformance with ISO 14001 following registration.
Sustainable Development	Protecting, maintaining and restoring the integrity, resilience and productivity of natural and social life-support services.
Work Instructions	Detailed instructions for completing specific tasks in specific work areas.

Acronyms

AF	air-to-fuel
ANSI	American National Standards Institute
ATNPC	Automatic Transmission New Product Center
Btu	British thermal unit
CAA	Clean Air Act
CAR	corrective action request
CEO	Chief Executive Officer
CEPA	Canadian Environmental Protection Act
CERES	Coalition for Environmentally Responsible Economies
CERLA	Comprehensive Emergency Response Compensation and Liability Act
CFR	Code of Federal Regulations
CFT	Cross-Functional Team
CRT	Certified Refrigerant Technician
CSP	Certified Safety Professional
CWA	Clean Water Act
DIS	Draft International Standard
DOT	Department of Transportation
EF	environmental forms
EMAS	Eco-Management and Audit Scheme
EMP	Environmental Management Program
EMR	Environmental Management Representative
EMS	Environmental Management System
EP	environmental procedures
EPA	Environmental Protection Agency
EPOC II	Emulsion Program for Overspray Capture
EQO	Environmental Quality Office
EWP	environmental work practices
FAO	Ford Automotive Operations
FES	Ford Environmental System
FMCP	Ford Motor Company Philippines, Inc.
FMS	flexible machining shop
FPS	Ford Production System
GRI	Global Reporting Initiative
ISO	International Organization for Standardization

kw	kilowatt
kwh	kilowatt-hour
LRQA	Lloyd's Register Quality Assurance
MISA	Municipal Industrial Strategy for Abatement
NOx	Oxides of Nitrogen
NPDES	National Pollutant Discharge Elimination System
PCB	polychlorinated biphenyl
ppm	parts per million
PRC	Parts Redistribution Center
psig	pounds per square inch gauge
RAB	Registrar Accreditation Board
RCO	regenerative catalytic oxidizer
RCRA	US Resource Conservation Recovery Act
RTO	regenerated thermal oxidizer
RO	reverse osmosis
RvA	Dutch Council for Accreditation
SARA	Superfund Amendment Reauthorization Act
scfm	standard cubic feet per minute
SF6	sulfur hexafluoride
SIC	Standard Industrial Classification
SOx	Oxides of Sulfur
TCM	total cost management
TNA	training needs analysis
UKAS	United Kingdom Accreditation Service
US	United States
VCA	Vehicle Certification Agency
VHO	very high output
VOC	volatile organic compound

Index

14001, Corrective and Preventive Action	9, 28, 54, 128, 137, 141, 148, 150, 158, 169-170, 175, 194, 197, 211-215, 217, 220-221, 223-224, 226, 252, 276, 281
14001, Environmental Policy	11-12, 23, 30, 39-40, 43, 45-47, 49, 51, 54, 61, 99, 125-129, 133-134, 137, 139, 141, 143, 151-157, 160, 167, 169-171, 173-174, 177-179, 192, 197, 205, 224, 235, 237, 261-262, 265, 267-270, 272, 277, 280
14001, Implementation and Operation	12, 127, 135
14001, Management Review	10, 12, 28, 31, 35, 39, 50-51, 54, 59, 75, 128, 137, 150-154, 159, 169-170, 176, 191-192, 197-198, 200, 204, 207, 211, 223, 225, 235, 237, 252, 275, 280
14001, Planning	10, 12, 24, 28-29, 53, 56, 62-63, 125, 127, 129, 143, 145, 182, 211, 214, 221, 226, 248, 277, 280
Agency Approvals	29, 197, 223, 235
Aluminum	53, 80-81, 261-263, 265
American National Standards Institute (ANSI)	53, 126, 283
Application, filing	159
Assessment, re-certification	164, 281
Assessment, registration	50-53, 160-161, 163
Assessments, special	164, 281
Audit, Environmental Management System	51, 128, 141, 149-153, 159, 169-170, 176, 212
Audits, internal	30-31, 59, 150, 213-214, 216, 277
Audits, internal environmental system	28
Australia	8, 56, 63, 73, 75, 122, 261-262
Automotive Consumer Services Group	106
Automotive-related services	
Th!nk	2
Qwik-Fit	2
Quality Care	2
Ford Credit	2
Award, Canadian Council of Ministers of the Environment Pollution Prevention	65
Award, Clean Corporate Citizenship	69

Award, Ford's Total Productive Maintenance	79
Award, Ford's Environmental	102
Award, Gold	77
Award, Governor's Pollution Prevention	79
Award, Wildlife Habitat Council	84-85
Belgium	262
Bentonite	63-64
British Standards Institution (BSI)	17, 275
Broadmeadows Facility	73, 122, 261
BS 7750	17, 56, 275
Business stakeholders	4, 121-122
Campaign material	46-48
Canada	25-26, 53, 65, 77, 84, 105, 262, 278
Committee, Allen County Local Emergency Planning	55-56
Committee, American Institute of Architects on the Environment	94
Committee, North Central Ohio Solid Waste Management District Policy	55
Communications, external	29, 49, 127, 138-139, 156, 173, 198, 200, 235, 237, 239
Community	4, 5, 55-56, 64-65, 92, 105, 111, 114, 134, 139, 152, 208, 232, 235
Connor, John	6
Contractor management	29, 275
Coolant	85-86, 90-91, 114, 116, 196
Core Procedures	26-27, 38-39, 44, 275
Core Team	6, 25-26, 30-31, 33, 35-36, 52-53, 278
Corporate Citizenship	5, 16, 21, 61-62, 69, 92, 112, 114
Corporate Environmental Policy Letter No. 17	20, 23, 274, 281
Corporate strategies	16, 19
Cross-Functional Team (CFT)	30, 40, 42-43, 54, 57-58, 171-174, 182, 186-191, 193, 196, 200, 205-208, 226, 231, 237, 238, 240, 243, 256, 276, 283
Detroit Edison	76-77
Documentation review	160
Documentation, EMS	28, 43, 127, 141, 156, 160, 170, 276
Document and data control	12, 29, 55, 127, 141-142, 148, 156, 169-170, 174, 197, 202, 220, 235, 242, 276
Documents, sample	167-168
Dunton Engineering Centre	84
Draft International Standard (DIS)	15, 27, 276
Edison Institute	6
Electricity	6, 64, 72, 75-77
Emergency planning	28, 56, 145, 182
Emergency Preparedness and Response	12, 127, 138, 141, 144-145, 156-157, 169-170, 174-175, 197, 204, 206, 220, 224, 226, 235, 252, 276
Emrick, Terry	56
Emulsion Program for Overspray Capture (EPOC II TM)	87, 283
Energy Management Efficiency	30, 277

Environmental aspects	10-12, 28-29, 34-36, 39-41, 44-45, 50, 54, 106, 112, 121, 126-127, 129-132, 134, 138-139, 141, 143-145, 154-157, 160, 167, 169-174, 177, 179-180, 194, 204-209, 223, 224, 226, 230-231, 233, 235-236, 240, 244, 248, 275, 280
Environmental Management Representative (EMR)	21, 31-32, 34, 43, 51, 170-171, 173-174, 176, 184, 192, 194, 196, 198, 205, 213-215, 220-184-191, 221, 223-224, 227, 230-231, 234, 237-238, 240-243, 249, 258, 260, 276-277, 283
Environmental Management System (EMS)	8-12, 17-18, 24-28, 30, 32-33, 35, 39, 43-45, 50-51, 58, 62, 75, 90, 101, 105, 112-113, 122, 125-129, 132-133, 135-142, 145-152, 154-156, 159, 160-164, 167-170, 172-174, 176, 178-179, 183, 192-197, 210, 212-213, 215, 220, 223-225, 230-231, 236, 241-243, 245, 249, 253, 270-271, 275-277, 279, 281, 283
Environmental Management Program (EMP)	3, 9, 28, 40-42, 46, 127, 129, 135, 137-139, 154, 167, 170, 172, 174, 200, 204-205, 207-208, 210, 224, 253, 277, 283
Environmental Objectives and Targets	9, 11-12, 24, 28, 35, 38-42, 45, 51, 54, 58, 63, 67, 126-130, 133-141, 143-145, 147, 150-155, 157-158, 160, 162, 167-172, 174, 179-180, 184, 188-189, 191-192, 194, 197, 204-205, 208-209, 223-224, 226, 230, 233, 235, 248, 252-253, 277-278, 280
Environmental Policy	11-12, 23, 30, 39-40, 43, 45, 46-47, 49, 51, 54, 61, 99, 125-129, 133, 134, 137, 139, 141, 143, 151-157, 160, 167, 169-174, 177-179, 192, 197, 205, 224, 235, 237, 261-262, 265, 267-270, 272, 277, 280,
Environmental Protection Agency (EPA)	79, 84, 121, 132, 283
Environmental Regulations	29, 34, 36-37, 106, 133, 146-149, 154, 171, 206, 227-228, 233, 279
Environmental Regulatory Compliance Assurance Program	29
Environmental target	38, 134, 207, 278
European Union (EU)	7-8, 133, 276
European Union's Eco-Management and Audit Scheme (EMAS)	8, 17, 56, 100, 133, 276
External communication	29, 49, 127, 138-139, 156, 173, 198, 200, 235, 237, 239
Federal-Mogul Corporation	121
Ford Automotive Brands	3
Aston Martin	3, 367
Ford	3, 80, 82, 102
Jaguar	3, 66, 102, 268
Lincoln	3, 82, 86-87
Mazda	3
Mercury	3, 69, 78, 80-82, 88
Volvo	3, 102
Land Rover	3

Ford Automotive Operations (FAO)	3, 20, 283
Ford Customer Service Division	119
Ford Dealership EMS Workbook	105
Ford Environmental Quality Office (EQO)	6, 19, 25, 31, 33-35, 52, 70, 115, 278, 283
Ford Environmental System (FES)	24-26, 30-33, 43, 45-48, 50-51, 54-56, 63, 65, 75, 109, 119, 164, 278-279, 283
Ford Land Development and Product Development Centers	119
Ford Rouge Center	88, 91-93, 270, 293
Ford, Henry	5-6, 88, 91
Ford, William Clay, Jr.	3-5, 15, 91, 94-95, 118
France	263
Germany	8, 17, 19, 56, 70, 94, 263
Global Testing Operations	119
Globalization	16-18
Green belt	65
GreenZone	106-108, 278
Hagenlocker, Ed	3, 20-21, 23, 109
Implementation Flow Chart	30, 58-59
Implementation Plan, EMS	32, 33-34, 276
International Organization for Standardization (ISO)	9, 126, 279, 283
ISO 14001	1, 3-12, 15-21, 23, 25-27, 30-33, 35, 43, 46-47, 50-59, 61-62, 65-66, 69, 75, 90, 97-102, 105-107, 109-114, 117-123, 125-126, 128-129, 132-135, 141-142, 146, 149-152, 154-165, 167, 170-178, 183, 199, 202, 204, 211, 217, 220, 223, 226, 228, 233, 235, 240, 242, 245, 248, 252, 255, 275-281
ISO 14001 Pocket Guide	46, 49, 52, 131, 136, 140, 146, 153
ISO 14004	126, 279
ISO 9000	7, 8, 9, 19-20, 24-25, 30, 53, 55, 101, 110, 114, 121, 125-126, 141, 147, 167, 279
ISO Mania (video game)	11, 57
ISO/TS 16949	7
Japan	19
Krygier, Roman	3, 112
Landfill, Woodland Meadows	77
Latin America	8, 25, 100, 278
Legal and Other Requirements	12, 34, 36, 39, 127, 132-133, 141, 145, 154, 169-172, 178, 181, 207, 224, 228, 237, 241, 255, 257
Lloyd's Register Quality Assurance (LRQA)	54, 56, 261-273, 281, 284,
Magnesium	80-81
Materials Management	12, 30, 208, 280
McDonough, William A.	91, 94
Mexican Ministry of Environment	94
Mexico	8, 26, 46, 56, 77, 94, 100, 113, 265, 278
Michigan Clean Corporate Citizen	69, 90, 122
Monitoring and Measurement	55, 112, 128, 130, 133-134, 142, 145, 147, 149-150, 158, 169-170, 175, 197, 204, 220, 223-224, 252-253, 280

Municipal-Industrial Strategy for Abatement (MISA)	66, 284
Nasser, Jaques A. "Jack"	3, 16, 94
National Water Commission	94
Natural Resources and Fisheries	94
New Zealand	261-262, 265
Nonconformance	12, 50, 128, 137, 141, 148-149, 150-151, 158, 160, 162-163, 167-170, 175, 194, 197, 211-213, 215, 217, 220-221, 223-224, 226, 252
Ohio Prevention First	81
Operational Control	12, 41-42, 127, 130, 134, 137-139, 141-144, 147, 157-158, 169-170, 174, 184, 186-191, 210, 224, 234, 253, 255, 280
Ozonation	65-66
Padilla, James	3, 114
Paint	6, 33, 64, 66, 68, 71, 73, 76-83, 86-87, 93, 112, 131, 180, 196, 262-264, 266-272
Paint overspray	60, 87
Paint sludge	6, 60, 80, 82, 87
Petrauskas, Helen	3, 109
Philippines	56, 265, 282
Pilot	53-54, 76, 91, 93, 105, 110, 120
Pilot Plants	53-54, 86, 110, 264, 281
Plan-Do-Check-Act	125, 127-128, 135, 145, 281
Plant, Broadmeadows Assembly	73, 122, 261
Plant, Browns Lane Assembly	66-67, 269
Plant, Dearborn Assembly	88, 93, 269
Plant, Essex Aluminum	262
Plant, Essex Engine	84-85, 262
Plant, Ford Atlanta Assembly	79, 268
Plant, Ford Casting	63-64
Plant, Ford Romeo Engine	82, 90-91, 271
Plant, Ford Woodhaven Stamping	75, 273
Plant, Halewood Body and Assembly	68, 73, 268
Plant, Hermosillo Stamping and Assembly	56, 77, 265
Plant, Lima Engine	53-56, 271
Plant, Lio Ho Assembly Engine and Casting	56, 267
Plant, Lorain Assembly	81, 271
Plant, Michigan Truck	18, 56, 60, 72, 74, 76, 82, 89, 271
Plant, Norfolk Assembly	79, 271
Plant, North Penn Electronics	53, 55
Plant, Oakville Assembly	53, 262
Plant, Ohio Assembly	78, 81-82, 271
Plant, Rouge Assembly	91, 93
Plant, Saarlouis Body and Assembly	56, 264
Plant, St. Thomas	77, 271
Plant, Taubaté Maintenance Engineering	64, 266
Plant, Twin Cities Assembly	78, 272
Plant, Van Dyke Transmission	53, 55, 68-69, 272
Plant, Wayne Assembly	18, 76, 272
Plant, Windsor Aluminum	53, 55, 263

Plant, Windsor Casting	65-66, 263
Plant, Wixom Assembly	86, 272
Powertrain Operations	3, 25, 64, 112, 261, 264
Pre-Assessment	54, 59, 159-161
Prevention of Pollution/ Waste Minimization	23, 29, 63, 81, 194, 208, 281
QS-9000	7, 101, 141, 147, 167
Records	29, 30, 43, 45, 128, 138, 141, 147, 149-151, 153, 158, 169-171, 173, 175-176, 185, 193, 197-203, 208, 212, 215, 222, 224, 227, 229, 231, 234, 238, 241, 243-247, 249, 253-254, 257, 282
Records Maintenance	30, 282
Recycle	5, 48, 62, 64-66, 71, 77, 78, 81-83, 87-90, 102, 107, 116-118, 120, 131, 144, 178, 183, 190
Recycle, cardboard	88-89, 117
Recycle, coolant	85-86, 90-91, 114, 116
Recycle, packaging	55, 62-63, 88-89, 117, 122, 144, 178, 183
Recycle, waste oils	117
Recycle, wooden pallets	89
Recycling Council of Ontario, Canada	77
Reduce	4, 8, 10-11, 35, 39, 55, 62, 65-69, 70-73, 76-83, 87, 91-93, 95, 97, 102, 106-107, 110, 112-115, 117, 178, 188, 190, 278
Regenerative thermal oxidizers (RTOs)	71-72, 86
Registered sites	261
Registration Process	116, 159-160
Retail System	106
Retail, Ford Dealership EMS Workbook	105
Retrofit	73
Reuse	60, 62, 63-65, 77, 81, 84, 91, 95, 107, 134, 178, 190
South America	115, 266
Spain	70, 266
Strelow, Roger	121
Structure and Responsibility	43, 127, 135, 138, 155, 153, 169, 170, 172
Supplier Environmental Requirements Manual	101-104
Supplier Survey	98-99, 101
Surveillance	11, 163-165, 282
Sustainability	1, 5, 61, 91, 94, 282
Switzerland	9
Taiwan	56, 267
Training	8-10, 12, 26, 30-33, 38, 41, 42-48, 51-55, 57-59, 63, 79, 100-101, 115, 117, 127, 130, 134, 137-139, 141, 143-145, 149-150, 155-156, 158, 167, 169-170, 173, 175, 192, 195-198, 200, 204, 212-213, 221, 224, 227, 235-236, 246-247, 250-251, 269, 272, 275, 278, 284
Training, Awareness and Competence	127, 134, 137, 139, 141, 144-145, 150, 155, 169-170, 173, 224
Training, Implementation	33, 38, 42-43, 196, 278
Training, Supplier Awareness	100
TUV Rheinland	54, 264, 265

United Kingdom (UK)	8, 53, 66, 78, 84, 267
United States (US)	7-8, 16, 18-19, 25, 53, 86, 105, 112-113, 116, 122, 126, 132, 159, 268, 278, 284
US Resource Conservation Recovery Act (RCRA)	82, 182, 195, 284
Vehicle Certification Agency (VCA)	54-56, 284
Visteon	25-26, 65
Volatile organic compound (VOC)	11, 71, 73, 77-79, 82, 86, 284
Waste, general	4, 8, 23-24, 29, 34, 43, 56, 60, 62-63, 74, 76-77, 80-83, 86, 94, 98-99, 101-102, 113, 115-118, 121, 145, 177-178, 182, 185, 190-194, 198, 201, 206-208, 232, 255, 257-258, 260, 275, 281
Waste, liquid	35, 63-64, 69, 78-79, 80, 82-83, 91, 117, 180, 182, 185, 190, 205
Waste, solid	5, 18, 35, 54-55, 63-64, 77, 81-82, 88, 122, 143, 147, 180, 182, 185, 190, 193, 205
Waste management	29, 62, 77, 79, 102, 182, 195, 233
Wastewater	36, 54, 63-70, 79-80, 83-84, 86, 90, 107, 132, 147, 180-181, 205, 232, 263-264
White House	94
Wildlife habitats	84

About the Author

Tim O'Brien

Mr. O'Brien is director of the Environmental Quality Office (EQO) at Ford Motor Company, which is responsible for environmental regulatory expertise, strategic planning, technical support, remediation and compliance assurance at Ford facilities in 26 countries, and for similar support in new and emerging markets.

A graduate of the University of Michigan and Detroit College of Law, he began his career with Ford with the finance staff, where he worked from 1973 to 1977. From 1977 to 1987, he worked in the Tax Accounting and International Tax Departments of the Ford Office of the General Counsel (OGC). From 1987 to 1993, Mr. O'Brien was a senior attorney in the Environmental Matters Practice Group of the Ford OGC, specializing in mobile source environmental issues. In 1993, he joined the Ford EQO as Air/Water Quality and Pollution Prevention Manager. He was appointed to his current position in January, 1995.

From 1995 to 1998, the EQO led Ford's initiative to become the first automotive company to have all of its manufacturing plants in the world certified to the ISO 14001 environmental management system standard. At the present time, Mr. O'Brien is leading the Rouge Heritage 2000 initiative to transform that site into the model of 21st century sustainable manufacturing.

Mr. O'Brien is a member of the Board of Directors at the Automobile National Heritage Area and the Wildlife Habitat Council. He is also a member of the Advisory Board of the University of Michigan-Dearborn Environmental Interpretive Center.